Distant Victory

Praeger Security International Advisory Board

Board Cochairs

Loch K. Johnson, Regents Professor of Public and International Affairs, School of Public and International Affairs, University of Georgia (U.S.A.)

Paul Wilkinson, Professor of International Relations and Chairman of the Advisory Board, Centre for the Study of Terrorism and Political Violence, University of St. Andrews (U.K.)

Members

Eliot A. Cohen, Robert E. Osgood Professor of Strategic Studies and Director, Philip Merrill Center for Strategic Studies, Paul H. Nitze School of Advanced International Studies, The Johns Hopkins University (U.S.A.)

Anthony H. Cordesman, Arleigh A. Burke Chair in Strategy, Center for Strategic and International Studies (U.S.A.)

Thérèse Delpech, Senior Research Fellow, CERI (Atomic Energy Commission), Paris (France)

Sir Michael Howard, former Professor of History of War, Oxford University, and Professor of Military and Naval History, Yale University (U.K.)

Lieutenant General Claudia J. Kennedy, USA (Ret.), former Deputy Chief of Staff for Intelligence, Headquarters, Department of the Army (U.S.A.)

Paul M. Kennedy, J. Richardson Dilworth Professor of History and Director, International Security Studies, Yale University (U.S.A.)

Robert J. O'Neill, former Chichele Professor of the History of War, All Souls College, Oxford University (Australia)

Shibley Telhami, Anwar Sadat Chair for Peace and Development, Department of Government and Politics, University of Maryland (U.S.A.)

Jusuf Wanandi, co-founder and member, Board of Trustees, Centre for Strategic and International Studies (Indonesia)

Fareed Zakaria, Editor, Newsweek International (U.S.A.)

Distant Victory

The Battle of Jutland and the Allied Triumph in the First World War

Daniel Allen Butler

Praeger Security International
Westport, Connecticut · London

Library of Congress Cataloging-in-Publication Data

Butler, Daniel Allen.
    Distant victory: the Battle of Jutland and the Allied triumph in the First World War / Daniel Allen Butler.
               p. cm.
    Includes bibliographical references and index.
    ISBN 0–275–99073–7 (alk. paper)
1. Jutland, Battle of, 1916. I. Title.
    D582.J8B95 2006
    940.4'56—dc22   2006015110

British Library Cataloguing in Publication Data is available.

Copyright © 2006 by Daniel Allen Butler

All rights reserved. No portion of this book may be reproduced, by any process or technique, without the express written consent of the publisher.

Library of Congress Catalog Card Number: 2006015110
ISBN: 0–275–99073–7

First published in 2006

Praeger Security International, 88 Post Road West, Westport, CT 06881
An imprint of Greenwood Publishing Group, Inc.
www.praeger.com

Printed in the United States of America

The paper used in this book complies with the Permanent Paper Standard issued by the National Information Standards Organization (Z39.48–1984).

10 9 8 7 6 5 4 3 2 1

Dedicated

to the

Memory

of

Ivan Harris

Chief Petty Officer, Royal Navy (Ret.)

1944–2004

"For all that, he was a man—

we'll not see his like again."

Contents

Author's Note	ix
A Note to the Reader Regarding Time and Distance	xiii
Prologue: Trafalgar	1
1 The Great War	7
2 Dreadnoughts, Battleships, and Battlecruisers	29
3 Strategies and Stratagems	53
4 The Price of Admiralty	73
5 Twisting the Lion's Tail	97
6 Gambit	125
7 "There's Something Wrong with Our Bloody Ships Today!"	143
8 The Thunder of the Guns	155
9 Steel Maelstrom	173
10 The Reckoning	185
11 The Fatal Blunder	199
12 Distant Victory	213

viii Contents

Epilogue: Scapa Flow   225

Appendix I: Royal Navy Order of Battle—the Grand Fleet at Jutland   231

Appendix II: Imperial Navy Order of Battle—the High Seas Fleet at Jutland   239

Sources   243

Index   247

Author's Note

Distant Victory is a work that I felt compelled to create. My interest in the Battle of Jutland dates back more than 30 years, and I was never completely satisfied with the accounts and explanations of who "won" the battle and why. As my own personal historical perspective developed, particularly my understanding that events do not happen in a temporal vacuum, but rather result from a myriad of preceding influences and produce an immense number of consequences, I came to understand the reason for my dissatisfaction. It was the limited perspectives of those historians who attempted to reduce Jutland to a simple function of arithmetic, totaling up and comparing losses and declaring a winner solely on that basis, rather than taking a longer view toward understanding what happened as a consequence of the battle.

It took me some time to realize it, but what I had done was run up against the ghost of Winston Churchill. The problem was that Churchill, with his exceptional gift for turning a phrase, was sometimes too subtle for the vast majority of later historians to fully comprehend. When he said that Admiral Sir John Jellicoe, the Commander-in-Chief of the Grand Fleet, was "the only man who could *lose* the war in an afternoon," he meant just that, nothing more. But for nine decades, lesser historians have misunderstood his epigram and took it to imply that if Jellicoe had the capacity to *lose* the war in an afternoon, he also had the capacity to *win* it in the same time span. Unfortunately for them, their readers, and history in general, this simply was not true—Churchill meant nothing more than what he actually said. The defeat, even the annihilation, of the High Seas Fleet would not have been sufficient to compel Germany to seek peace with the Allies. It would have been a severe blow to German morale, true, but Germany's ability to wage war would have remained unaffected even if every German battleship and battlecruiser lay at the bottom of the North Sea.

Not so with the Royal Navy: a serious defeat of the Grand Fleet, Britain's collection of battleships anchored at Scapa Flow at the northern mouth of the North Sea, would have spelled the end of Britain's war effort in a matter of weeks. The Grand Fleet kept the High Seas Fleet effectively locked up in the North Sea: denied access to the North Atlantic and the opportunity to prey on Britain's shipping lanes, the German fleet was essentially impotent. Any reduction in British naval strength severe enough to allow the High Seas Fleet to escape its North Sea prison would have meant disaster for Great Britain, hence Churchill's observation about Jellicoe.

But there were two questions about Jutland that no one ever seemed to ask or answer: why, after Jutland, did the Germans never again face the Grand Fleet in battle? Why did Germany instead turn to unrestricted U-boat warfare against civilian shipping, a course of action that she knew would bring the United States into the war against her?

The answers to those questions are why *Distant Victory* was written.

The real origins of *Distant Victory* can be found in my years as an undergraduate student, as discussions with the late Dr. Paul G. Fried, of Hope College, Holland, Michigan, and Dr. Lynn Mapes, of then–Grand Valley State College, now Grand Valley State University, Allendale, Michigan, both professors of history, started me down the road to developing my own capacity for historical analysis and critical thinking. I was fortunate in that these two gentlemen had the greatest influence on my education and my thinking. Neither of them felt compelled to force their own interpretations on me; both of them encouraged me to think openly and freely. This book owes its origins to them —I owe them my gratitude.

The story of the Battle of Jutland is, in many ways, a modern epic, and it seemed at times that the research needed to retell it correctly would have to be of epic proportions—and it very nearly was. While not exactly a cast of thousands, there were scores of people, at institutions of every description, in four countries scattered across two continents, who made some kind of genuine, material contribution to this work. I would like to thank them all, and single out those persons and institutions whose assistance were particularly significant.

As any writer will readily acknowledge, good librarians and archivists are the people who make a writer's work possible. Consequently, I want to acknowledge my debt to the librarians, archivists, and pages of the following libraries, museums, and archives: The U.S. Library of Congress, Washington, DC; the Broward County Library System, Fort Lauderdale, Florida; the Orange County Library System, Orlando, Florida; the University of Michigan

Author's Note

Library System, Ann Arbor, Michigan; and the libraries of Florida State University, Tallahassee, Florida. Once again the staff at the Van Wylen Library at Hope College in Holland, Michigan, as well as the librarians and student assistants at the Grand Valley State University libraries in Allendale, Michigan, were tireless in their efforts to aid me in locating old, out-of-print books through the Michigan University Library System.

The Bundesarchiv in Koblenz, Germany, is the repository for much of the diplomatic correspondence of Imperial Germany, as well as the surviving logs of the warships of the High Seas Fleet, while the British Public Records Office is the repository of all of the unclassified British Admiralty files from the Great War. The staff at each of these institutions were often worth their weight in gold, as those in Germany were always ready to assist in translating some of the more difficult technical passages that defied my (very) rusty German; those in Great Britain took particular delight in interpreting the sometimes rather turgid British "officialese" when my modern "American English" was not up to the demands of First World War–vintage "English English."

I would be remiss if I failed to acknowledge my debt to three specific museums. First is the Mariners' Museum of Newport News: as I have said elsewhere, this is a museum staffed by men and women who know ships and the sea, and so can give insights and perspectives on a subject that might otherwise escape many a land-bound historian. The National Maritime Museum in Greenwich, England, on the other hand, has no equal anywhere in the world for the breadth and depth of its resources or its accumulated knowledge of ships and the sea; it is literally impossible to write about British naval history without access to its archives.

Finally, the Imperial War Museum is the *non plus ultra* of military historians: research into the First World War, land or sea, simply begins and ends here. In each of these institutions I conducted some major or at least a significant portion of my research, and in each I was always received with consummate professionalism and courtesy. Over the course of several years and many visits, the faces and names would often change, so that now I can only dimly recall some of them, but to each and every one, I extend my genuine and sincere gratitude.

A special mention is deserved of certain individuals whose contributions to this work merit singling out. My editor at Praeger, Elizabeth Demers, had such an enthusiasm for *Distant Victory* from our very first conversation that it made the long hours required to complete this book worth every bit of the effort. Trish Eachus once more took time out from her own writing to do yeoman work in research and proofreading; once more the result was her usual sterling job. Peter Griffes offered moral support and physical resources that literally allowed *Distant Victory* to be written. Eileen Wojahn

xii Author's Note

provided valuable inspiration, sometimes in ways of which she was totally unaware; in a sense she gave me cause to finish this book. Eileen also has one of the most incisive minds I have ever encountered, and her ability to spot a flawed or weak argument or a lapse in logic is unparalleled. Every author should have someone like "Eily" in their life to keep a critical eye on their work.

Most particularly, I want to direct a special "thank you" to the man to whose memory this book is dedicated, the late Ivan R. Harris, Chief Petty Officer, RN (Ret.), who passed away in January 2004 at the all-too-young age of 59. Ivan was a wellspring of insight into the workings and traditions of the Royal Navy and never hesitated to share his knowledge of ships, the sea, and naval service in general. Ivan had a knack for making clear the differences—some subtle, some startling—between the reality of life in "the Andrew" as compared to how it is often portrayed in print and on-screen. I cherish the memories of the nights when we saw our womenfolk off to bed, then left the cap off the Balvenie bottle, and talked until the wee hours of the morning. Looking back, they seem too few in number, and the memories are now priceless. Fair winds and following seas, Ivan.

In every case, the generosity of the people and institutions mentioned contributed in some substantial way to *Distant Victory*. Without them this book would never have been completed. How I availed myself of the information or support—or both—that they provided makes me responsible for how I used it. If I have done so erroneously, the fault is entirely mine. As always, I would not have it any other way.

A Note to the Reader Regarding Time and Distance

While some references to time in the text are general (e.g., "around 8 o'clock that morning") any mention of a *specific* time of day in the text is recorded in 24-hour military time, e.g., 4:15 PM becomes 1615 hours, and is based on Greenwich Mean Time. Likewise, all distances are recorded in nautical miles. It will be helpful to remember that a nautical mile is longer than a statute mile on land—6,000 feet against 5,280 feet. Thus at sea, 2,000 yards is equal to one nautical mile; for those readers who are accustomed to the metric system, one nautical mile is equal to 1.852 kilometers.

Prologue

Trafalgar

The time was approaching noon on October 21, 1805; the place was an expanse of open sea off Spain's Atlantic shore between Cadiz and Gibraltar. Two fleets of warships, each sailing under clouds of white canvas, were slowly converging. It was not a mutually agreed-upon convergence: one fleet was desperately trying to escape, the other determinedly intent on overtaking. Weather—and superior seamanship on the part of the latter fleet—decreed that the escape attempt would fail and that two fleets would meet a few miles off a little-known inlet on the Spanish coastline called Trafalgar Bay.

The fleet that was fleeing was a combined Spanish and French force commanded by Admiral Pierre Villeneuve. The ships were part of an intricate plan developed by the French Emperor Napoleon Bonaparte to give him naval supremacy in the English Channel for the four days he deemed necessary to transport the 100,000 troops *Le Grande Armee* from Boulogne to the English shore at Dover and accomplish the conquest of Great Britain. Consequently, Villeneuve was under orders to avoid an engagement with the Royal Navy, instead bringing his command intact into the Channel. Villeneuve did not have to be told twice to avoid a fight, for he had no stomach for facing the murderous, close-range broadsides of the British ships of the line. His crews, he knew all too well, were pitifully trained, poorly motivated, and woefully inexperienced; they would be no match for the veteran officers and ratings of the Royal Navy. Now, as he pressed to the northwest under all possible sail, Villeneuve saw that a battle was inevitable. Even before the first gun fired, he knew the battle was lost.

The overtaking fleet was, of course, British, under the command of Vice Admiral Lord Horatio Nelson, the most enigmatic and charismatic officer ever to tread a Royal Navy quarterdeck. He was also the most tactically gifted commander "the Andrew"—as the lower-deck ratings called the Royal Navy —had ever known. For more than two years Nelson had worked to bring about the battle that was just moments away. The whole strength of the Royal Navy, from the Admiralty in London, where the guiding hand of Admiral Sir John Jervis, Earl St. Vincent, positioned the squadrons of the fleet, to the small, swift frigates and sloops that patrolled the waters off the European ports where the components of Bonaparte's navy took shelter, had been bent toward this day, this hour. The battle that was about to be fought was the very reason for being for the Royal Navy.

The role of the Royal Navy has traditionally been defensive: rarely used as an instrument of colonial expansion, its primary mission was to protect the British Isles, Britain's overseas possessions, and the sea-lanes that connected them. While France had for centuries been England's enemy, the two nations had rarely openly threatened each other's sovereignty or territorial integrity. Now, with the rise of Bonaparte, all that had changed. Determined that all of Europe must accede to his will, Napoleon had introduced the "Continental System," a primitive form of Common Market, which compelled the nations of Europe that were under French domination, a condition that encompassed most of the Continent, to trade among themselves, at the same time forbidding any imports without the express permission of the Emperor himself.

The idea behind the Continental System was to drive the economy of Great Britain, which Bonaparte scorned as "a nation of shopkeepers," into ruin, compelling the British to accept Napoleonic suzerainty. Great Britain resisted with great success, in the process expanding her overseas markets and her overseas possessions, as France's former colonies, all but cut off by the Royal Navy, fell like plums into London's lap. Bonaparte decided that the obstinate English could be brought to heel only by force, and so decided on invasion.

But to invade England his army had to cross the English Channel, and to be able to do so required naval supremacy—a preponderance of naval power in the Channel that the Royal Navy could not hope to defeat in time to prevent the Grande Armee from making its crossing. Drawing ships from Holland and Spain, and combining them with the French fleet, Napoleon believed he could accomplish exactly that. Thus Villeneuve's orders were given to avoid any action with the British until his ships had reached the Channel and rendezvoused with the rest of the gathering French fleet.

They were orders with which Villeneuve was more than prepared to comply: his ships had spent months, sometimes years, tied up at their moorings in French and Spanish harbors, where their crews' morale decayed, their sailing skills eroded, and their gunnery declined. The French admiral was painfully aware that the Royal Navy's men-o'-war were, ship for ship, easily the equal of two, three, or even four French or Spanish warships of equal size. Spending endless months at sea—before Nelson had returned to England for what was to be the last time earlier that autumn, he had spent more than a year aboard his flagship, HMS *Victory,* without setting foot on land—the British crews practiced their gunnery drills relentlessly, while simply keeping station off the French and Spanish coasts had honed their sailing skills to the point of perfection. Knowing that a straightforward fight with Nelson's fleet was folly, Villeneuve hoped to be able to evade the British, but the winds that morning favored the Royal Navy, and so *Victory* and her 26 consorts were able to close with the fleeing French and Spanish warships.

Disdaining complex evolutions or a long range artillery duel, Nelson trusted his seamen's skill and courage, following his own dictum that "No captain can do very wrong if he places his ship alongside that of an enemy." Setting a course that would take *Victory* into the very heart of the opposing fleet, cutting it in two and then drawing up alongside the nearest enemy vessel, Nelson was determined to fight the battle muzzle to muzzle, battering the French and Spanish ships into submission, confident that neither their officers nor crews could endure the cannonade of the British broadsides and return them in kind.

In little more than four hours it was over. One by one the British warships followed *Victory* into the van of the enemy fleet and began remorselessly pounding it to pieces. Often able to rake their enemies—systematically firing a broadside in a foe's relatively vulnerable bow or stern—before drawing alongside them, the British gun crews were able to get off three, sometimes four, rounds for every one the French or Spanish returned. The sheer volume of fire quickly took its toll, as the cannon balls, some weighing as much as 32 pounds each, smashed bulwarks, upended gun carriages, and tore into decks. Grapeshot, which turned the huge muzzle-loading cannons into titanic shotguns, cut bloody swaths across the gun decks, while up above sharpshooters stationed in the mast tops took careful aim at enemy officers.

Solid shot thudded into hulls, or tore apart railings and gangways, releasing flurries of lethal splinters. Masts creaked, cracked, and toppled, yardarms crashed onto decks below, and rigging coiled and twisted about the wreckage. The great guns kicked and rolled back against their restraining tackle, as the crewmen went through the carefully rehearsed and endlessly drilled routine of sponging out, ramming a fresh charge of powder down the barrel, driving home another round shot, priming the gunlock, and firing it. Many sailors would permanently lose their hearing as a consequence of this day's action, but they fought on with an almost superhuman endurance. It would prove too much for their French and Spanish foes.

When the smoke had cleared and the thunder rolled away, the British had all but annihilated the French and Spanish fleet. It was the greatest of all of Nelson's victories, but it came at the price of his life. Struck down earlier by a sharpshooter's bullet, Nelson died just as the battle was reaching its climax, moments after being told of the extent of his triumph. Of the 33 ships of the line under Villeneuve's command, 18 had struck their colors and surrendered, a 19th had caught fire and had blown up, while most of the survivors were heavily damaged. Not one British ship had been lost. The cost was high: nearly 1,700 British officers and seamen were casualties, a quarter of them killed; for the French and Spanish it was a horrible toll: nearly 7,000 casualties, 4,000 of them dead, with another 7,000 captured. For all practical purposes, the French and Spanish navies ceased to exist. Villeneuve himself would become a belated casualty of the battle, taking his own life within a matter of months as undeserved charges of cowardice were laid against him.

The threat of invasion was dispersed with thunderous finality: the day before Nelson's annihilation of Villeneuve's fleet, the Grande Armee had won an amazing victory over a combined Russian and Austrian army at Austerlitz. The French had marched from their camp at Boulogne more than a month before the clash at Trafalgar, but the crushing French defeat there meant that even should the Grande Armee return to its Channel encampment, the French would never be able to assemble the numbers of ships required to seize control of the Channel and bring the troops across. The war against Bonaparte would go on, but Great Britain would never again be confronted with the threat of a hostile army barely 20 miles from her shores, waiting to make the leap across the Channel. As Admiral the Earl St. Vincent observed, "I don't say they can't come, I only say they can't come by sea."

But the war *would* go on: Nelson's victory at Trafalgar would make it possible to continue the war, but by itself it would not be enough to topple the Emperor. Abdication, Elba, the Hundred Days, and St. Helena all lay nearly ten years in the future. Yet, while before Trafalgar the fall of the First Empire was dimly perceived as inevitable by only a few, after the battle it no longer seemed impossible. The myth of French invincibility had been broken. A decade would pass before the road to Austerlitz would finally lead Bonaparte to Waterloo, but it began on the Spanish shore, at Cape Trafalgar.

More than a century would pass before Great Britain again faced a challenge as grave as that posed by Bonaparte, and again the Royal Navy was called upon to be the instrument of Britain's salvation. In 1914, with the German High Seas Fleet poised across the North Sea to spring on British shipping and ravage Britain's supply lines, the battleships of the Grand Fleet were deployed against it in anticipation of another great battle of annihilation. It would take almost two years to bring that battle about, and when

Trafalgar

the Grand Fleet and the High Seas Fleet collided at Jutland on May 31, 1916, in an afternoon of tumult and fury, when the smoke had cleared and the thunder rolled away, the outcome was quite different. Instead of the widely expected destruction of the German battle fleet, the British lost more ships and suffered greater casualties than did the Germans. Rather than a battle of annihilation, to many observers on both sides of the North Sea Jutland appeared to be hardly more than a skirmish of indecision.

But the results were the same: Jutland dictated that Germany would lose the First World War. After the battle, reeling from damage that was almost beyond the ability of German shipyards to repair, the High Seas Fleet would never again openly challenge the Grand Fleet. Instead, the German Naval High Command would turn to a controversial new weapon, the submarine, to cut Britain's sea-lanes and starve the British Isles into defeat. In doing so Germany would bring the United States, hitherto an always uneasy and often not-quite-neutral nonbelligerent, into the war on the side of the Allies, irretrievably turning the balance of power against Germany and making her own defeat a certainty.

Yet for nearly nine decades, the Battle of Jutland has been presented as a tactical victory for Germany, or at most a draw, as three generations of historians have focused on the immediate results of the battle but failed to look beyond them and comprehend its subtle strategic aftermath. Like Trafalgar, Jutland could not and did not immediately bring down Great Britain's enemy. But like Nelson's victory 11 decades earlier, in time it made Great Britain's victory inevitable. When the Allies triumphed in November 1918, it was due in no small part to decisions made and choices taken as a consequence of what happened at the Battle of Jutland. Tactical loss or tactical draw—in the end it did not matter for Great Britain—strategically Jutland was a victory. It was just a distant victory.

Chapter 1

The Great War

Late on the night of August 4, 1914, wireless sets in Royal Navy ships all over the world began sparking with the dots and dashes of a fateful message:

Admiralty to all HM Ships
and Naval Establishments

Signal
4 August 1914
11 pm Admiralty
COMMENCE HOSTILITIES AGAINST GERMANY

The warships receiving this instruction were patrolling the waters of the North Sea, steaming up and down the English Channel, or roaming the waters of the Mediterranean, the North and South Atlantic, or the vast reaches of the Pacific, searching for German vessels. The dreadnoughts of the Grand Fleet waited with steam up on their anchorage at Scapa Flow should the German High Seas Fleet sortie into the North Sea, while the Battle-cruiser Squadron was making ready to patrol off the German coast. Reserve ships were manned and ready for action, while auxiliaries were steaming toward British ports where they underwent the transformations that made them part of the fleet.

It was an amazing display of preparation, training, technical competence, and strategic thinking: any chance that Germany may have had in those first hours of the war of achieving strategic or tactical surprise against the British was lost, and with it vanished Germany's best chance of winning the naval war against Great Britain. In short, the Royal Navy stood tall while the German

High Seas Fleet dithered. It was a lost opportunity that ultimately decided the course of the war.

It began on June 28, in a street in Sarajevo, Bosnia, when a young man named Gavrillo Princzip shot and killed the Archduke Franz Ferdinand, heir to the throne of Austria-Hungary, along with his wife. The assassinations served as the trigger that released tensions that had been building in Europe for nearly a century, and what should have been a private quarrel between Vienna and Belgrade quickly spiraled out of control into a continent-wide conflagration. A little more than a month after the shootings, a tragedy of errors saw Russia, Germany, Austria-Hungary, and France go to war as a complex and tangled skein of alliances and diplomatic maneuvers quickly and irretrievably unraveled.

As unimaginable as Europe's rush toward self-destruction may seem, what still seems all but impossible to truly comprehend more than 80 years later is how enthusiastically the peoples of Germany, France, Austria-Hungary, and Russia rushed to war, the ecstatic crowds thronging the *Unter den Linden*, the *Champs de Elysees*, the *Ringstrasse*, or the Red Square cheering as their respective governments declared war, or how readily the young men were prepared to march off to the sound of the guns, to the strains of *Deutschland uber Alles*, *le Marseillaise*, or "God Save the Tsar." What should have been an isolated quarrel between Austria-Hungary and Serbia instead became the means to an end for settling old scores, asserting new hegemony, or confirming existing preeminence.

For Germany this war was a God-sent opportunity to settle scores with a revivified France and secure German dominance—economic, political, and military—of the Continent for generations. For France it was a chance at fulfilling the national dream of *revanche* on the despised Boches and reclaiming the "lost" provinces of Alsace and Lorraine. Russia was presented with an opportunity to restore the international prestige she had lost in the Russo-Japanese War in 1905 and solidify her self-appointed role as protector of all Slavic peoples in Europe. The aging, creaking Austro-Hungarian Empire, whose confrontation with Serbia had snowballed into the continent-wide conflict, was determined to crush once and for all the nationalistic aspirations of the tiny Balkan states while reasserting her status as a great power.

But for one nation, the coming of war was an agony. Watching intently but having no real interest in becoming part of this growing conflagration, Great Britain desperately tried to mediate a peaceful settlement, but to no avail. True, there was an increasingly dangerous and bitter naval race going on between the Royal Navy and the High Seas Fleet, as the British perceived Germany's maritime ambitions to be a threat to the Royal Navy's dominance of the world's oceans, on which Britain's economy depended, a perception that

The Great War

the Germans were only to happy to reinforce. And it was also true that there had been extended staff talks between the French and British armies to coordinate a response should Germany invade France. And it was further true that Britain had been signatory to an international treaty signed in 1839 that guaranteed the integrity of a neutral Belgium. But so far, by the first day of August 1914, the German Navy had not stirred from its berths in Kiel and Wilhelmshaven, German troops had not crossed the French border, and Germany, as heir to Prussia's diplomatic obligations, had also been a signatory to that 1839 treaty and had always honored it. While there was concern in Whitehall that Britain might be drawn into the war against her will, there seemed to be little cause for believing it would actually happen. That was to change, abruptly and irrevocably, that afternoon, when word reached the Foreign Office that at 3 o'clock that morning, German troops had invaded Belgium, surging forward in a huge mass of field grey toward the fortress city of Liege. Swiftly, an ultimatum was sent to Berlin, announcing that if German troops had not begun their withdrawal from Belgium by noon on August 4, a state of war would exist between Great Britain and Imperial Germany. The officials in Berlin's foreign ministry on the Wilhelmstrasse were aghast: the Chancellor, Theobald von Bethmann-Hollweg, had assured everyone that Britain would never go to war over an 80-year-old treaty that was hardly more than "a scrap of paper."

The Germans did not even bother to respond. Instead, they kept pouring more and more troops into Belgium, along with mammoth cannon, specially designed years before by Krupp and Skoda, to reduce the Belgian forts that ringed Liege and blocked their advance. The Germans were bound by that strategic dogma that has become enshrined in the lexicon of popular history as the Schlieffen Plan: the rigid and inflexible deployment of Germany's armies, designed to crush France in six weeks, before the mobilization of Russia's huge army could be completed, allowing the whole of German might to be massed in the east to face the expected Russian onslaught, eliminating Germany's worst nightmare—fighting a two-front war.

The provisions of the plan necessitated the violation of Belgian neutrality to guarantee the success of the German army, allowing three-fourths of the German forces—1.25 million men—to swing behind the French armies positioned along the Franco-German border and descend on them from the north, rolling up the French lines like a bloody carpet. Twelve noon passed on August 4 without word of any intention of a German withdrawal, and so the orders went out to dispatch the British Expeditionary Force, the BEF, to Belgium, there to take up positions on the left of the French Seventh Army and prepare to meet the German juggernaut.

The main body of the BEF began shipping across the Channel on August 12. Every day for the next week an average of 13 ships sailed each day from Southampton to Le Havre or Boulogne. One hundred and forty thousand men were safely transported, the largest movement of troops by sea in history up to that time. The single busiest day was the last day, August 18, when 34 transports crossed the channel in a single 24 hour span. Three days later the six divisions of the "ptibles" were assembled and moved toward the front; on August 25, they met the German army at Mons.

But carrying the BEF to France was not the end of the Royal Navy's role in the redeployment of the British army. September saw 39 battalions of regulars stationed in India brought back to Great Britain, where they became the 27th, 28th, and 29th Divisions; three territorial divisions were sent to India to take their place. Two divisions of Canadian troops were convoyed across the Atlantic in October, while in November 30,000 Australian and New Zealand volunteers were brought up from "down under" to the Suez, where in Cairo they were formed into the Australia and New Zealand Army Corps, soon to gain immortality as the ANZACS. In all that time and all that travel, not one British, Canadian, Australian, or New Zealander soldier lost his life to enemy action at sea. It had been the largest army redeployment by sea in history, and one of the greatest, though almost forgotten, displays of the meaning and potential of sea power.

Germany's only chance of winning a swift, decisive—and relatively bloodless—victory in the opening weeks of the war was to intercept these convoys and do as much damage as possible. Instead, timorousness on the part of the German High Command left the High Seas Fleet riding at anchor in Wilhelmshaven and Kiel. Not a single British soldier lost his life being transported to France; it was Germany's single greatest strategic blunder of the entire conflict.

While the High Seas Fleet's impotence was due in no small part to a cautiousness that bordered on cowardice with the German Naval Staff, it also stemmed from the German Army's *Generalstab* (General Staff) attitude that the BEF was so small as to be almost not worth consideration—indeed, Kaiser Wilhelm II had referred to it as a "contemptible little army." Amused, the officers and rankers of the BEF adopted this sobriquet as a badge of honor and styled themselves "The Old Contemptibles." German derision notwithstanding, those seven divisions were the finest troops Europe had ever seen or would ever see, and when they met the oncoming waves of field grey on August 22, they handed the advancing Germans setback after bloody setback for the next month, retreating only when their exposed flanks were threatened, their numbers slowly but irrevocably dwindling, as the supporting

French armies, bleeding and demoralized, reeled from the shock and surprise of the German assault.

Fatal delays were inflicted on the unforgiving timetable of the Schlieffen Plan's schedule for advance, and, when the German II Army was within sight of Paris, a hastily assembled French army, not letting the time bought so dearly by the BEF go to waste, made a desperate stand on the River Marne, then launched a devastating counterattack that threw the now-weary Germans back some 40 miles, with the exhausted armies finally coming to a halt on September 22.

But by now Britain's "little red Army" was fast becoming a "little dead Army," and while reinforcements from the distant garrisons of the Empire finally began to reach France, it was clear to everyone that the BEF had been decimated. At the same time, it slowly dawned on the generals and politicians alike, and even more slowly on the general public, that something had gone terribly wrong in the calculations that had been made and the assurances given before the troops marched off to war.

The troops, everyone had been assured, would be home before the leaves fell—in six weeks' time, eight at the most. But when the leaves fell, they only covered the fresh graves of the dead or swirled into the newly dug graves of those still dying. Then the cry was that the war would be over before Christmas, but Christmas came and went, and there was no end in sight, of either the war or the casualty lists. After the first clash of arms in Belgium and on the French frontier had swept the Germans to the gates of Paris, and the aptly named "Miracle of the Marne" had pushed the advancing *feld grau* tide back, a series of sidestepping maneuvers westward had begun, as each army sought to work its way around the other's flank. Already a thin, snake-like line of trenches, growing more and more elaborate with each passing week, was being dug from the Swiss border to the Channel, depriving each side of the opportunity to maneuver, as the opposing armies strengthened their positions and began looking for a way to break the enemy's lines.

Soon entire military traditions were being overthrown. It began to dawn on the Germans that here was a problem no amount of *Generalstab* intellect could think its way out of. The French realized that no amount of *elan* could defeat well laid out patterns of German artillery fire. The British saw that their tiny BEF, so tragically mauled in the battles in Belgium when facing overwhelming odds, could never be resurrected and that, to build the army of the size required to honor her obligations to Belgium and France, the entire resources of the Empire would need to be mobilized.

By the spring of 1916, what had developed became the lasting memories of the Great War. Methods of living and dying that could find parallels only in the darkest passages of writers like Edgar Rice Borroughs, Jules Verne, H.G.

Wells, or Howard Phillip Lovecraft as trenches evolved into sophisticated systems of defensive positions, listening posts, dugouts, bunkers, and communication cuttings. The Germans, during their retreat from the Marne, had generally seized the high ground, the better to keep a wary eye on developments on the Allied side of the lines, and began to construct increasingly elaborate defensive positions, content to lob artillery shells into the enemy trenches and leave any offensive action to the Allies.

It was a grim prospect. The Allies really had no choice: as long as the Germans occupied Belgium and parts of France, peace was impossible—they had to be forcibly ejected. Time and again the French and British armies surged forward against the waiting German defenses—and each time found some hellish new innovation that cut them down by the thousands. Machine guns proliferated, giving even small units incredible amounts of firepower, what J.F.C. Fuller called "the concentrated essence of infantry." Huge entanglements of barbed wire appeared, with barbs the size of a man's thumb, the better to catch on uniforms, accouterments, and flesh, pinning the hapless victims long enough for the chattering machine guns to find them. Mine throwers made their debut, hurling packages of explosives into enemy trenches, often wrapped with a covering of metal shards, watch springs, cogwheels, or nails.

Soldiers began to learn that sounds could be dangerous—the steady mechanical rattle of the Spandau machine gun that made a weird, half-human half-metallic sighing as spent shell casings were ejected; the hissing roar of the *flammenwerfer*, the flamethrower, one of Germany's new weapons of terror; the unforgettable "click-clack, clack-click" of a round being chambered in a Lee-Enfield rifle; the short, sharp scraping of the primer cord being drawn from the handle of a potato masher hand grenade. And always the shells: There were shells that whistled, shells that warbled, shells that whizzed; some chugged like freight locomotives, others whined like banshees, and still others whispered in flight. There were shells that whistled before they exploded, shells that exploded then the whistle caught up, shells that whistled and moaned but never seemed to explode—and there was always the one you never heard—the one that got you.

Even the colors were lethal: red Very lights at night signaling corrections to artillery bombardments; green or yellow mists snaking along the ground, the terrible tendrils of phosgene or mustard gas; white on a man's gums or blue on his feet announcing the presence of trench mouth or trench foot; black on a wounded soldier's body declaring that gangrene had already set in.

The slaughter was appalling for both sides. In the First Battle of Ypres, in October 1914, where wave after wave of German infantry, many of them university students advancing arm-in-arm singing patriotic songs, was cut down by the deadly accurate British rifle fire, one German division lost over 9,300 men out of strength of 12,000—*in a single morning.* The British lost 60,000 men killed or wounded in the first day of the Somme, July 1, 1916, while the ten-month long charnel house of Verdun cost the French and Germans together more than 700,000 lives.

In the postwar years, the commanding generals on both sides were pilloried as mindless brutes who could conceive of no alternative but to feed endless masses of men into a vast killing machine, in the hope that the enemy would run out of troops first. It was actually all very simple to the generals, as the popular refrain went, just supply them with enough troops so that the enemy could not kill them fast enough and victory was assured. Actually, it was far more complicated—and in its complications, far more tragic—than that.

In plain fact the commanding generals, much maligned as incompetents as they are, and many of them deservedly, never meant to slaughter the finest generation of young men their nations would ever produce. Certainly none of them ever enjoyed it, no matter what the slanderers might say in later years. The hard, painful truth was that they were unprepared for the war they found themselves given the responsibility of fighting. For years it had been a tenet of military faith, and correctly so, that the day of the frontal assault was over— the American Civil War and the Franco-Prussian War had first demonstrated that truth, and the Russo-Japanese War of 1905 and the Balkan War of 1912 had only reinforced the lesson. Modern firepower made frontal assaults too costly, for infantry in even a hastily prepared defensive position could hold off several times their number of attacking troops, inflicting unacceptable losses in the process. So for decades the emphasis had been placed on conducting wars of maneuver, which gave an army the opportunity to turn a foe's flank and achieve a decisive result in battle without having to resort to the terrible waste of frontal attacks. What was never anticipated was this war where maneuver was impossible, where there were no flanks to turn, and where the dreadful frontal assaults were the only option remaining to them.

Every aspect of European military thought had been devoted to the pursuit and exploitation of mobility, which gave the capacity to maneuver, from the German *Aufmarch* (mobilization) plan and the railroad timetables of the German troop trains, to the design of French artillery equipment. What no one clearly foresaw, though Alfred von Schlieffen came closer than anyone, was that the sheer mass of modern armies negated the advantages of mobility. When the dying von Schlieffen muttered (and he really did), "Let the soldier on the farthest right brush the [English] Channel with his sleeve," he was acknowledging that only by engaging in sweeping maneuvers on a scale of which no one had ever before dreamed could mobility be decisive, for on a narrow front the sizes of the two armies prohibited any kind of war of maneuver.

But even von Schlieffen, whose creativity was more the result of hard work than real genius, never conceived of a war where maneuver would be *impossible*. Maneuver, to the generals of the Great War, was decisive—by definition it had to be. And in truth it was, for when the great maneuver of the Schlieffen Plan failed in September 1914, a decisive result had been reached, though no one knew it at the time. The decision was that the Germans would not take Paris this time and so knock France out of the war. That had been the objective of the vast sweep of the Schlieffen Plan, and it failed. Hard on the heels of its failure came one of the greatest General Staff blunders of all time, for the Germans had no contingency plan to fall back on should the vaunted Schlieffen Plan *not* deliver Paris into their hands. Even worse, as a direct result of the Plan, Germany now had to number Great Britain among her enemies, a consequence of the invasion of Belgium.

What this meant was the series of sidesteps toward the Channel that became known as the Race to the Sea were hastily improvised and executed, rather than part of a developed strategy. When the race was over, the result was two sets of opposing armies, organized, trained, and equipped to fight wars of maneuver, deprived of any opportunity to do anything but bludgeon away at each other in an endless series of bloody frontal assaults. For the generals it was a nightmare: they literally had no idea what else to do. The Western Front was a scenario outside all of their experience, German, French, or British, and in a desperate attempt to do something, the only course of action left to them was to continue to pound away at the enemy, hoping against hope that someone, somewhere, might break through and return mobility to the battlefield.

What happened time and again was that, after an artillery bombardment that lasted for hours, sometimes days, or even weeks, the Tommies and *poilus* clambered over the top of their trenches and crawled to their jump-off tapes, lying in the mud until the second hands of their officers' watches touched zero hour, then they stood up, the British to the sound of the officers' whistles, the more romantic French to bugles blaring the *Pas de Charge,* and began their methodical advance across the shell-torn mudscape that stretched between the opposing lines of trenches and became known as No Man's Land. The Germans, usually having weathered the barrage in the relative safety of their deep dugouts, emerged to assume their prepared positions and bring down a withering hail of rifle, machine gun, and artillery fire on the advancing troops.

The results were inevitable: more often than not, there were not enough soldiers left alive among the attackers to take the objective and hold it, or if

The Great War

the Allied troops did reach their goal, the cost was prohibitive—one advance of barely 700 yards took three weeks at a cost of nearly 30,000 lives. Even when there were no titanic battles being fought, nearly 5,000 men were being killed every day by sniper fire and random shelling, though on such days the communiqués issued to the public read, "All quiet on the Western Front." The British, methodical as ever, referred to such losses as "normal wastage."

What makes it all so incomprehensible three generations later is that the soldiers accepted it so willingly—even cheerfully. Millions fought stoically, with a quiet, unassuming belief in the essential rightness of their nations' causes that has long since vanished. Somehow, even after all the absurdities of World War II, Korea, Viet Nam, and Iraq (though none are remembered for being as absurd as the First War), there is still a rose-tinged nimbus of romance that surrounds the Great War. It was the songs—"Keep the Home Fires Burning," "Pack Up Your Troubles," "Till We Meet Again," and everyone's favorite, "Tipperary." It was the traditions—in England, newly commissioned subalterns visiting an armorer to have their swords sharpened before leaving for France, much as Henry V had done; the French cuirassier regiments and squadrons of German *uhlans* looking as if they had just stepped out of a Phillipoteaux painting of the Napoleonic Wars. It was black and silver saber knots, spiked *Pickelhauben* helmets, and French gunners resplendent in black and gold tunics. It was the grandeur of an age that was, in fact, its shroud.

France and Germany had armies of conscripts, it is true, but conscription had been a national institution for generations—what made these conscripts conspicuous was how few tried to evade their responsibility. In Great Britain the situation was even more astonishing: not until 1916, when Britain was compelled to field the largest army the Empire had ever mustered to carry out the Somme Offensive, did the British Army have to resort to a draft to fill its ranks. These young men, rightly called the flower of European youth, were the most idealistic the world would ever see, untainted by the cynicism and affected, postured disdain of later generations. Instead, they steadfastly believed in *Ein Kaiser, ein Volk, ein Reich,* or *Liberte, Egalite, Fraternite!* and *Vive la Republique!,* or fighting for king and country. What Europe was killing, no matter how willing the victims, was the vitality that has left later generations listless and disillusioned, the fire that had driven the Continent having been quenched forever in a carnage whose scale was unthinkable. By the end of May 1916 nearly 2 million soldiers once clad in khaki, feld grau, or horizon bleu were dead or missing on the Western Front, while another 4 million had been wounded. And the bloodiest years were yet to come....

All the while as the carnage mounted on the Western Front, at sea the Great War was being fought just as viciously, just as ruthlessly, and sometimes just as brutally, as on land, but because it was far more methodical and deliberate it would never be cloaked in the romantic nonsense that made the land war—and in particular the Western Front—at once so fascinating and so repulsive.

It was in Captain Alfred Thayer Mahan's work, *The Influence of Sea Power Upon History,* one of the most influential books written in the last 200 years, that the concept of "sea power," long intuitively understood by the navies of the world, was articulated in a clear and coherent form. Mahan defined sea power as a nation's capacity to use the world's oceans to transport the flow of raw materials and finished goods necessary to sustain a nation's economy in peacetime, as well as transport troops and supplies in wartime, while simultaneously denying that capability to the enemy. No nation has more thoroughly understood or expertly executed that concept throughout its history than Great Britain.

Probably the most convincing demonstration of that understanding was the results produced by the flurry of orders and deployments issued by the Admiralty in the first weeks of the war. The Imperial German Navy was impotent to interfere with the movements of the British troop convoys; all 42 of the fast liners meant to be converted into commerce raiders were trapped in German or neutral ports—or sunk on the high seas; and aside from Admiral Maximilian von Spee's Far East Squadron I in the Pacific and a pair of German cruisers in the Mediterranean, the whole of the High Seas Fleet was bottled up in Kiel and Wilhelmshaven. It was a situation due in no small part to the combined circumstances of the German Navy's failure to put to sea before Great Britain declared war, and the Grand Fleet being perfectly deployed just as the war broke out.

The Royal Navy's incredible state of readiness was the result of the prescience of the First Lord of the Admiralty, Winston Churchill. July had found the Royal Navy in the middle of its annual maneuvers, part of which was a practice mobilization of the entire fleet, including reservists. Churchill kept a careful watch as the crisis on the Continent precipitated by the assassination on June 28 of Archduke Franz Ferdinand, heir to the throne of Austria-Hungary, grew and expanded until it seemed that war might sweep across the whole of Europe. When the maneuvers ended on July 25, rather than disperse the fleet, Churchill sent only the second-line reservists home and kept the battle squadrons of the Grand Fleet concentrated in the waters of the North Sea.

By contrast the German Navy's preparations for war were so incompetent as to be almost comical. No sooner had France declared war on Germany than Admiral Alfred von Tirpitz, Secretary of the Navy, wanted to convert Germany's fast liners into their merchant cruiser guise as swiftly as possible and

The Great War 17

send them out into the sea-lanes to prey on enemy shipping; the Kaiser, Wilhelm II, refused to consent. Next von Tirpitz urged that the High Seas Fleet be ready to put to sea at any moment so that it might take advantage of any strategic opportunities that might present themselves should Great Britain come into the conflict. Again he was denied. Von Tirpitz, caught in a purely administrative office with no actual operational control over the navy he had created, could only fume impotently, while the commander-in-chief of the High Seas Fleet, Admiral Friedrich von Ingenohl, and his chief of staff, Vice Admiral Hugo Friederich von Pohl, two men whose dilatory tendencies approached cowardice, counseled prudence to the Kaiser, which in his eyes meant avoiding a clash with the Royal Navy. Von Ingenohl's timidity allowed the Royal Navy to establish an ever-increasingly effective blockade of the North Sea, Germany's only outlet to the world's oceans. While a screen of light cruisers and destroyers kept a careful watch on the approaches to the German fleet anchorage at Wilhelmshaven, other British ships were on patrol, stopping and seizing any merchant ships with cargoes bound for Germany. At the same time the Grand Fleet waited patiently for a sortie by the High Seas Fleet to force the issue and break the blockade in a climactic confrontation of dreadnoughts. That the Royal Navy would have ample warning of any such attempt by the High Seas Fleet only made the task of maintaining the blockade easier. That it was the Germans themselves who were unwittingly providing the warning was probably the best kept secret of the war. And thereby hangs a tale, for the ability to read German ciphers had a decisive effect on the course of the war.

In the early hours of August 4, 1914, a small British cable ship, the *Telconia,* was cruising back and forth in the waters near Emden, where the German and Dutch borders meet at the North Sea. Dragging a grappling hook behind her, the cable ship dredged up five underwater telegraph cables and, one by one, cut them. These were the German transatlantic cables, Germany's secure links with her overseas embassies and consulates. Now Germany was forced to rely on wireless to communicate with her agents and diplomats overseas, depending on the security of her codes and ciphers to prevent prying enemy ears from listening in. The German cipher systems—there were ciphers for naval, military, and diplomatic usage—were among the most complex in the world, and repeated tests by the Germans themselves had assured Berlin that they were impenetrable.

That may have been true, but they were not beyond being compromised. The Royal Navy's prewar director of Naval Intelligence, Rear Admiral Henry Oliver, had established a chain of wireless monitoring posts around the British Isles, with the intention of using cross bearings they obtained to monitor the movements of German ships at sea. At the same time he set up a small, secret section of scholars and cipher experts who were given the task of breaking the German codes, which eventually evolved into the shadowy organization known as "Room 40" after the location of their offices in the Old Admiralty Building. This proved a task beyond their abilities, but in an incredible string of bad luck for the Germans, in the first three months of the war the British were able to recover copies of three of the most widely used German code books. The diplomatic cipher was recovered from the wreckage of a destroyer sunk in the North Sea trying to run the British blockade and deliver the code book to the German Embassy in the United States. The cipher for German zeppelins, merchant vessels, and small ships was taken from a freighter captured by the Royal Australian Navy in the Pacific. But the greatest prize of all was a copy of the German High Seas Fleet naval cipher, which contained all the codes used by the German capital ships as well as the U-boats.

In the predawn darkness of August 26, 1914, the German light cruiser *Magdeburg,* on patrol in the Baltic, ran aground in the Gulf of Finland near Russian Estonia. Her captain strove mightily to free his ship, even enlisting the help of a German destroyer, which failed to pull the cruiser free. Knowing that *Magdeburg* was a sitting duck and Russian warships would arrive on the scene soon after sunrise, the German skipper decided to scuttle his ship. Part of the scuttling procedure was to destroy any code books and cipher equipment, the responsibility of the cruiser's signal officer. Three copies of the Naval Code were either burned or thrown overboard before the German crew abandoned ship aboard, but when boarding parties from the Russian light cruisers *Palladia* and *Bogatyr* inspected the stranded warship, they discovered a fourth copy in the *Magdeburg's* safe, apparently forgotten by everyone aboard. Showing a rare generosity for the Russians in those days, the Imperial Russian Navy sent the code book to London by fast cruiser, reasoning that the Royal Navy could put it to the best possible use.

The cipher books were rushed to Room 40, where they came under the authority of the new director of Naval Intelligence (DNI), Captain William Reginald Hall. Captain Hall arrived at his post of DNI fresh from the bridge of a battlecruiser and ran his department in the quaint fashion that had made his ship one of the most efficient in the Royal Navy by declaring that peacetime standards and habits were no longer acceptable. When he came to the office of DNI, Hall knew next to nothing about cryptography or intelligence gathering, but with typical thoroughness he had within a few short months mastered his new profession as few ever have. It was not long before he was building an intelligence network that had few rivals and no peers. From working hand in glove with Scotland Yard chasing German spies to keeping the Foreign Office informed about Middle East intrigues, Hall had a finger in every shadowy pie that threatened the Empire. As Barbara Tuchman put it in *The Zimmerman Telegram,* "Like God in the British national anthem, Hall was ready to confound the politics and frustrate the knavish tricks of Britain's enemies. He was ruthless, sometimes cruel, always resourceful."

Hall's direction of Room 40 proved a priceless advantage, for Britain's war effort, her very existence, depended on the steady flow of food, goods, and materials from overseas. Any interruption of Britain's shipping lanes would be devastating; if they were cut, it would be fatal. The final piece of the cryptographic puzzle fell into place when a lead-lined chest was recovered from the North Sea by a British fishing vessel on November 30, 1914. In it were supplemental codes and ciphers of the German Navy, but more importantly were charts marked with the High Seas Fleet's top-secret position grid, which was used to monitor the movements of friendly warships and merchantmen.

The German grid was duplicated and set up on a large table, ten feet on a side, in the Operations division of the Admiralty, and quickly became known as "The Plot." Using a unique grid-square system, a German warship could signal its exact position within two or three miles simply by informing Berlin that it was at such-and-such a section of grid square so-and-so, giving the combination of letters and numbers that identified that specific section of the map. Since position signals were sent daily from every German warship at sea, U-boats, and surface ships alike, by reading these signals and marking the positions given on the Plot, the Royal Navy knew from day to day the exact location, within one or two miles, of every German ship at sea. It proved to be a critical advantage, for in the early months of 1915 the war at sea took a new and nasty turn as the number of British merchant ships being sunk by German U-boats began to increase alarmingly. What Great Britain now faced was not a crisis, but the beginnings of a threat to her survival.

On October 20, 1914, naval warfare had entered an entirely new era when *U-17,* cruising submerged 14 miles off the Norwegian coast, surfaced alongside the British merchant ship *Glitra* and ordered her to stop. After the *Glitra's* crew had safely taken to the lifeboats, *U-17's* crew opened the ship's sea cocks and scuttled her. It took 20 minutes for the *Glitra* to sink, and, while no lives had been lost, it was a turning point in naval warfare—she was the first merchant ship ever sunk by a submarine.

For all of its implications for merchant shipping, the event was overshadowed in both the public's and the Royal Navy's consciousnesses by a more terrifying incident that had taken place a month earlier. On September 22, 1914, like ducks in a shooting gallery, three British armored cruisers, *Hogue, Aboukir,* and *Cressy,* were torpedoed and sunk by *U-9.* They were not the first British warships to be sunk by a German submarine—that unhappy distinction belonged to HMS *Pathfinder,* a light cruiser torpedoed and sunk in the

North Sea on September 3 by *U-21*. But the implications as well as magnitude of the disaster that befell the three cruisers far overshadowed the loss of a single light cruiser. Assigned to, of all things, an antisubmarine patrol in a section of the North Sea known as the Broad Fourteens, the three cruisers were big (12,000 tons), and heavily armed with twelve 6-inch guns each, but they were all nearly 15 years old, slow with nearly worn-out engines, and had very poor, almost nonexistent underwater protection. Within the space of two hours all three cruisers were sent to the bottom, taking with them more than 1,400 British sailors and the legend of British naval invincibility.

The Royal Navy was stunned. Suddenly the Grand Fleet began to believe it was seeing submarines everywhere, even in Scapa Flow, alarms being raised on at least three different occasions, the climax coming on October 17, when the entire fleet put to sea as destroyers dashed about, firing guns at anything that resembled a U-boat. Not that the German Naval High Command was particularly quick on the uptake in understanding the significance or the potential of *U-9's* exploit. The strategy, planning, and doctrines of the German Navy were so firmly fixed on the idea of one great cataclysmic clash of fleets that the Germans were at first oblivious to the fact that *Kapitanleutnant* Otto Weddigen had given them the key that released German naval power from its North Sea prison.

For it was an unavoidable reality that, despite all the confidence, ability, and quality of ships and crews they commanded, the German Naval High Command was utterly unable to *force* the Royal Navy into a decisive battle. The whole balance of naval power had been determined by two overriding factors, one industrial, the other geographic. In both instances, Germany came out second best.

First, of course, was Britain's enormous numerical superiority in capital ships, coupled with the industrial capacity to maintain it. Britain boasted nearly twice as many slipways capable of building battleships as Germany, while maintaining a huge standing army was a burden Great Britain's foundries and arsenals never had to bear.

The second, geographic, factor was in some ways even more fundamental to the impotence of the High Seas Fleet. Great Britain sat astride the only two routes that the German Navy had to the North Atlantic, through the English Channel or up through the North Sea and around Scotland. Neither proved to be practical, since the Channel was a natural choke point, easily sealed off by Royal Navy mines and submarines. Meanwhile the Grand Fleet, moored at Scapa Flow in the Orkneys, sat waiting at the entrance to the North Sea, waiting for the High Seas Fleet to steam into its grasp. As Grand Admiral Karl Doenitz, a destroyer captain in the Great War, wrote in his memoirs,

The High Seas Fleet was denied its normal radius of action—to steam into the North Atlantic, where alone a decision was possible. Only [when it was] in the North Sea our fleet presented no danger to the Grand Fleet. The Royal Navy then had but to put into operation the war plans envisioned before 1914.

Doenitz was referring to the fact that the Royal Navy wholeheartedly embraced the concept of the blockade as the definitive expression of sea power. By sealing off the Channel and the North Sea, it cut off all imports into Germany—most importantly food, since Germany was not able to produce enough for her own needs, and nitrates, which were essential to the manufacture of explosives, of which Germany possessed no natural sources. The Germans devised stratagems for countering the Royal Navy's original plans, where cruisers and destroyers cruised a few miles outside German waters, while the van of the fleet kept station over the horizon, but the British Admiralty threw a spanner in the High Seas Fleet's works even before the war broke out when it realized that the Grand Fleet need only prevent the Germans from breaking out of the North Sea. By stationing the Grand Fleet at three distant anchorages in Scotland the Royal Navy effectively sealed off the North Sea, catching, as the Duke of Wellington would have put it, "a damned big rat in a damned small bottle!"

Now all that seemed about to change as the submarine appeared to be rewriting the rules of naval warfare. The submarines had given them the key that released German naval power from its North Sea prison: the U-boats allowed the German Navy to outflank the Grand Fleet technologically. Most perilous of all for Great Britain, by early 1915 the German U-boats suddenly became more dangerous to merchant shipping than they had ever been before.

What had happened was simple: on February 15, 1915, Germany issued a declaration that not only changed the course of the war at sea, but also changed the basic nature of warfare forever. The German Foreign Office had sent a cable to every neutral capitol in Europe, as well as every country in North and South America, that read:

The waters surrounding Great Britain and Ireland, and including the whole of the English Channel, are proclaimed to be a War Zone. On and after the 18th of February 1915, every enemy merchant ship found in the said war zone will be destroyed without it always being possible to avert the dangers threatening the crews and passengers on that account. Even neutral ships are exposed to dangers in the war zone, and in view of the use of neutral flags ordered on January 31st by the British government and of the accidents of naval war, mistakes may not always be avoided and they may be struck by attacks directed at enemy ships.

Accompanying the declaration was a list of safe zones in which neutral ships could travel to Europe, none of which, of course, led to a British port.

Simply put, the Germans felt that the British had pushed them too far. Beginning in October 1914, a steady stream of orders had issued forth from the Admiralty to British merchant captains regarding their conduct if and when they were attacked by a German U-boat. First, it was made a criminal offense for a captain to stop his ship if ordered to do so by a German submarine. Then merchant skippers were given orders that required them, if they were challenged by a U-boat, to not only refuse to stop, but to attempt to engage the submarine with whatever armament the merchant ship had, or if it were unarmed, to attempt to ram the U-boat. Finally, all British merchant ships were ordered to paint out their funnels' colors and names and to fly false flags whenever possible to make identification as difficult as possible. More provocative—and more dangerous to the U-boats—was the increasing number of British merchant ships that were carrying deck guns that were quickly turned on any German U-boat attempting to conduct a "stop-and-search" attack according to the requirements of international law.

While the presence of the deck guns was becoming increasingly obvious, the Germans learned of the inflammatory orders entirely by accident, when *U-21* stopped the *Ben Cruachan* on her way to Liverpool on January 31, 1915. A prize crew from the U-21 found the orders along with the ship's papers before sending the *Cruachan* to the bottom. The German government reacted so sharply and so swiftly in no small part because the Admiralty orders were making a mockery of the German Navy's attempt to carry out its submarine campaign according to the dictates of the Cruiser Rules.

The Cruiser Rules were a naval "search and seizure" etiquette dating back to the days of Henry VIII in the early 1500s that governed a warship's conduct toward unarmed merchant ships, meant to protect passengers and crew, as well as prevent the accidental destruction of neutral vessels.

However, the protection the Cruiser Rules offered to ships, cargo, passengers, and crew applied only to *unarmed* freighters and merchant ships. By January 1915, however, many British merchant ships were "defensively" armed as a measure of protection against submarine attack, usually with a pair of 12-pounder guns, as the British called their 3-inch gun, although some ships carried guns with calibers as large as 6 inches. A single hit from a 12 pounder could cripple a U-boat, while a hit from a 6-inch shell would blow a submarine out of the water. Surfacing and challenging a ship carrying such an armament left the U-boat dangerously exposed to an attack itself, to which the U-boat had no reply but to torpedo the merchantman without warning.

The thought of surfacing amid a flurry of 3-, 4-, or even 6-inch shells whistling past their ears did not appeal to the U-boat crews. Learning that even

The Great War

unarmed freighters were expected to try to ram U-boats on sight caused the U-boat commanders to argue that the British measures had made further adherence to the Cruiser Rules a practical impossibility, and any attempts to do so would needlessly lose boats and crews. They wanted to be able to sink British ships on sight, without warning, and they wanted neutrals warned that they sailed in British waters at their own peril. Taking their argument to the Naval Staff, they found a surprising ally in Vice Admiral von Pohl, who enthusiastically endorsed the idea, in particular because it offered an opportunity to strike hard at Britain's supply lines while presenting no risk to his precious battleships and battlecruisers. Von Pohl took the suggestion to the War Staff, where von Tirpitz voiced strong objections. He believed that allowing the U-boats to sink ships on sight would have a strongly adverse effect on neutral opinion and would be "more far-reaching in its effect on neutrals than a [surface] blockade, and considerably more dangerous politically." It was von Tirpitz's opinion that, while the world understood and respected the legitimate nature of Britain's blockade of Germany, it did not understand the legitimacy of a German policy of unrestricted U-boat warfare.

Von Pohl then came up with what he believed to be a novel solution: why not mimic the British and declare the waters around the British Isles to be a war zone, much like Britain's announcement of the North Sea as a "military area" in October 1914? Germany would provide neutrals with instructions and routes to avoid the war zone. Since this would not interfere with neutral shipping but merely reroute it, there would be no contradiction with Germany's policy that the British blockade was illegal. The Kaiser himself endorsed the idea, and the appropriate memoranda were drawn up and sent out to the German embassies around the world on February 5.

The U-boats wasted no time in putting the proclamation into effect. Between February 18 and March 28, 25 ships were sunk by U-boats, 16 of them torpedoed without warning. Of a total of 712 crewmen from those 16 ships, 52 were killed, though not a single passenger out of 3,072 involved were even injured. It was a not unenviable record, but it could not last forever.

On March 28, 1915, the 5,000-ton steamer *Falaba,* bound for Liverpool, was torpedoed by *U-28* after refusing to obey the U-boat's order to halt. The ship's cargo of explosives blew up in sympathetic detonation, sending the ship to the bottom in minutes. Among the 104 lives lost was Leon C. Thresher, an American citizen, the first American to be killed in the war at sea. That incident seemed to act as a sort of trigger as suddenly the conduct of the U-boats underwent a transformation from gentlemanly to barbarous in a matter of days. A whole series of neutral ships were sunk in March and April—two Norwegian ore carriers, the *Regin* and *Nor,* a Swedish freighter, the *Hanna,* and the *Duoro,* a Portuguese coastal freighter. On April 10, the

24 Distant Victory

6,000-ton steamer *Harpalyce*, boldly marked with the words "Belgian Relief Commission" and flying a prominent white flag was torpedoed without warning; the ship sank so rapidly that 17 members of her 44 man crew were trapped and drowned before they could reach the lifeboats.

All of this was leading up to the single most barbaric act of the war, the destruction of the *Lusitania*. At 2:10 PM on May 7, 1915, *U-20*, under the command of *Kapitan-Leutnant* Walther Schwieger, put a single torpedo into the liner's starboard side. It was a deliberate act, the *Lusitania's* profile was unmistakable, and Schwieger had tracked the ship for over 30 minutes before taking his shot. The torpedo struck the ship on the starboard side, abreast of her first funnel, and, within seconds, the ship took on a sharp list, then was shaken from stem to stern by a violent internal explosion deep within her bow. Steam lines burst in the boiler rooms and engine rooms, making it impossible to stop the ship or steer her toward shore, while the momentum of the 33,000-ton liner making 18 knots continued to drive her forward, pushing her bow deeper into the water and making it all but impossible to launch the lifeboats. Panic broke out on her decks as passengers and crew scrambled desperately for whatever illusory safety they could find as the ship quickly heeled over to starboard and vanished in 18 minutes.

When the final totals were tallied, out of 1,959 people on board, passengers and crew, 1,198 had been killed, 128 of them Americans. The news of the *Lusitania's* sinking was cause for a national celebration in Germany: in Berlin the Kaiser declared a national holiday. In Great Britain, the news of the *Lusitania's* destruction was a bitter blow to the entire nation. In Liverpool and London, riots broke out as mobs savaged German-owned businesses—or even those with merely German-sounding names. Many naturalized British citizens of German birth were forced to seek police protection, as were some nationals of neutral countries who were mistaken for Germans in the hysteria: several were accosted and beaten bloody in the streets of the British capitol.

The rest of the world was aghast at the news of the sinking. The *Lusitania* was not some obscure tanker or merchantman that had been torpedoed by accident. She was arguably the most famous and in some ways the best-loved ship in the world. It was impossible for Germany to claim that this was anything other than a deliberate act. How America would react to the sinking, and how Germany would explain it, riveted the attention of the chancelleries and foreign offices of the nations of the Central Powers and the Allies alike. The question on everyone's mind and lips was whether or not the United States would go to war with Germany.

When the Germans had first declared a war zone around the British Isles, President Woodrow Wilson had issued a stern warning to the Kaiser's government, promising that Germany would be held "strictly accountable" for any

The Great War

25

American lives lost through the actions of the German U-boats. Though the meaning of "strict accountability" was somewhat ambiguous, the phrase had a vaguely threatening ring to it, implying that there was some real if undefined limit to America's tolerance of the U-boat campaign. Through deft and sometimes duplicitous diplomacy Acting Secretary of State Robert Lansing was able to prevent the destruction of the *Lusitania* from becoming a *causus belli* between the United States and Germany, but it became clear to observers on both sides of the Atlantic that another such incident could well provoke the United States into going to war with Germany.

Suddenly—and rather belatedly—appalled at what had been done in his name, and rightfully fearful of the reaction of the American people, Kaiser Wilhelm decided that it was necessary to call off his undersea dogs. In late June 1915, orders went out over his signature to the U-boats to strictly observe the Cruiser Rules, and in any cases of doubt as to the identity of a target to err on the side of caution and break off an attack. These instructions triggered a rancorous argument between the German government and the German Navy that stretched out over the following ten months; its resolution led directly to the great clash of dreadnoughts, which is called the Battle of Jutland, and from there to the United States' declaration of war on Germany.

In any event the U-boats were making a mockery of Wilhelm's Imperial posturing. On August 19, the 16,000-ton White Star liner *Arabic* was 60 miles out of Liverpool, headed up around the north coast of Ireland bound for New York, when she was sighted by *U-24*. Knowing that the *Arabic* was an unarmed passenger ship, the U-boat's commander put a torpedo into her anyway. She sank in a little over ten minutes, taking 44 of her passengers and crew to the bottom with her, three of them Americans. The next victim to follow the *Arabic* was another liner, the *Hesperian,* sunk on September 4, also in direct defiance of the Kaiser's orders not to attack passenger liners. Thirty-two lives were lost; the submarine responsible was *U-20,* still under the command of Walther Schwieger. In a macabre twist, the *Hesperian* was carrying one of the last victims of the *Lusitania* to be recovered and identified—an American—back to the United States for burial.

On November 7, 1915, *U-38* stopped the Italian liner *Ancona* with the traditional warning shot across her bow. It was the only concession to the Cruiser Rules the U-boat made that day. Once the *Ancona* had stopped, and while the terrified passengers and crew were frantically trying to take to the lifeboats, the submarine's gun crew calmly began indiscriminately shelling the ship, hitting the hull, decks, and superstructure with little regard for the civilians aboard who were desperately trying to save their lives. The ship sank in less than an hour: 208 passengers and crew were killed.

This was the last straw for the Kaiser. It was impossible to say which angered him more: that his orders were being openly flouted by the U-boat commanders or that they were courting disaster by offering the Americans even more provocation. Since midsummer the furious debate between his Chancellor and Foreign Minister on the one hand and the officers of the High Seas Fleet—von Tirpitz and the U-boat commanders in particular—on the other had raged at fever pitch. Von Tirpitz, von Pohl, and the U-boat commanders all made their cases with a forcefulness that bordered on *lese-majeste,* insisting in their audiences with Wilhelm that the U-boat was an instrument of "self-defense" that Germany was compelled to use because of the British blockade. When the German government attempted to present this argument to the world, however, it was astonished to find that neutral nations, the United States in particular, rejected it out of hand. President Wilson was adamant in insisting that Germany give up what he described as an "inhumane" weapon.

In August the Chancellor, Theobald von Bethmann-Hollweg, persuaded Wilhelm that the U-boats should attack no passenger ships without first making every effort to determine their nationality. Von Tirpitz and the naval chief of staff, *Kapitan* Gustav Bachmann, argued that it was von Bethmann-Hollweg's responsibility to make Germany's case clear to the world: the German submarines were being compelled to adopt the tactics they were using in response to the Royal Navy and the British government playing fast and loose with the interpretations of international law. Trying to observe all the details of international law or making exceptions for particular types of ships played straight into the hands of the British, who seemed to be rewriting the rules of search and seizure on a daily basis, and whose distant blockade of Germany was, by German definition, illegal. It was tantamount to asking the German Navy to fight with its hands tied.

Yet Wilhelm, and even more so von Bethmann-Hollweg, understood that while the details of international law were too complex and convoluted for most Americans to grasp, those same Americans had no difficulty in imagining the face of a drowned child who died as a result of a U-boat attack. In mid-March 1916, the Chancellor was able to have some of von Tirpitz's ministerial powers removed, which prompted the Navy secretary's resignation but strengthened von Bethmann-Hollweg's position in trying to restrict the U-boats' freedom of action. When, less than a week later, the cross-channel steamer *Sussex* was torpedoed with the loss of 80 lives, four of them American, Wilhelm's worst fears seemed to be coming true, as President Wilson sent a sharply worded note of protest to Berlin, warning the Kaiser and his government that "unless the Imperial Government should now immediately declare and effect an abandonment of its present methods of submarine warfare against passenger ships and freight-carrying vessels, the Government of the United States can have no choice but to sever diplomatic relations."

Bluntly put, the U-boats had brought America and Germany to the brink of war. The Kaiser had little choice: on May 4, 1916, he issued an Imperial Order directing that no more unresisting passenger liners or merchantmen were to be attacked without warning and without giving those aboard time to safely take to the lifeboats.

Now that the U-boats were effectively limited to attacking purely military targets, if Britain's overseas lifelines were to be cut, they had to be severed by the guns of the High Seas Fleet. The time had come for the long-awaited confrontation between the German battleships and battlecruisers moored at Wilhelmshaven and their counterparts riding at anchor in Scapa Flow, the dreadnoughts of the Royal Navy.

Chapter 2

Dreadnoughts, Battleships, and Battlecruisers

In 1860 the Royal Navy launched a ship that has come to be regarded as "the first battleship of the modern age," HMS *Warrior*. Though she resembled a conventional wooden-hulled ship of the line, with three square-rigged masts and an auxiliary steam engine, in every aspect of her design and construction that mattered she was a complete break from the naval traditions of the past. Steam-powered, with the masts rather than the engine meant for auxiliary power, screw-propelled, with mounting guns that fired explosive shells rather than solid shot, and built of iron from the keel up, *Warrior* was faster, more maneuverable, better protected, and more powerfully armed than any of her contemporaries. She embraced the best of the successful new technologies of the Steam Age, making every other warship in the world obsolete, and introduced what was for the next nine decades fundamental elements of warship design.

And yet it is astonishing to see how the most profound significance of *Warrior's* introduction into the British fleet has been, for the most part, overlooked. By simultaneously embracing all of the successful developments in contemporary naval technology, she gave lie to the myth that has come to be perpetuated about the nineteenth century Royal Navy, that it was an utterly hidebound, fossilized service with an institutionalized dislike of anything new or innovative. Far from it: almost every innovation in tactics, weapons, designs, and equipment that was embraced by the world's navies in the nineteenth and twentieth centuries was introduced or developed by the Royal Navy. Conservative the British Admiralty certainly was—hidebound and fossilized it was not.

It was not that the admirals of "the Andrew," as the Senior Service was called, dreaded *any* change and innovation; what they dreaded was embracing the *wrong* one. It is something of an article of faith among those who have no real understanding of either warfare or military and naval affairs that senior officers, generals and admirals alike, are always incorrigible opponents of change, progress, new technology, and new weapons, fiercely clinging to the ways and means of battle that they knew in their youth, and fiercely resistant to any innovation that might disrupt their comfortable, predictable, well-ordered ways of combat. What was good enough for Waterloo or Trafalgar, they supposedly argued, was good enough for the present, an attitude that leads to their castigation by the proponents of whatever tactic or invention is being espoused.

Certainly "tradition" and bureaucratic inertia—along with a granted lack of imagination on the part of more than a few senior soldiers and sailors—played a part in the real as well as perceived lack of technical progress in the armed forces of the Great Powers in the nineteenth century. But, while field marshals and fleet admirals of that era are often lampooned for their refusal to embrace developing technologies that were experiencing great success in the civilian world, the mockery displays an ignorance of the powerful forces at work that inhibited changes in weaponry and tactics.

Such a derisive attitude overlooks one vital detail: the weapons and tactics to which the hidebound conservative officers allegedly clung, limpet-like, *worked!* "We've always done it this way!" was not merely an excuse given to avoid change, it was also a declaration that the weapons and tactics in question were the result of hard-won and often bloody experience. All competent officers, whether soldiers or sailors, understand that, in order to succeed in their profession, they must be willing to expend material and sometimes lives, but no competent officer is ever willing to expend either needlessly. War was not a mere intellectual exercise: it exacted a toll in flesh and blood as well as powder and steel.

There is a term that gained popularity in military circles in the late twentieth century, though the concept is older than the Roman legions: "soldier proof." It has become a given that if any weapon or piece of equipment can be broken, then some soldier, sailor, airman, or marine will find a way to break it. No doubt some of the first iron swords issued to Athenian hoplites were broken or bent within days of their issue, and the rankers' habit of at one time or another somehow breaking every piece of equipment in sight has been a plague on armed forces ever since. Consequently, weapons and the means of using them—tactics—that are above all else reliable become coveted by military leaders. No general or admiral wants to go into battle with weapons that might not work or rely on tactics that are flawless in theory but impossible to execute in action. "Back to the drawing board" may be an acceptable response to failure for an engineer, but for leaders in wartime, there is no such benign equivalent: failure means battles lost, which in turn means lives, territory, wealth, even nations, lost as well.

In the morning of the Industrial Revolution, when new inventions and technologies were appearing on an almost daily basis, successfully guessing which inventions and technologies that might have military applications would prove practical, workable, and reliable required something approaching genius. Genius is, as Otto von Bismarck once observed, hearing the distant hoofbeat of the horse of history and then leaping to catch the passing horseman by the coattails. The problem for the Royal Navy in the nineteenth century was deciding at which horse and horseman to lunge, since for every new concept and technology that ultimately became successful there were dozens that proved to be dead ends. It was a task that required not genius, but clairvoyance.

The retention of masts and sails on warships long after the introduction of steam power is a popular target of critics bent on lampooning the Victorian Royal Navy, with their arguments often echoing the idea that the ships' captains and the Admiralty's senior officers disdained steam power simply because they preferred the sails on which they had been brought up in the Andrew.

Unlike a certain number of older officers who *did* want to cling to masts and sails, younger officers coming up through the ranks were a different story: they were quite prepared to embrace steam power, but at the same time they were being trained to be extremely practical. Well into the 1880s steam was still not a wholly reliable system of propulsion, and the lack of power that plagued those early steam engines is best illustrated by a brief passage from Rudyard Kipling's *McAndrew's Hymn,* written in 1894:

> *I mind the time we used to serve a broken pipe wi' tow.*
> *Ten pound was all the pressure then—Eh! Eh!—a man wad drive;*
> *An' here, our workin' gauges give one hunder' fifty-five!*

Thus for much of the age of the Victorian Navy, steam engines were chronically underpowered—and short ranged as a consequence—while their reliability was often questionable. Even the crack transatlantic liners of the day used their sails as auxiliaries to their steam power plants.

Until the 1880s, technical progress was in such a constant state of flux that the ships of every major navy were a rather motley collection of various designs, the brainchildren of a melange of theories regarding firepower, protection, and the best layout of a ship's armament. Armor grew in thickness at the same time guns grew in bore, as the constant seesaw of supremacy between gunpower and protection rocked back and forth, while ships began sporting secondary and even tertiary batteries, until it seemed that every space on board where a gun could be mounted was occupied by one. Main guns began to be housed in revolving turrets, which experience on both sides of the Atlantic had proven to be the superior method of mounting. At the same time, though, positioning gun turrets along with masts and rigging so that there was minimal interference between them and the guns' fields of fire was a challenge that no naval designer of the era really successfully surmounted. The ancient tactics of ramming even enjoyed a brief vogue during one of the periods when armor was stronger than guns, and hulls specially strengthened with ram bows were built; several serious peacetime accidents resulted in one ship ramming and sinking another.

By 1892, however, much of the nonsense and flights of fancy in naval design had, for the Royal Navy at least, been winnowed out, and the class of battleships introduced that year became the template for every other navy in the world for the next decade. This was the seven-ship *Royal Sovereign* class, the brainchild of Sir William White, one of the greatest naval architects of all time. The *Royal Sovereign* design mounted a main armament of four heavy guns mounted in pairs in a barbette at each end of the superstructure, with a secondary battery positioned amidships. Turrets replaced the barbettes in subsequent classes. The protection plan was well thought-out, and although she was larger than any battleship previously built, at 14,150 tons, *Royal Sovereign* was capable of 17½ knots, making this class the fastest capital battleships afloat.

Nine successive classes of battleships followed the *Royal Sovereign's* layout and were essentially nothing more than improvements on the basic design. This trend lasted through the two ships of the *Lord Nelson* class, the last British battleships built before the introduction of HMS *Dreadnought*. While it was imitated by every other major navy in the world, with the exception of the French, who continued to make strange excursions into the naval neverland, by 1905 it was ripe for replacement by a design specifically formulated to take advantage of the technical developments of the previous decade. It was at this moment that Admiral Sir John Arbuthnot Fisher turned the whole of the naval world on its collective ear.

Known among ordinary seamen as well as the public who adored him as "Jackie," Fisher has been called "the greatest British admiral since Nelson," and in terms of his influence and effect on the Royal Navy, it is a fair description. But while Nelson was a fighting admiral, Fisher was a strategist and administrator, and in a sense was closer in the role he played to that of Admiral John Jervis, First Earl St. Vincent, who was the mastermind behind the strategy that culminated in Nelson's victory at Trafalgar.

Dreadnoughts, Battleships, and Battlecruisers

Born in Ceylon in 1841, the son of an infantry officer who turned plantation owner, John Fisher had entered the Royal Navy as a midshipman at the age of 13 and had worked his way up through the officer ranks, commanding his first ship at the age of 35 and his first battleship at 36. He progressed through various fleet commands, all of them with marked success, but his finest hour was between 1904 and 1910 when he was First Sea Lord. In those six years he reorganized the Royal Navy, most significantly by first establishing a Reserve Fleet and then by reducing the number of the Royal Navy's far-flung squadrons, instead concentrating the whole of the fleet's battleship strength into a newly created Home Fleet, which was then redesignated, appropriately enough, the Grand Fleet. He scrapped or sold old, obsolescent ships, freeing up experienced men and money for new units; conceived and built the dreadnought battleship; introduced submarines and the 13.5 inch gun; overhauled the navy's education and training programs; and oversaw the construction of 161 warships, including 22 new battleships. It was an astonishing performance; most astonishing of all was his masterpiece, HMS *Dreadnought*.

Fisher was fiery tempered and passionate, given to great angers and great kindnesses. With dark, almost black eyes and a curiously Oriental face, he characterized himself as "ruthless, relentless, and remorseless." He certainly was unforgiving when dealing with officers who crossed him professionally; he saw to it that their careers were effectively ended. He had the advantage of almost always being right—consequently few officers, or civilians for that matter, dared to cross him. But he was usually right because he was a genius, and more importantly he was one of those tantalizingly rare geniuses who could instantly identify which new weapons and weapon systems would be successful and then pursued their development relentlessly. It is worth noting that he was one of the first British naval officers to grasp the potential first of the torpedo, then of the submarine; at the same time he was one of the earliest advocates of long-range gunnery training for the Royal Navy and was among the first to champion director fire.

While Fisher had a passion for efficiency and organization, they were always the means to an end, never ends in themselves. He never lost sight of the purpose of both—to improve and enhance the fighting qualities of the Royal Navy. He believed passionately in the need for the ships of the Royal Navy to be able to strike hard and effectively at their foes, and in the first decade of the twentieth century, as in the previous 400 years, the dominant weapon at sea was still the great gun.

Fisher understood this, for all of his prescience about torpedoes and submarines. Gunnery became his ultimate passion, and anyone who shared it was beyond reproach: he once remarked about a fellow admiral on whose character critics cast various aspersions: "I don't care if he drinks, gambles, and

34 Distant Victory

womanizes—he hits the target!" During his tenure as First Sea Lord, he carefully guided the careers of officers who had specialized in gunnery so that in time of war they were in positions of leadership, prepared to carry the battle to the enemy.

At the same time, in Fisher the Royal Navy was fortunate to have the right man in the right place at the right time, for he possessed the vision to perceive the confluence of several design and technological developments that resulted in what amounted to a revolution in naval construction, tactics, and strategy. Fisher, whose boundless energy, *bonhommie*, and drive never concealed the fact that he possessed a truly first-class intellect, perceived an approaching revolution in naval warfare, as technology and tactics converged to compel a new design in battleships that was as complete a break with past designs as *Warrior* had been almost a half-century earlier. With characteristic energy, he pounced on it.

Every warship design is a compromise effected between three competing factors: speed, protection, and firepower. The most successful designs are those that strike the best balance among the three; they are interrelated and to some degree mutually exclusive, hence the need for compromise. In order to achieve high speed, a large power plant consisting of big, powerful engines fed by banks of boilers is required, which dictates hull size—the larger the power plant, the larger the hull. To keep enemy shells from damaging this power plant, the hull must be protected by armor, which is heavy, and increased weight means decreased speed. In addition to the space required for the boilers and engines, the guns, shell hoists, and magazines have to be accommodated within the hull and protected as well, meaning even more weight. Speed can be increased only by employing larger engines or decreasing the weight of the guns and armor; reducing the armor means less protection and an increased probability of the ship being damaged or even sunk by enemy shells, while decreasing the number of the guns reduces the warship's ability to deal serious damage to its opponents. What Jackie Fisher was about to do was introduce the most effective and successful compromise among these competing factors in naval history.

The reasoning behind the proliferation of multiple calibers in main, secondary, and tertiary batteries aboard battleships in the 1890s, along with steady increases in the bores of those guns, was that the prevailing tactical doctrines of the late nineteenth century encouraged engagement at any and all ranges. The heavy guns of the main battery were to deal "knock-out blows" to the enemy, while the more rapidly firing medium- and light-caliber guns of the secondary and tertiary batteries were meant to overwhelm an enemy with a "hail of fire" intended to wreak havoc on the superstructure and upperworks and at the same time cause critical casualties among the enemy crew.

Dreadnoughts, Battleships, and Battlecruisers

Unfortunately for this doctrine—or the lack of one—it led toward problems with spotting the fall of shells necessary for the range corrections that would ultimately produce hits. A gun captain, firing his weapon, watched for the spout of water sent up by the fall of the round he had just fired or, ideally, for a hit on the target. Knowing the time it took for a round of a given caliber to travel the known distance, as determined by range-finding equipment, between the firing ship and its target, the gun captain then made corrections in his gun's bearing and elevation to compensate for his shell's arrival short of or over the target, ahead of or behind it. But the hail of fire so popular with Victorian naval architects and armchair experts produced a curtain of shell splashes, which more often than not obscured the target, making accurate observation and correction a near impossibility. The two ships of the last class of "traditional" Victorian-era battleships, *Lord Nelson* and *Agamemnon,* carried main batteries of four 12-inch guns, along with ten 9.2-inch pieces; the French, Italian, and Japanese navies all introduced ships virtually identical to them. Even under conditions of perfect visibility, at the ranges that the Royal Navy expected to engage its enemies—10,000 yards or more —the shell splashes of a 12-inch shell were virtually indistinguishable from those of a 9.2-inch round. In the middle of a battle, with smoke, spray, mist, fog, rain, or some combination of all of them surrounding the firing ship and its target, such a distinction simply could not be made, permitting accurate gunnery at little more than point-blank ranges.

The solution to the problem appears to have occurred more or less simultaneously to several navies and naval architects: combine the concept of the hail of fire with a main armament of guns of uniform caliber and mount them in greater numbers than ever before carried by a battleship. Starting around 1903, naval designers in Great Britain, Italy, Japan, and the United States all began work on plans for ships with main armaments of eight or more 12-inch guns, double the main battery carried by a traditional battleship. Vittorio Cuniberti, chief naval constructor for the Kingdom of Italy, is generally credited with first articulating the idea of the "all-big-gun" ship in the 1903 edition of *Jane's Fighting Ships,* although Admiral Fisher claimed in his memoirs that *he* had conceived the idea as early as 1900 while still in command of the Mediterranean Fleet. In any case, who originated the concept and when is irrelevant, for Fisher's vision and inspiration transcended that of all of his contemporaries. He decided that a speed advantage of at least three knots was necessary for the new battleship; while that was hardly a stroke of genius, how he chose to accomplish it was. Since the introduction of steam engines that powered oceangoing ships, they had all been one form or another of a reciprocating engine; this included every battleship built for the Royal Navy up to this time. After consulting the finest technical minds in Britain, Fisher was determined that his new battleship would be powered by turbines instead.

Reciprocating engines were made up of a series of cylinders, ranging from as few as two in number to as many as ten, inside of which heavy steel pistons were moved up and down by steam pressure. A connecting rod attached to a crankshaft converted the piston's vertical motion into rotary motion, which then turned the propellor shaft. This meant that every time the shaft made a single revolution, the piston had to be moved downward, its momentum stopped, then moved upward, and its momentum halted again at the top of the stroke—the whole process being repeated sometimes as many as 120 times a minute. The pistons, rods, and shaft were subjected to a constant, extraordinary pounding, compounded by the number of cylinders in the engine. The brass bearings carrying the loads between piston and connecting rod, and connecting rod and crankshaft, required constant attention and adjustment —it was not unknown for hoses to keep steady jets of water playing on an overheating bearing during prolonged high-speed runs. The vibration created was bone-shaking, the noise deafening, and the clouds of steam the engines emitted were blinding. A reciprocating engine room was a dangerous place, the decks slick with oil and water, making footing treacherous, and as the machinery was open, falling into the maw of a thrashing collection of connecting rods, crankshafts, and counterweights was a constant peril. The din made carrying on normal conversation difficult, and hearing orders shouted down from the bridge through a voice tube or over a telephone was often a dicey proposition.

Turbines produced their power through rows of carefully designed blades attached to a central rotor. When steam was ducted against the turbines, the entire rotor assembly spun, its motion steady, constant, and turning in only a single direction. This made the contrast of the engine room of a turbine-driven ship with that of one powered by reciprocating engines astonishing. Gone were the huge expanses of exposed, noisy moving machinery, with all of their attendant hazards. Turbines were far quieter, they caused no clouds of steam to fill the engine spaces, and the vibration they created was remarkably mild compared with the pounding of the great masses of metal being shunted back and forth in a reciprocating engine. Even more significant was that the rotor of the turbine was connected directly to the propellor shaft, so steam acted directly on the shaft, resulting in very little wasted motion or loss of power, and vastly reduced stresses on the moving parts.

There was another significant advantage that turbines offered over reciprocating engines: smaller size. The only way to significantly increase the power output of a reciprocating engine was to make it larger, either by increasing the size of the cylinders and the length of their stroke or by increasing their numbers. There were practical limits, though, to this process; increased cylinder size and length of stroke meant increasing the height, which took up volume inside the ship. Increasing the number of cylinders simply increased the overall length of the entire engine. Already there were engines that stood almost 40 feet tall and 80 feet in length, with cylinders more than 8 feet in diameter. Any dramatic increase in the horsepower produced by such engines would require a corresponding increase in size; there was the real possibility that the engines might actually become too big for the hulls they were meant to be driving.

For turbines, the key to increased power was an increase in the number of blades attached to the turbine rotor. While this could be done by increasing a given rotor's diameter, it was more easily and efficiently accomplished by simply lengthening the rotor, increasing the number of rows of blades. By eliminating the need for pistons, connecting rods, and crankshafts, turbines could be built that were much smaller than a piston engine with a similar power output; as a rule of thumb, a turbine required roughly half the space of its reciprocating counterpart. This meant smaller engine rooms, which allowed for better watertight subdivision, increasing a ship's survivability. It also freed space for more boilers, which in turn provided more steam for the turbines, driving the ship even faster.

Taken together, turbine power and all big-gun armament, the design produced by the Admiralty at Fisher's direction instantly made every battleship built to that point obsolete. The keel of the new warship was laid in the Royal Navy Dockyard at Portsmouth on October 2, 1905, and the First Sea Lord was determined that she would be completed and commissioned in a year. By the following February the hull was ready for launching, and on February 10, His Majesty King Edward VII broke a bottle of champagne across the new ship's bow, loudly declaring, "I christen you *Dreadnought!*" as the hull began its slide down the ways.

Less than seven months later, on October 1, 1906, one day shy of a year from the laying of her keel, HMS *Dreadnought* went to sea for the first time. So radical in her appearance, yet at the same time so undeniably powerful compared to all other battleships afloat, it was clear to even the most casual observer that she was ushering in a new era of naval power. She was 527 feet in length, with a beam of 82 feet and a displacement of 18,100 tons. Her ten 12-inch guns were sited in five twin turrets, one placed forward of the bridge, one on each side of the ship abreast of the forward funnel (a position known as "wing" turrets), and a pair in tandem on her long quarterdeck. For protection against destroyers and torpedo boats she mounted twenty-seven 12-pounder quick firing guns, and five 18-inch torpedo tubes added an extra offensive punch. So complete was her superiority and so profound her influence on battleship design that "dreadnought" became the generic term for every battleship that was built subsequent to her.

The ship was not without her critics. There was a tremendous row in Parliament when her construction was announced, in particular from David Lloyd George, who condemned her as "a piece of wanton and profligate ostentation," demanding to know why the ship had been authorized when in effect it reduced the rest of the Royal Navy to obsolescence. "We declared, 'Let there be dreadnoughts.' What for? We did not require them, nobody was building them, and if anyone had started building them, we, with our greater resources, could have built them faster than any country in the world." Nor was Lloyd George the ship's lone critic: naval experts, designers, and architects across Britain scrutinized her and found *Dreadnought's* design wanting in some respect, often because she did not incorporate their particular pet concepts or theories. Sir William White, who had designed many of the Royal Navy's earlier battleships, joined forces with Admiral Sir Charles Beresford, an influential Member of Parliament, in denouncing "putting all one's eggs in one or two vast, costly, majestic but vulnerable baskets." But the experts, along with Lloyd George, were wrong: little more than a month after *Dreadnought* joined the fleet, the Imperial Japanese Navy commissioned the all big-gun *Satsuma,* and a year later the United States Navy commissioned the USS *South Carolina* and *Michigan,* two ships of an "all big-gun" design whose construction had, unknown to Fisher and the Admiralty, actually begun *before* that of HMS *Dreadnought.* Clearly the concept embodied in *Dreadnought* was an idea whose time had come. Fisher had, in fact, produced a superior design, for both the *Satsuma* and *South Carolina* classes were powered by reciprocating engines, rather than the turbines that propelled *Dreadnought,* and as a consequence were significantly slower.

Dreadnought herself proved to be one of a kind, as operational experience with the fleet soon began to highlight defects in some of her details, from the siting of the mainmast abaft the forward funnel, where smoke interfered with spotting, to problems with her steering engines, which were underpowered. When a class of new ships was authorized in 1906, rather than simply build repeats of *Dreadnought,* the Admiralty revised her design, resulting in the three slightly larger ships of the *Bellerophon* class. Some 500 tons heavier than *Dreadnought,* the *Bellerophons* carried the same armament of ten 12-inch guns in the same five-turret arrangement. The three ships of the *St. Vincent* class that followed next repeated this layout, but the ships themselves were more than 1000 tons heavier than *Dreadnought,* most of the additional weight being given over to added armor.

One of the flaws in *Dreadnought's* design was that when firing a broadside the wing turret on the opposite side of the ship could not be brought to bear,

Dreadnoughts, Battleships, and Battlecruisers

depriving her of the use of two guns. It was no trivial matter: the British 12-inch naval rifle was an outstanding weapon. With a range of over 20,000 yards (ten miles) and firing a shell weighing 850 pounds, the 12-inch gun could wreak havoc on its targets. If all ten of *Dreadnought's* guns could be brought to bear, she could have thrown 8,500 pounds of metal and high explosive at her enemies; as it stood, with a broadside of only eight guns, that figure was reduced to 6,800 pounds. By 1908, when the next class of dreadnoughts was being designed, the challenge for the Admiralty architects was to find a way of bringing all the guns these ships would mount to bear on as many bearings as possible, in particular allowing them to fire on either broadside.

It was not as simply resolved a problem as it might have seemed at first glance. The obvious answer, putting all of the gun turrets on the ship's center line, was unfeasible: gun turrets take up a lot of space, both above and below deck, and placing all the guns on the center line would drastically increase the length of the hull required. This was not possible because at the time the Royal Navy possessed no dry docks or fitting-out basins capable of accommodating hulls exceeding 600 feet in length.

The solution produced on the *Neptune* class was twofold. First, the designers put the wing turrets in echelon amidships, with the portside turret slightly ahead of the starboard one, and breaks in the superstructure that allowed each turret to fire across the deck onto the opposite beam. The second part of the solution lay in superimposing the two aft turrets, an arrangement that the American success with the *South Carolina,* whose four turrets were sited in two superimposed pairs, one forward of the superstructure, the other one aft of it, demonstrated the practicality of the concept.

The next class was known as "second-generation" dreadnoughts, for they introduced the first major increases in armament as well as displacement. The four ships of the *Orion* class were each more than 23,000 tons, carried much heavier armor than their predecessors, and abandoned the tried and true 12-inch gun for a new design of 13.5-inch caliber. By this time the navy had enlarged its dry docks and basins and was able to accommodate larger hulls, so all ten guns mounted by each of the *Orion*-class ships were carried in center line turrets, giving vastly increased fields of fire to all of their guns.

The switch to the 13.5-inch gun was, of course, part of a process that had begun centuries earlier in the days of fighting sail, the effort to build bigger and more powerful ships than those of an enemy; *Dreadnought* herself was the embodiment of this idea. But, although the new gun's increase in size over its predecessor sounds modest, it was, in fact, enormously more powerful. The weight of an artillery projectile increases geometrically in relationship to the dimensions of the gun's bore, so while a 12-inch shell weighed a not-inconsiderable 850 pounds, the added 1.5 inches in bore meant that the

40 Distant Victory

13.5-inch shell massed a formidable 1,250 pounds, an increase of almost 50 percent. A full ten-gun salvo from an *Orion*-class dreadnought hurled over six tons of metal and high explosive towards enemy ships as far away as 25,000 yards—more than 12 miles. Just as impressive, as experience was gained with the new 13.5-inch gun, was the discovery that it was incredibly accurate and remarkably reliable, two invaluable characteristics for naval ordnance.

The two classes of dreadnoughts that followed the *Orions,* the *King George V* class and the *Iron Dukes,* each of four ships, were essentially improvements of that design, in much the same way that the *Bellerophons* and *Neptunes* were improvements on the original *Dreadnought.* What followed them was a class of ships that came to define the modern battleship even more completely than did *Dreadnought.* So great was their physical, emotional, and visceral impact that for three generations they were the embodiment of the Royal Navy itself: the five ships of the *Queen Elizabeth* class.

By building larger hulls than any previous class of dreadnoughts, reducing the main battery from five twin turrets to four, giving them hotter-burning oil-fired boilers instead of coal-fired units, which produced more heat and thus more steam, resulting in higher speeds than had ever before been achieved by a battleship, and being armored on an unprecedented scale, the *Queen Elizabeth* class approached the perfect balance of speed, protection, and firepower. Six hundred forty feet in length, 91 feet in beam, with a displacement of 30,000 tons, these newest dreadnoughts were at once awesome yet elegant, terrible in their power yet graceful in their lines. They may well have been the handsomest battleships ever built.

One characteristic that set them apart from all other dreadnoughts but was invisible to observers was their speed. The decision to switch from coal firing to oil firing did not come easily to the Admiralty, and again it was not tradition or conservatism that lay at the root of the Royal Navy's reluctance. The heavy, black bituminous mined from seemingly inexhaustible veins in the South Wales valleys was the finest fuel coal in the world. More importantly, its source was secure: short of physically invading the British Isles and occupying the coal fields, no enemy could deny fuel to the Royal Navy. Oil was a different story: Britain had no domestic source of fuel oil; sources had to be found overseas. But because oil burned so much hotter than coal, it permitted higher pressures in the steam head generated by the boilers, which meant that the turbines could be spun faster, increasing the ship's speed. This meant that the *Queen Elizabeth* class could reach speeds never before dreamed of for battleships: 25, even 26, knots. Such a speed advantage was priceless: it was so compelling an argument that Winston Churchill, who had been appointed First Lord of the Admiralty just a few months prior to the laying of the *Queen*

Elizabeth's keel, had little trouble persuading Parliament to authorize £12,200,000 to acquire a controlling interest in the Anglo-Persian Oil Company, as well as build the necessary storage facilities and tank farms to assure the Royal Navy a secure supply of oil. No battleship in any navy on the planet could escape the *Queen Elizabeths,* and once engaged, no battleship or dreadnought could stand up to them.

If the Royal Navy's 12-inch gun was impressive—and it was—and the 13.5-inch was magnificent, the British 15-inch guns mounted on the *Queen Elizabeth* class were nothing short of awesome. They were the largest guns then carried by any battleship of any navy in the world, and the most powerful. Because of their immense size—each barrel was over 52 feet long and the entire gun assembly weighed 100 tons—a major drama had played itself out at the British Admiralty when the decision was made to produce them.

All other factors being equal, the size and number of guns a warship is to carry dictates the size of the ships' hull, as well as the proportions of its framing and bulwarks; the hull must be capable of supporting not only the weight of the guns but also absorb the shock of recoil when they are fired. In the autumn of 1911 the successor to the *Iron Duke* class was already on the drawing boards with a projected armament of ten 13.5-inch guns when Churchill learned that a new 15-inch gun was being developed. There was still time to rework the new warship design to accommodate the new weapon, but no prototypes of the gun had yet been built, so no one knew if it worked properly or not. Instinctively Churchill felt it imperative that these new ships carry the largest, most powerful guns available to them, but risked the ruin of an entire class of dreadnoughts if the new 15-inch gun were anything less than a spectacular success.

His anxiety was founded in no small part because of his own position: he would be the person held responsible should the new gun prove a failure. Impetuous and headstrong for all of his intelligence and brilliance, Churchill knew he was mistrusted by politicians of both the Liberal and Conservative Parties for his refusal to put party loyalty above the dictates of conscience and personal conviction, and there were more than a few fellow members of Parliament who openly regarded him as little more than a political opportunist. "Fancy if they [the new guns] failed. What a disaster. What an exposure," he later wrote of his decision to authorize the redesign of the new class of ships to take the new guns. "No excuse would be accepted. It would all be brought home to me—'rash, inexperienced,' 'before he had been there a month' and producing 'this ghastly fiasco,' 'the mutilation of all the ships of the year.' What could I have said?" Admiral Fisher came to the First Lord's support, reminding him with typical forcefulness that the whole purpose of any dreadnought's existence was to hit enemy ships as hard as possible and keep on hitting them. To deprive the new ships of such powerful weapons, according to Fisher, would amount to treason against the Empire. Feeling reassured by the older man's confidence and determination, Churchill ordered the guns built and the new dreadnoughts modified to carry them.

Experience with the new guns proved the wisdom of Churchill's gamble, as the design proved to be extraordinarily reliable, highly accurate, and devastating in its effects. The 15-inch projectiles, each weighing 1,938 pounds, hurled out to a range of 35,000 yards—nearly 18 miles—were half again as heavy as those fired by the 13.5-inch, and dwarfed the rounds fired by the 12-inch. Even with her battery reduced by one turret from what had been the standard ten-gun armament for a British dreadnought, *Queen Elizabeth* could deliver a broadside of nearly eight tons; firing at a rate of one broadside every 60 seconds, she pulverized her opponents. It was these guns that prompted Churchill to offer this tellingly graphic metaphor to Parliament in May 1912 while describing the power of these guns:

> ...to imagine a battle between two great modern iron-clad ships, you must not think of...two men in armor striking at each other with heavy swords. It is more like a battle between two eggshells striking each other with hammers.... The importance of hitting first, hitting hardest, and keeping on hitting...really needs no clearer proof.

Classified as "fast battleships," the *Queen Elizabeth* class was formed into a separate squadron and attached to the Royal Navy's Battlecruiser Squadron, based at Rosyth in Scotland's Firth of Forth, to augment the fighting power of the Grand Fleet's scouting arm. What was apparently overlooked by everyone was the subtle—and dangerous—irony of this assignment: with their unparalleled firepower, protection, and speed, the *Queen Elizabeth*–class dreadnoughts made obsolescent the very ships they were meant to support—the British battlecruisers.

The "battlecruiser" was Admiral Fisher's other brainchild of the first decade of the twentieth century. While he firmly believed in the combination of dreadnoughts, destroyers, and submarines as the key to dealing with enemy battle fleets, he was also aware of the vulnerability of Britain's shipping lanes to a *guerre de course*, a war on merchant shipping. Battleships could not protect the sea-lanes at the same time they were being concentrated to face the enemy fleet. Consequently, the need for cruisers to protect Britain's merchant shipping was a priority: despite being one of the submarine's earliest advocates, Fisher was aware of the type's limitations in speed and range, while destroyers lacked firepower and protection. Cruisers were the answer.

The first true "cruisers" were built around 1880. Direct descendants of the frigates of the days of sail, cruisers were large, swift, oceangoing warships, smaller in displacement than battleships but significantly faster. With top speeds usually between 28 and 30 knots, and carrying a battery of 8 to 12 medium guns (usually of 4-inch to 6-inch bore, though the largest of the breed carried 8-inch guns) the role of the cruiser was to serve as the eyes of the main battle fleet, scouting ahead and alongside it, giving prompt and accurate reports of the size and location of any enemy ships sighted. When operating in an independent role, detached from the fleet, they were to hunt down enemy merchant ships or defend friendly merchant vessels from marauding enemy cruisers.

These two missions—scouting for the fleet and protecting friendly shipping while at the same time raiding enemy commerce—soon led to the development of two types of cruisers. The first was known as the "armored cruiser," typically between 10,000 and 15,000 tons displacement, usually mounting a 6-inch battery of guns; their designation came from the belts of side armor, ranging from 2 to 4 inches in thickness, that were fitted along their hulls above and below the waterline. They were extraordinarily large ships, sometimes as much as 200 feet longer than contemporary battleships —but had extremely narrow beams: the fastest armored cruisers were capable of speeds approaching 30 knots. These ships were designed to serve as a screening force to drive off overly inquisitive enemy cruisers and to shield the battleships from attacks by enemy torpedo boats. The Royal Navy built 42 armored cruisers between 1885 and 1907, when the type was supplanted by the battlecruiser.

The other type of cruiser was known as a "protected cruiser," which was something of a misnomer, as they carried very little protection other than the shell plating of their hulls and superstructures. Protected cruisers' displacement could range from anywhere between 2,000 and 14,000 tons; they were considerably smaller than their armored cruiser cousins in every dimension. Seagoing slugfests were not their mission: the tasks assigned to protected cruisers were patrolling trade routes, escorting troopships and important merchant vessels, and hunting down enemy shipping and commerce raiders. One hundred and one protected cruisers were built by the Royal Navy between 1885 and 1907.

The introduction of quick-firing guns of up to 8-inch caliber—firing two, three, sometimes four rounds per minute—compared to the slow rate of fire of the 11- and 12-inch pieces, usually one round a minute, offered the tantalizing possibility of a fast ship armed with rapid-firing guns taking on and defeating a slower, heavily armed ship with only a few big guns and a battery of small 4- or 5-inch quick-firers. Rapid-firing guns, it was argued in some naval circles, could wreak havoc on her decks and gun positions before the battleship's main battery could even be brought to bear or find the range. This meant, so the argument went, that armored cruisers might actually have an advantage over battleships at some ranges.

In Italy and Russia designs were put forward for ships armed exclusively with 8-inch guns, which were seen as the ideal combination of rapid fire with the ability to penetrate substantial armor. Generally, however, the world's navies settled on a more-or-less standard design for armored cruisers that mounted a large gun, usually a single 8- to 10-inch weapon, in turrets fore and aft, with rows of medium caliber guns ranged amidships, intended to demolish the enemy's upperworks and lighter batteries, while the turret-mounted big guns delivered the "knockout punch" to the enemy hulls.

There was a time when these new armored cruisers seemed the coming thing, and one French admiral, Francois Fournier, argued in the mid-1890s that they were in fact "universal" ships that could fulfill the role of battleships as well as protecting—or raiding—merchant ships on the high seas. It is possible that Fournier's thinking influenced Fisher, who is known to have read the French admiral's writings, when the British admiral was formulating the concept that eventually became the battlecruiser.

Speed had always been an obsession of Fisher's, leading him once to lay down the famous dictum that "Speed is armour." His belief, and it was not unrealistic, was that a fast ship could dictate the terms of a naval action by being able to choose the range at which it would be fought. If the enemy tried to close in, a fast ship could open the range at will; if the enemy attempted to flee, a fast ship could always overtake. And, of course, the faster a ship moved, the more difficult it was for the enemy to find the range in order to hit and do damage.

In this perspective the idea of an exceptionally fast and well-armed "supercruiser" standing off and destroying a slower enemy battleship at ranges where the battleship could not effectively return fire had a certain appealing logic. The next link in Fisher's chain of reasoning was not quite as convincing: because it would be harder to hit, the supercruiser would not need as much armor as a battleship, and the weight saved could then be given over to heavier guns and faster machinery. To Fisher, as good as *Dreadnought* was, she was still just a better battleship; his concept of the supercruiser was an echo of Fournier's "universal" ship, a "New Testament," as Fisher called it, in warship design.

Similar in size and main armament to the dreadnoughts, they would be significantly faster—but significantly less well-protected. The high speed he envisioned—25 knots or more—could be achieved only by radical increases in shaft horsepower, which in turn required huge power plants and consumed coal in prodigious amounts—all of which required space. In order for the design to be seaworthy, sacrifices had to be made somewhere, and it was in armor that Fisher made them. Unlike *Dreadnought,* which struck a remarkable balance in the naval design triumvirate of speed, guns, and protection, or *Queen Elizabeth,* which approached perfection in that balance, Fisher proposed a distinctly unbalanced design, where firepower and speed were paramount and protection was a distant third.

Fisher was untroubled by flying in the face of centuries of naval wisdom. Believing as he did that "speed [coupled with heavy firepower] was its own best protection," he envisioned an operational doctrine for his "large armored cruisers," which popular usage soon designated "battlecruisers": they would be able to outgun or outrun any enemy warship. The battlecruiser's armor, though thin, would be sufficient to withstand the smaller caliber guns of a conventional armored cruiser or protected cruiser, while its superior speed would allow it to outrun any battleship or dreadnought it might encounter.

It did look good on paper. Of course, had Fisher clearly thought through the entire idea, he might have perceived its inherent flaws. Perhaps the most pernicious was the confidence he placed on speed: making a target more difficult to hit did not make it impossible to hit. Sooner or later the law of averages would catch up with one of his supercruisers, and she would be struck by one or more of the enemy's shells. Being so much more lightly armored than a true dreadnought, the battlecruiser would suffer proportionately greater damage. An enemy might be able to achieve only two or three hits on a battlecruiser, but they might prove sufficient to cripple or, given the right circumstances, even destroy her.

And what if other navies began building battlecruisers of their own? The whole premise of success for the battlecruiser was its superiority over traditional armored cruisers; it was folly to think that once the battlecruiser made its appearance, other navies would persist in constructing obsolete ships. When another navy began building battlecruisers, that advantage would disappear, and the Royal Navy's new ships would be as vulnerable to their foreign counterparts as armored cruisers had been to theirs. Should a British battlecruiser engage an enemy battlecruiser, neither would have an advantage: both would be heavily armed, both would have high speed—the whole philosophy of the battlecruiser, that it could outrun what it could not outfight, would collapse, as would, most likely, both ships in a battle of mutual annihilation.

Unconcerned by these questions, possibly never even asking them, Fisher ordered construction begun on the first three battlecruisers, HMS *Invincible, Inflexible,* and *Indomitable,* in the spring of 1906. At 560 feet in length, they were 30 feet longer than *Dreadnought,* though some ten feet narrower in beam, 78 feet to *Dreadnought's* 88; their displacement was almost identical to *Dreadnought's.* Their real difference lay in their speed. Designed for

25 knots, they purchased the extra four knots at a cost of double the horsepower *Dreadnought* required to make 21. The 46,000 shaft horsepower was produced by the steam generated by 31 boilers—*Dreadnought* required only 18. In order to make space for the extra boilers and their coal bunkers, the *Invincibles'* armament was limited to four twin 12-inch gun turrets, spaced almost equally along the length of the ship, the center two in echelon as on the *Neptune* class dreadnoughts.

For the speed Fisher demanded, a further penalty had to be paid. The *Invincibles* were far less well-protected than *Dreadnought,* their 7-inch armor belts, which in places tapered to as little as 4 inches, being less than two-thirds as thick as *Dreadnought's* and less than half of that on a *Queen Elizabeth.*

The follow-on class, the *Indefatigables,* were, like the *Bellerophons* that followed *Dreadnought,* simply improved *Invincibles,* mounting the same armament and carrying the same armor, but with more powerful engines and slightly higher speed. The introduction of the 13.5-inch gun meant that the next class of battlecruisers would have to be completely new designs, as the *Indefatigables* took their particular layout as far as it could go.

This "second generation" of British battlecruisers were immense ships; known as the "Big Cats," they were named *Lion, Princess Royal, Queen Mary,* and *Tiger.* At 700 feet in length, with a beam of 88 feet, and a displacement of 28,000 tons, they were among the largest ships in the world at the time of their building. Carrying the same ten-gun 13.5-inch armament of the second generation of dreadnoughts, their armor was only marginally better than that of the *Invincibles* and *Indefatigables.* Their speed, however, was astonishing. Designed for 26 knots, each of the quartet exceeded 28 knots on their sea trials. Long, low, and sleek, they were handsome ships—but time proved them to be very fragile.

They looked like dreadnoughts and were armed like dreadnoughts, so it was not long after the battlecruisers began joining the Grand Fleet that the inevitable happened. In early 1913 the Battle Cruiser Squadron was formed, detailed with the task of screening the Grand Fleet and providing a powerful reconnaissance force. It was *Brassey's Naval Annual* that first articulated the problem: "…an admiral having *Invincibles* in his fleet will be certain to put them in the line of battle where their comparatively light protection will be at a disadvantage and their high speed of no value." In other words, no fighting admiral worth his tarnished gold braid would be able to resist the temptation to add their guns to his battle line. The then-commander-in-chief of the Grand Fleet, Admiral George Callaghan, confirmed this when the Battle Cruiser Squadron was created, writing that their mission was "to engage enemy battle cruisers in a fleet action, or, if none are present, by using their speed to cross the bow of the enemy [dreadnoughts] and engage the van of his battle fleet." In the right hands, it might prove to be a priceless tactical innovation; in the wrong hands, this doctrine could be a recipe for disaster.

On the other side of the North Sea, the launch of *Dreadnought* came as nothing short of a profound shock to the admirals of the German High Seas Fleet. In 1860 when the Royal Navy launched HMS *Warrior,* the German Navy, like the German Empire, did not even exist. It took three wars and a coercive peace treaty with France to accomplish the latter, while building a truly seagoing fleet out of the rather ragtag coast defense force that the Kingdom of Prussia had possessed took decades longer. It was not until 1898 that Germany began building proper battleships, and when she did they were merely Teutonic versions of the *Royal Sovereign* class and its successors.

A series of navy laws passed by the Reichstag beginning in 1898 committed the Imperial Navy to an ambitious program of warship construction specifically directed at confronting the Royal Navy for supremacy on the world's oceans. The first two classes of battleships had already seen extensive sea duty, and the third, the *Deutschland* class, had been completed only the year before *Dreadnought* was launched. The new British warship caused more than consternation within the German Naval High Command: it threw the High Seas Fleet's entire strategic and operational planning into disarray, creating a disruption in naval construction that the German Navy was never quite able to overcome.

What had happened was simple enough: the next class of German battleships, successors to the *Deutschlands,* had already been laid down, and construction on the first ship of the class, *Nassau,* was already well advanced. Designed to be an all big-gun ship, mounting a dozen 11-inch guns, she was vastly inferior to *Dreadnought* in almost every respect. When *Dreadnought* went to sea and comprehension of her destructive capabilities began to dawn on the German admiralty, work on the *Nassau* class was abruptly halted while the admirals debated what modifications were necessary to keep *Nassau* and her sisters from becoming obsolete before they were even launched. More than a year passed before work was finally resumed on the *Nassau* class, precious time that was irretrievably lost, for by then the next class of British dreadnoughts, the *Bellerophons,* was already under construction.

If *Dreadnought* had not been built, *Nassau* might have been the ship to usher in the "all big-gun" ship era. Her main armament, 12 guns mounted in six twin turrets, was a variation on what had been the standard battleship layout for the previous two decades. One turret was situated at each end of the superstructure, while a pair of turrets were sited on each side of the ship; the arrangement if viewed from above resembled an elongated hexagon. The pairs of wing turrets on each side replaced the secondary batteries that had previously occupied those positions, and the arrangement gave the *Nassaus* the same broadside as *Dreadnought*—eight guns. But it was acquired with the price of the extra weight and complexity of those two additional turrets.

Moreover, the German 11-inch gun, while powerful, was not the equal of the British 12-inch, which outranged the German weapon as well as firing a shell weight half again that of the 11-inch gun. But what was really crippling to the *Nassau* class was Germany's inability to produce reliable marine turbines. Powered by a trio of triple-expansion reciprocating engines— *Dreadnought* was driven by a quartet of turbines—the top speed of the *Nassau* was barely 20 knots, fully a knot or more slower than the British ship.

Not that *Nassau* had no advantages of her own. In particular, her compartmentation and underwater integrity were better than *Dreadnought's*, meaning that she could better survive damage from shellfire as well as mines or torpedoes. But even those qualities had a price. The *Nassau* class, along with every subsequent class of German dreadnought, was cramped inside. Crew quarters were scattered wherever space for them could be found, rather than being sited near the ratings' action stations in spaces designed for crew accommodation; ventilation and lighting were often poor as well. This was because the German ships, despite the title of the High Seas Fleet, were not really designed for the waters of the North Atlantic; their hull forms were better adapted to the short swells of the North Sea and the Baltic rather than the long reaches of the open ocean. Their crews spent more time ashore living in barracks than they did aboard their ships. British ships had much better "habitability," as the term went: crews lived aboard their ships, their messes were larger than those on German warships, and quarters were located close to action stations. The ships themselves, longer and less beamy than their German counterparts, were designed with an eye to extended deployments steaming in the worlds' oceans.

When the *Nassau* and her sisters joined the High Seas Fleet in 1909 and 1910, fully a year after their original projected completion dates, they were quickly followed by the quartet of ships of the *Heligoland* class. Rather than follow the British practice of improving existing designs, the Germans chose to introduce a ship that had little in common with the *Nassau* class save for the layout of their main guns. Improvements were made in the siting of the new class's engine and boiler rooms, although they still relied on reciprocating engines. Significantly larger overall than the *Nassaus*, the *Heligolands* were able to mount 12-inch guns, and their greater beam allowed the wing turrets wider arcs of fire. Built with the same extensive watertight subdivision as the *Nassaus*—more than one observer likened their lower decks to a honeycomb of compartments—the *Heligoland* class ships proved capable of absorbing tremendous damage without sinking. The ability to take damage and remain

Dreadnoughts, Battleships, and Battlecruisers

afloat and an effective fighting unit was known as a ship's "lifing," and as the British learned throughout the Great War, German ships were without equal in this respect.

Yet the cold, hard truth was that, while they were trying to catch up to the British, not only in numbers of ships built, but in the ships' capabilities, the Germans were actually falling behind. Not until the third class of German dreadnoughts was introduced did the High Seas Fleet possess ships that were equal or superior to the original *Dreadnought*. When the *Kaiser,* lead ship of her class, joined the fleet in 1912, she mounted ten 12-inch guns sited in five twin turrets, was turbine powered, and was capable of speeds approaching 23 knots. In one aspect *Kaiser* was actually superior to *Dreadnought*—all five of her turrets were capable of firing to either beam, giving her a ten-gun broadside compared to the British ship's eight; this was accomplished by imitating the echelon arrangement of the midship's turrets introduced on the *Neptune* class. Longer, broader, and heavier than the *Heligolands,* the *Kaisers* were soon known as good sea boats: their stability in all but the roughest seas, as well as their ability to respond quickly to helm and engine orders, made them popular postings among German sailors and officers alike. The *Kaiser's* only drawback was not any inherent design flaw but rather a consequence of lack of foresight on the part of the Imperial Navy's Ordnance Board. While the German Naval High Command managed to convince itself that the 11-inch gun was the equal of the British 12-inch, when, in fact, it was not, the two navies' 12-inch guns matched up fairly equally. The problem was that while the Germans were mounting 12-inch guns the British were introducing the first class of 13.5-inch gun-armed dreadnoughts, the *Orions.* Amazingly, the Imperial Navy had no designs in hand for a larger-bore follow-on: when the main armament of the *Queen Elizabeth* class was made public, Fried. Krupp of Essen, the great steelmaker and gun manufacturer who provided the High Seas Fleet's ordnance, had to scramble to design a weapon of similar bore for the ships that were built as a reply. These were the *Bayern* class, very obviously German copies of the *Queen Elizabeths; Bayern,* though, did not join the fleet until the summer of 1916. By that time the Royal Navy had eight 15-inch gunned ships in service.

Unfortunately for the Imperial Navy, the last class of German dreadnoughts completed before the beginning of the Great War continued the institutional inferiority of the German fleet. Armed with ten 12-inch guns mounted in five center line turrets, the *König* class was the best-balanced, best designed dreadnoughts the Germans built. All five of their gun turrets were sited on the ship's center line, with the forward and aft pairs of turrets in superfiring positions, giving unparalleled arcs of fire. Like all the German warships their subdivision was complex and thorough, but even with their large size—26,000 tons—they were still cramped and uncomfortable. If the German dreadnoughts were inferior to their British counterparts in most major respects—and despite the later claims of British critics and German apologists, apart from the extensive subdivision of their hulls, there was nothing in their construction that was markedly superior to the work of British shipyards—the Imperial Navy's battlecruisers were a different story altogether.

Apparently Admiral Alfred von Tirpitz, State Secretary for the Navy, a position roughly corresponding to Britain's First Lord of the Admiralty, took the time to think through all of the implications of the battlecruiser concept. While he and the fiery Jackie Fisher shared much in common in their devotion to their profession and their respective fleets, von Tirpitz grasped the flaw in Fisher's reasoning that Fisher, dazzled perhaps by his own genius, never quite saw. Once Britain built battlecruisers, it was imperative that Germany have them as well.

Their response to *Invincible* was SMS *von der Tann*. Two thousand tons heavier than *Invincible* on a hull of similar dimensions, *von der Tann* mounted 11-inch guns, sited in four twin turrets arranged identically to *Inflexible's*. Turbine powered, she was just as fast as *Invincible*, and she carried a hidden advantage over her British counterpart: the additional tonnage she carried as well as the weight saved by mounting the smaller 11-inch guns was given over to armor, *von der Tann's* main belt and deck armor being very nearly equal to that of *Dreadnought's*.

This level of protection set the standard for the three subsequent classes of German battlecruisers: *Moltke* and her sister *Goeben* were essentially improved *von der Tanns*, while *Seydlitz* was an improved *Moltke*. Both classes had an additional pair of 11-inch guns sited in a fifth turret aft, and both were even more heavily armored than *von der Tann*.

The last German battlecruisers to be completed before the war began were the sister ships *Lützow* and *Derfflinger*. Their design reverted to an eight-gun main armament, but the guns were now the same 12-inch bore as the dreadnoughts of the High Seas Fleet. Armored almost as heavily as a dreadnought, although they were classed as battlecruisers (*schlachtkreuzer*), these two ships were closer in concept to the "fast battleship" as typified by the Royal Navy's *Queen Elizabeth*. Again in common with the German dreadnoughts was a heavily subdivided hull and extensive watertight compartmentation. And like their dreadnought cousins, their design was more suited to the waters of the North Sea than the open expanses of the Atlantic Ocean.

When war came, then, in August 1914, the Royal Navy was able to put to sea with 22 dreadnoughts; the five *Queen Elizabeths* joined the fleet over the next two years. They were supported by ten battlecruisers. Progress and development of these massive and powerful ships had been so rapid that by this time *Dreadnought* was no longer considered a first-rank fighting ship: she was relegated to service with the Channel Squadron, which was expected to see very little action. Less than ten years after she had made every other battleship ever built obsolete, obsolescence threatened to overtake *Dreadnought* herself.

Across the North Sea the High Seas Fleet boasted 17 dreadnought battleships, accompanied by five battlecruisers (*Moltke's* sister ship *Goeben* was stationed in the Mediterranean). The first ships of the *Bayern* class were not ready to join the fleet until 1916.

As the two immense fleets squared off across the North Sea when the Great War erupted in August 1914, all of Europe and much of the rest of the world waited breathlessly for the clash of titans that everyone knew must come sooner or later; it was only a matter of how it would be brought about. Now that the British and German navies had their fleets of dreadnoughts and battlecruisers, what remained to be seen was whether or not either nation had any idea what to do with them.

Chapter 3

Strategies and Stratagems

In 1890, a rear admiral retired from the United States Navy, Alfred Thayer Mahan, published a brilliant book called *The Influence of Sea Power on History*. Beginning with the Punic Wars between Rome and Carthage two centuries before Christ, Mahan forcefully and convincingly argued that the decisive factor in the most important wars in history—those that changed the flow of civilization's development—had been sea power, that is, the ability of one nation's navy to control strategic waterways and deny their use to the enemy, primarily through blockade. Mahan's thesis culminated in his representation of the decisive nature of the French blockade at Yorktown precipitating Cornwallis's defeat by Washington in 1783, and his demonstration that the Royal Navy was the one opponent Napoleon Bonaparte was never able to decisively defeat, while the Royal Navy's blockade of Europe had strangled the Continent's economy until Europe rose in anger to bring down Napoleon's empire.

In some ways Mahan was a seagoing von Clausewitz, who maintained that strategy was the method by which one nation imposed its will upon an enemy. Mahan's reasoning was logical, his examples persuasive, and his presentation eloquent. There was one flaw in Mahan's work—oversimplification: it gave the impression that sea power alone was the decisive influence on history, whereas the combination of sea power and land power had always been necessary to achieve the victories he described. Had it not been for the Continental armies, paid for with British gold, which repeatedly confronted Bonaparte and eventually toppled him, Nelson's victory at Trafalgar would have been glorious but hollow. While "that far-off line of storm-beaten ships on which the eyes of the Grand Army never looked stood between Napoleon and the dominion of the world," as Mahan described the Royal Navy's ships of the line, they could not themselves bring the Grand Army to bay. A truer conclusion, which Mahan actually approached but did not quite articulate, though the British inherently understood it, was that land power, when confronted with land and sea power combined, will always lose; while sea power alone cannot assure victory, but merely prevent defeat. Given the brilliance of Mahan's presentation and the obvious nature of the conclusions drawn from the examples he gave, this lapse was easily overlooked, and so Mahan's theories had profound effects on the British and German admiralties.

Of course, Mahan's ideas were so well received in London and Berlin because they could be interpreted to allow each nation's navy to draw exactly the conclusions that it wanted. For the British, Mahan's work was scholarly proof of what the Royal Navy instinctively had known for centuries, that a fleet superior in numbers and training to any and all possible opponents ensured command of the sea, with all the consequent strategic and economic benefits that command entailed. Throughout the nineteenth century the Royal Navy held to a policy of maintaining a fleet as large as the combined strength of any two possible enemies' navies (France and Russia were the usual suspects) in order to execute a strategy of blockading the enemy's coast while being able to simultaneously maintain a battle fleet at sea. Known as the Two Power Standard, it was the product of an empirical process that had evolved from hard-won experience in decades of warfare against dozens of enemies. Mahan's work simply made this article of faith, for that is what it really was, seem to be premeditated, an act of remarkable foresight on the part of their Lordships in Whitehall.

The doctrine of blockading an enemy coastline inherent in the Two Power Standard was simply the manifestation of Mahan's thesis of sea power. By bottling up an enemy's fleets, both merchant and naval, in port, and sweeping the seas of whatever remnants escaped before the blockade closed in, the blockade would allow the British merchant fleet unlimited access to the world's trade while at the same time denying it to the enemy.

This seemingly simple state of affairs had even more impact in the closing years of the nineteenth century than they did in Bonaparte's day, for by then no modern industrialized nation was economically self-sufficient: whether it was food for the populace or raw materials for the factories, some vital import could be cut off from an antagonist by the British fleet, ensuring that some crippling disruption would eventually occur. Should frustration spawned by the shortages build to the point where the enemy chose to sortie against the Royal Navy, the preponderance of strength possessed by the British fleet assured that, once the smoke of battle had dissipated and the wreckage was cleared away, the blockade still remained in place, now even more tightly than before.

Thus a blockade was a powerful form of naval warfare, though hardly glamorous and never swift, nor was it without risk. The Royal Navy's blockade of Napoleonic Europe, for example, lasted for 20 years, and there was always the chance that one of the blockaded nation's powerful trading partners might take exception to the loss of trade as well as the infringement on their rights to free passage. International agreements in the last years of the nineteenth century and the opening years of the twentieth century had gone far toward clearly defining the means and methods of accomplishing a blockade, while at the same time clarifying the status of neutral nations and their shipping in blockaded waters. Most nations accepted these definitions, although there were a few holdouts who insisted on complete freedom of the seas, most notably the United States, which held that its citizens had the right to travel wherever and whenever they chose, on any vessel of their choosing, with complete immunity from interference or attack. It was a position that eventually led to confrontation between the United States and the German Empire.

In the case of a war between Great Britain and Germany, a British blockade of German ports had the potential to devastate the Teutonic economy. Before 1914, a quarter of Germany's food was imported from overseas, in particular meat, fish, eggs, and dairy products. The United States sent 1.5 million tons of wheat into German ports annually, along with 3 million tons of feed grain. America also supplied two-thirds of the copper used by German industry and all of the cotton used by German textile mills. Half of the nitrates used by German agriculture and industry came from overseas—this last was a critical vulnerability, for nitrates were an irreplaceable component in the manufacture of high explosives and propellant charges for artillery rounds.

Every industrial nation was similarly vulnerable to blockade—France, for example, while self-sufficient in food production, was woefully deficient in the raw materials needed by modern industries, particularly ores. If the blockading fleet was at once larger than the forces opposing it, and it was intent on merely maintaining a blockade rather than seeking battle, it was painfully obvious that a small navy could not effectively intervene against a larger fleet to end the blockade. Consequently, the more ambitious Continental navies— Russia, France, and in particular Germany—began to explore ways of breaking the power of a blockade. The Russians were never able to develop a coherent naval policy, since the nation was in the midst of widespread social and economic upheaval while the army was given priority in reform, reorganization, and reequipment. In France Mahan's ideas resulted in the *Jeune Ecole,* the New School, a sort of doctrinal trip into a naval neverland of torpedo boats, quick-firing guns, and submarines that were often more dangerous to their crews than to an enemy; before it had run its course, this school of strategic thought reduced the French Navy to third-rate status, a blow from which it never fully recovered. In Germany, as might be expected, the method by which naval doctrine was developed was considerably more well-thought-out, and in the decades before the Great War, the German Navy and its strategy were synonymous with one man, Alfred von Tirpitz.

With his bald pate, forked beard, and determined gaze, the popular image of von Tirpitz has become something almost menacing, even sinister, as if he were anticipating the furies soon to be loosed on the world and was determined to unleash them no matter what. Nothing could be further from the truth: von Tirpitz was a patriot in the best sense of the word, and the steeliness in his expression was a product of his determination to do his utmost to see his country assume a place of world leadership. In many ways he was Germany's equivalent of Admiral Sir John Fisher, and their geniuses often paralleled one another.

Born on March 19, 1849, Alfred Tirpitz—the enobling "von" did not come until he was 51—was the son of a Prussian lawyer and judge, his childhood typically German middle class. An indifferent student, he saw service in the Prussian Navy as an escape from the grind of academia. Once enrolled as a cadet, Tirpitz, age 16, spent his first days at sea in the English Channel during Prussia's War of 1866 against Austria. There were no actions to be fought then, nor were there any during the Franco-Prussian War four years later. As a consequence, the Prussian War Ministry refused to allow the promotion records of the officers and men to list their service during the conflict as "wartime service," an embarrassment that von Tirpitz never forgot nor forgave.

Moving up to the rank of *Leutnant,* von Tirpitz began specializing in torpedoes in 1877, followed by a further specialization in torpedo boats a few years later. Given the responsibility for designing the new ships, as well as developing the tactics they would employ, Tirpitz came to work closely with Navy State Secretary Georg von Caprivi, which gave him his first taste of politics. In 1887 he was introduced to Crown Prince Wilhelm, who as Kaiser Wilhelm II became Tirpitz's political sponsor and champion. The next year he was given his first seagoing commands, the cruiser *Preussen* followed a year later by the cruiser *Württemburg.* In 1890, still a rather junior *kapitan,* he was appointed Chief of Staff of the German Baltic Squadron. Invited one evening to dine with the Kaiser and several senior officers at Kiel Castle, Tirpitz listened as Wilhelm, now enthroned as the Kaiser, asked for ideas on developing a proper navy for the newly minted German Empire. After hearing all of the senior officers' proposals, the Kaiser announced in a disgusted tone, "Here I have been listening to you arguing for hours that we must put an end to all this mess, and yet not one of you has made a really positive suggestion." Tirpitz boldly spoke up and declared that Germany must build battleships.

His comment struck a responsive chord in the Kaiser, who, nine months later, appointed Tirpitz as the Chief of Staff of the Naval High Command in Berlin, and personally commissioned him to develop a plan for constructing an oceangoing navy for Germany, as well as to produce a strategy for its employment in wartime. Once in Berlin he assembled a staff of like-minded colleagues and went to work with a fierce determination. His experience at sea convinced him that the German Navy had no naval strategy. Producing a book of tactical exercises, which he presented to the Kaiser on December 1, 1892, Tirpitz asserted that previous naval policy had resulted in an "aimless" strategy and a "heterogeneous collection of vessels from which one could not confidently expect any mutual cooperation in the event of war."

Tirpitz's accusation was based on experience: while developing his tactics, he had attempted to utilize the active ships in the German fleet, and in doing so found a hodgepodge of designs, displacements, gun sizes, speeds, and steaming ranges. In order for a fleet to be effective in wartime, it had to function as a unit, and could do so only if its component ships shared common characteristics in their capabilities and performance. Tirpitz argued for building battleships, organized into proper battle squadrons, which could meet an enemy fleet face-to-face. His arguments seemed to fall on deaf ears, however, and by 1895, Tirpitz, tired of the endless vacillations by the Kaiser, the Reichstag, and the Naval High Command, had enough and in disgust requested a transfer to sea duty. It was granted, and he spent the next two years as commander of the German Far East Squadron, based in Tsingtao, China.

It is worth noting at this point, as Tirpitz unknowingly stood on the threshold of the professional pinnacle of his career, that he was no seagoing von Schlieffen, devoid of any sentiments or sensibilities not wholly devoted to warfare and naval affairs. While he was "aggressive, ruthless and domineering" while at work at the Admiralty (he once acidly remarked to a young officer more fond of court life in Berlin than standing watches on the bridge of a warship, "You have very white hands for a man who hopes to command a cruiser!"), outside of his office he was polished and urbane. He was appreciative of subordinates who worked hard and was intensely devoted to his wife and two daughters.

He was also no Erich von Ludendorff, glacial, detached, hiding a highly neurotic personality behind a facade of impassivity and disdain. Tirpitz had flaws: he was highly emotional, and was sometimes subject to extreme mood swings; he was also something of a hypochondriac, although he was able to control it so sufficiently that it never appeared to interfere with his work. Like Jackie Fisher in the Royal Navy, he lived for his beloved navy; above all, like Fisher, Tirpitz was determined to prepare the Imperial Navy to do more than just show the flag—he was preparing the fleet to fight.

58   Distant Victory

Like most German sailors of his day, Tirpitz greatly admired the Royal Navy—in fact, it is not inaccurate to say that he was somewhat in awe of the British fleet. This may have been due in part to his anglophilia, for he was very much enamored of most all things English. It was as a cadet that he first encountered the depth and consequences of Great Britain's maritime and naval tradition: decades later he recalled in his memoirs how:

> Between 1864 and 1870 [the Prussian Navy's] real supply base was Plymouth, where Nelson's three deckers and the great wooden ships-of-the-line of the Crimean War lay in long rows up the river. Here were felt ourselves almost more at home than in the peaceful and idyllic Kiel, which only grumbled at Prussia.... In the Navy Hotel at Plymouth we were treated like British midshipmen.... Our tiny officer corps looked up to the British Navy with admiration.... We grew up on the British Navy like a creeping plant. We preferred to get our supplies from England. If an engine ran smoothly...if a rope or a chain did not break, then it was certain not to be the home-made article, but a product of English workshops—a rope with the famous red strand of the British Navy....

For its part, the Royal Navy looked on the fledgling German navy with a fondness that a big brother reserves for a younger sibling, encouraging its ambitions and supporting its growth, all the while never imagining it ever becoming strong enough to seriously threaten Britain's naval supremacy.

The German sailors, for their part, were eager to emulate "the Andrew." German officers readily adopted British naval traditions, the Admiralty's design bureaus openly copied British warships and equipment, while the Naval Staff openly readily followed the British example in organization and logistics. Even the uniforms worn by German seamen were curiously reminiscent of the jumpers donned by British "Jack Tars." It was not simply an example of mindlessly slavish mimicry: the Germans were modeling themselves after the greatest navy in the history of the world in the belief that such imitation would produce an attitude of professionalism and competence. What the Prussian and later German fleets could not accrue through experience, it was hoped, it would acquire through imitation. If the German Navy languished in the shadow of the German Army, kept there by generals jealous of their prerogatives and prestige, it was not for lack of spirit on the part of the German sailors.

When Wilhelm II ascended to the throne in 1889, he had already developed an admiration of his own for the Royal Navy, and within a half a decade of his becoming Kaiser he was considering plans to expand the German fleet into a significant seagoing power. In June 1904, he confided to King Edward VII at a dinner aboard the Imperial yacht *Hohenzollern,*

> When, as a little boy, I was allowed to visit Portsmouth and Plymouth...I admired the proud English ships in those two superb harbors. Then there awoke in me the wish to build ships of my own like these someday, and when I was grown up to possess as fine a navy as the English.

It was an extraordinarily candid admission on Wilhelm's part, who usually attributed the motivation of all of his ambitions to Divine Right and his consciousness of Germany's mission to rule the world.

In the first five years of his reign, however, Wilhelm seemed unable to make up his mind exactly what sort of navy he actually wanted. Incorrigibly belligerent—one observer remarked that "Wilhelm was always playing at war"—and suffering from a severe inferiority complex regarding his English cousins all the while he was admiring and attempting to emulate them, he was determined to build a High Seas Fleet that would command respect for his newly created empire. That was not an unreasonable position for the Kaiser, or any other head of state, to take: at issue was the form the navy that Wilhelm was to build would take. As the German economy began to grow in the last quarter of the nineteenth century, Germany suddenly found herself possessing the second-largest merchant marine in the world—only Great Britain's was larger. Suddenly Germany's economic interests were worldwide, and it was only sensible that some measure of protection be available to them and to the hundreds of German ships that were carrying cargoes to and from every corner of the globe.

This, of course, was an essential part of Mahan's thesis about sea power, and it became painfully obvious that Germany's huge merchant fleet was vulnerable to attack by even a third-rate navy. For decades, though, the German merchant marine had enjoyed the tacit understanding that it was under the protection of the Royal Navy, an understanding that had its foundation in the days of Waterloo, when the British and Prussians had formed the alliance that defeated Napoleon once and for all. It was this understanding that had allowed the German merchant fleet to grow to such an enormous size without simultaneously requiring the German Empire to construct a fleet for its protection.

For the vast majority of the German people, this was a perfectly acceptable state of affairs. It was the army that was popular both with the public and with the German aristocracy. After all, it had been the army, not the navy, that had fought three victorious wars and unified the German Empire. With a perennially hostile France, hell-bent on revenge for the humiliations of 1871, to the west and the hulking menace of the Russian army to the east, every *pfennig* spent on the army seemed to be money well spent. There seemed to be no sense in wasting money on warships that would almost certainly have little or no influence on the course of any future war in which Germany might find herself caught up. Despite Wilhelm's ambitions, for the first decade of his reign the whole idea of a powerful German navy rarely met more than a lukewarm reception among the German people.

The German people were wrong and the Kaiser was right, although in a fashion typical for him he went overboard in his determination to build a strong navy. The Germans began to doubt the durability of their understanding with Great Britain during the Boer War, when a number of German merchant ships were temporarily detained by the Royal Navy on the suspicion—erroneous as it turned out—that they were carrying arms and supplies to the Boers, and as Britain began methodically settling her old quarrels with France and Russia, Germany's traditional enemies. Should a war break out with Germany and Britain on opposite sides, the German merchant fleet was essentially defenseless and could be swept from the world's oceans in a matter of a few weeks by the Royal Navy. Even if Germany were to be involved in a war that found Britain neutral, the Royal Navy would still be compelled under international law to withdraw its protection of Germany merchant shipping, leaving it easy prey to whatever naval forces Germany's foe might possess.

Wilhelm listened as his economic and naval advisors explained these facts of life to him, and the conclusion to which he finally came was, given his bombastic personality and martial prejudices, inevitable. He was determined that Germany would build a fleet that, while perhaps not superior in numbers to the Royal Navy, would be of such quality that the British would be afraid to bring it to battle. Once he had decided that, as he declared to the Reichstag, "Germany's future lies upon the water!" there was only one officer in the entire German Navy whom the Kaiser believed could accomplish such a task: Tirpitz.

Less than two years after he was posted to Tsingtao, Tirpitz was recalled to Berlin to take up the office of Naval State Secretary, the German equivalent of the United States Secretary of the Navy or the Royal Navy's First Lord of the Admiralty. Now an admiral, Tirpitz immediately began formulating a policy for expansion of the German Navy that allowed it to become a powerful tool in formulating and executing German foreign policy. With the explicit blessing of the Kaiser, Tirpitz presented the German Reichstag with a series of Navy Bills in 1897, 1900, and 1903 that wrote the expansion of the Navy into German law, and then rammed them through.

In Tirpitz, the subtleties of Mahan's theories and conclusions found a receptive and dedicated disciple. Within Mahan's theorems about the necessity of a nation to maintain a credible battle fleet in order to exert sea power and thus influence world events lay the corollary of the "risk fleet." A risk fleet, in short, was a navy that was not large enough to decisively defeat a numerically superior opponent, but ship for ship it was qualitatively the better fleet and so could threaten to inflict unacceptable losses on its foe, should the two fleets meet in battle, and at the same time could utilize the superiority of its individual ships to erode its enemy's numerical superiority through attrition tactics in smaller engagements. The effectiveness of the smaller navy is then dramatically increased, since a blockading fleet must avoid large scale actions that do not promise decisive results, as it cannot risk the possibility of losses that reduce the effectiveness of the blockade, hence the term "risk fleet." With Imperial Germany's colonial ambitions necessitating a blue water navy to support it, and the growing assumption that Britain and Germany would find themselves on opposing sides of any coming European war, the attractions of such a navy for Germany were considerable.

The first Navy Bill was actually a rather modest affair, specifying a balanced fleet of 19 battleships organized into two battle squadrons, with an appropriate number of supporting cruisers and destroyers. But if the fleet Tirpitz requested was modest, its purpose was quite the opposite, for with it the admiral was laying the foundation for a challenge to Great Britain's naval supremacy. On June 15, 1897, Tirpitz presented to the Kaiser a 2,500-word memorandum stamped *Streng Geheim*—"Most Secret"—bearing the cumbersome title "General Considerations on the Constitution of Our Fleet According to Ship Classes and Designs." The title sounded dull; its contents were anything but. Within it were four distinct declarations with which Tirpitz laid out in clear and concise terms the concepts and doctrines that governed German naval strategy for the next two decades. The logic was relentless, the phrasing uncompromising, as Tirpitz's made his case for a powerful navy:

> For Germany, the most dangerous naval enemy at the present time is England.
>
> Our fleet must be constructed so that it can exert its greatest military potential between Heligoland and the Thames.
>
> The military situation vs. England demands battleships in as great a number as possible.
>
> Commerce raiding…against England is hopeless because of the shortage of [overseas] bases on our side and the great number on England's side, so that we must ignore this type of war against England in our plans for the constitution of the fleet.

Within the eight pages of Tirpitz's memorandum lay the seeds of an arms race with the Royal Navy, which 17 years later was in part responsible for Germany and Great Britain finding themselves at war with one another, and two years after that produced the clash of battleships history came to know as the Battle of Jutland.

The Navy Law of 1897 was passed by the Reichstag after a sharp, prolonged debate: what Tirpitz was proposing was, in fact, putting naval expenditures outside of the Reichstag's control. He was proposing that the budget for the navy be fixed and unalterable for the next eight years, a situation many Reich deputies found to be a disquieting diminution of their constitutional power. Opponents fought the Navy Bill for more than a month; in the end, though, enough support within and without the Reichstag was mustered to compel passage of the Navy Law of 1898, which soon became known as the First Navy Law.

The Naval State Secretary let it be known that he was satisfied with the provisions of the law, when, in fact, Tirpitz was preparing to demand a fleet so powerful that the greatest naval power in the world would think twice before challenging it. That demand came the following year, with the passage of the Second Navy Law. While the two battle squadrons authorized by the First Law gave the Imperial Navy a fleet powerful enough to confront any other navy save Great Britain's, they were no threat to Britain's maritime supremacy. This is not so with the Second Navy Law, which superseded the First Law less than a year after the initial bill had passed. The Second Navy Law called for a doubling of the size of the fleet initially authorized: when its projected completion date was reached in 1920, the High Seas Fleet would be the second largest battle fleet in the world; moreover, the Second Law's language left no doubt as to the purpose of this expansion. While Great Britain was never explicitly mentioned, phrases such as "an enemy who is more powerful at sea," "a great naval power," and, most tellingly, "the greatest naval power in the world," left little doubt as to the purpose of the new fleet. The preamble of the Second Navy Law removed any uncertainty:

> To protect Germany's seat trade and colonies in the existing circumstances, there is only one means: Germany must have a battle fleet so strong that even with the greatest seapower as an adversary, a war against it would involve such dangers as to imperil his own position in the world.
>
> For this purpose it is not absolutely necessary that the German battle fleet should be as strong as that of the greatest naval Power, because a great naval Power will not, as a rule, be in a position to concentrate all its striking forces against us. But even if it should succeed in meeting us with considerable superiority of strength, the defeat of a strong German fleet would so substantially weaken the enemy that, in spite of a victory he might have obtained, his own position in the world would no longer be secured by an adequate fleet.

Just as the Two Power Standard had codified the strategy of blockade for the Royal Navy a decade earlier, now Tirpitz's Second Navy Law codified his theory of a risk fleet. The great irony, which no one saw at the time, was that it was all the result of a bit of semantic sleight of hand. Tirpitz had from the beginning of his naval career wanted the High Seas Fleet to have battleships; in order to justify having them, he had to present a credible danger to Germany's merchant marine. Tensions between Germany and Great Britain during the Boer War gave him his chance—he was able to present the British as the threat: in order to fight the Royal Navy the High Seas Fleet needed battleships. Now that German battleships were being built, to continue to justify their existence, as well as the construction of new ships, the threat had to continue to be Great Britain, no matter what the dictates of diplomacy or political common sense might say. Thus an antagonism toward Great Britain was institutionalized in Berlin, in spite of whatever the British or German governments might actually want. Moreover, the risk fleet concept served only to heighten that antagonism: the "risk" in the concept was not merely that run by Great Britain of serious, possibly even decisive, losses should the Royal Navy ever do battle with the High Seas Fleet; there was also the risk to Germany that the British might be unwilling to tolerate so powerful a foreign fleet so close to the British Isles and attempt a preemptive strike at Germany's naval bases, sinking or crippling much of the fleet while it was at anchor. The British had done it before, destroying the Danish fleet at Copenhagen in 1801 to prevent it from falling into French hands.

That Tirpitz adopted a naval policy that could invite such a drastic response from the British demonstrated one other vital flaw in his strategy: he truly did not think through the consequences of constructing a fleet specifically built to challenge the Royal Navy. Britain's dependence on sea-borne trade and the maintenance of British sea power was absolute: deprived of her navy and her merchant marine, Great Britain and the British Empire would simply cease to exist. The British populace grasped this concept with an understanding so instinctive it almost seemed that they were born with it. When the Anglo-German naval race spawned by Tirptiz's two Navy Laws had been running for more than a decade, Winston Churchill summed up the fundamental differences between British and German naval aspirations in an address to an audience in Glasgow:

> The purposes of British naval power are essentially defensive. We have no thoughts…of aggression and we attribute no such thoughts to other Great Powers. There is however this difference between the British naval power and the naval power of the great and friendly Empire…of Germany. The British Navy is to us a necessity and, to some points of view, the German Navy is to them more in the nature of a luxury. Our naval power involves British existence…. It is the British Navy which makes Great Britain a great power. But Germany was a great power, respected and honored, all over the world before she had a single ship.

While the German press and some factions in the Reichstag howled with outrage at Churchill's description of the High Seas Fleet as a "luxury," the British Prime Minister, H.H. Asquith, admitted it to be "a plain statement of an obvious truth."

Tirpitz had, in fact, blundered, and blundered badly, first in antagonizing the British by appearing to threaten them, and then in institutionalizing that antagonism by continuing the expansion of the High Seas Fleet with the express purpose of challenging the Royal Navy for maritime supremacy. Yet neither Tirpitz nor the Kaiser saw the admiral's policy as a blunder: Tirpitz believed that he had enhanced and enlarged German power and prestige, as with one masterstroke he had transformed Germany from a continental power, a status granted by virtue of her huge and efficient army, into a world power, by the introduction of an enormously powerful battle fleet. The Kaiser agreed, and when the Second Navy Law passed in February 1900, he rewarded Tirpitz by elevating him to the Prussian nobility: the admiral now styled himself Alfred *von* Tirpitz. Surprisingly, given its ambitious—and as a consequence expensive—program, the Second Navy Bill passed the Reichstag with less opposition than did the first, although the defiant minority was still vocal and loud.

Perhaps this should not have been surprising: public enthusiasm for the German Navy had been whipped out of virtually nothing to a near frenzy in the space of a few years through various official, quasiofficial, and private organizations, most prominent among them being the Navy League (*Flotteverein*), which acted as a semiofficial mouthpiece for the Imperial Navy as well as the German industrialists who built it. Already the German military and German industry were locked in the deadly embrace that was not broken for nearly half a century, until the ruins of the Third Reich lay collapsed across the rubble of the Second. When the Second Navy Bill became law, it specified that the High Seas Fleet would have four battle squadrons of eight ships each, plus two flagships, and four additional battleships as a reserve. The target date for completing this huge expansion of the fleet was 1920.

The original battle fleet called for by the First Navy Law, 19 battleships, was a textbook expression of Mahan's risk fleet theory: while too small to have any realistic chance of defeating the Royal Navy, it was sufficiently large to be able to inflict serious damage on the British fleet before being overwhelmed itself. In that sense it was a perfect instrument of foreign policy, for it gave Germany an alliance value she had previously lacked, while not directly threatening any other nation. This in part accounts for the German public's willingness to pay for an even larger fleet—since the First Navy Law had expanded Germany's prestige, it seemed to follow that an even larger navy would further enhance Germany's position in the world.

But a 38 ship battle fleet threatened to meet the Royal Navy as an equal, a circumstance the British could not—and would not—tolerate. The British government quietly let it be known that it was prepared to expand the Royal Navy's construction program to whatever degree was necessary to ensure Britain's continued maritime supremacy. Von Tirpitz, in turn, knowing that in the event of a war between Britain and Germany the Royal Navy would swiftly establish a blockade of the German coast, instructed the German Naval Staff to begin developing plans that would allow the High Seas Fleet to surprise and catch isolated squadrons of the Royal Navy on blockade duty, with the objective of gradually eroding Britain's numerical superiority to the point where the German and British fleets could meet as quantitative equals.

There were flaws von Tirpitz never suspected existing in the assumptions on which he built this strategy, the most significant being in his belief that the ships of the High Seas Fleet were superior to those of the Royal Navy in construction and their ability to absorb punishment. It was a conceit that the German Navy foisted on the world so convincingly even the Royal Navy believed it—at least until after the First World War, when tests and extensive examination of surrendered German ships showed that aside from their more extensive internal subdivision, there was nothing superior in design, materials, or methods used in constructing the German battleships.

The other great flaw was von Tirpitz's falling victim to the failure that Napoleon (who was eventually undone by the same mistake) called "painting pictures," that is, assuming that an enemy did exactly what one expected and wanted them to do, rather than preparing for whatever they were capable of doing. In his case, von Tirpitz blithely assumed that the Royal Navy was incapable or unwilling to adapt its strategy of blockade to the realities of modern, steam age, steel age warfare.

Refusing to cooperate with von Tirpitz's plans, the Royal Navy threw a spanner in the works by abandoning the close blockade strategy to which it had been wedded since the eighteenth century, instead turning to a strategy of distant blockade in the eventuality of a war with Germany. In terms of its practical effects on the German economy, there was little to choose from between either strategic posture; in terms of its effects on the High Seas Fleet's planning, it threw von Tirpitz's entire strategy of the risk fleet into a cocked hat.

In a close blockade, the disposition of forces responsible for maintaining the blockade differed little from the days of fighting sail. Light units, in this case cruisers and destroyers rather than frigates and sloops, patrolled close to the enemy shore, paying particular attention to ports and naval bases. Should an enemy ship try to sail for the open sea, it was quickly intercepted and captured; should a force of enemy warships attempt to sortie, the light units quickly reported this to the main fleet, which was keeping station off the enemy coast, just over the horizon. The fleet steamed up, engaged the enemy ships, and defeated them; in execution the strategy was not all that different from what Nelson had used in bringing about the Battle of Trafalgar.

A distant blockade was, from a strategic and operational perspective, an entirely different proposition. Instead of maintaining its battle squadrons relatively close to the enemy coast, a fleet conducting a distant blockade stood off in sheltered waters, leaving only a light screening force to watch over the enemy fleet, relying on timely reports of any sortie by the enemy and at the same time denying access to the enemy's ports through the use of cruisers and destroyers. The only time the blockading battle fleet needed to expose itself to danger was when the enemy fleet actually sailed out to do battle.

Two new inventions prodded the Royal Navy into abandoning the close blockade: the torpedo and the mine. When Robert Whitehead invented the "automobile torpedo" in 1868, it was an erratic mechanical novelty propelled by compressed air, carrying an 18-pound warhead to a maximum range of barely 300 yards. Improvements rapidly followed, however, and by the turn of the century hydrogen peroxide had replaced compressed air as the propellant, warheads had grown to over 100 pounds, ranges exceeded 1000 yards, and the introduction of gyroscopic stabilization finally allowed torpedoes to run straight at fixed depths. By August 1914, the typical torpedo—there was little to choose from between the various navies' equipment—had a range of as much as 11,000 yards, carried a warhead of nearly 400 pounds of high explosive, and ran at speeds exceeding 30 knots.

Jackie Fisher had been one of the first senior British officers to truly grasp the threat of the torpedo. He had twice served as director of HMS *Excellent*, the Royal Navy's torpedo instruction school, and gunnery remained his primary obsession; he never lost sight of the weapon's destructive potential.

What made the torpedo so deadly a weapon was that by detonating underwater, it took advantage of hydrostatic dynamics, which made a torpedo's warhead much more effective than a comparably sized shell. Because water, unlike air, is essentially incompressible, the shock wave created by an exploding torpedo is transferred to the target ship's hull with little or no loss of power, unlike a shell burst, which dissipates much of its explosive force into the surrounding air. Consequently, the extent of the damage done is much greater; at the same time, because the explosion takes place under water, if it ruptures the hull, it immediately allows the sea access to the ship, while hits from shells usually often open compartments to the sky.

Mines were huge containers, usually spherical in shape, holding as much as a ton of high explosive detonated by contact fuses, attached by cables to a heavy weight that sank to the seabed and kept them in place. Because they were immobile, they were used to deny access to specific areas, usually the approaches to ports and harbors, or were sown in "fields" across heavily traveled sea-lanes. Being so much larger than a torpedo, a mine's explosive capacity was much greater as well: it usually took multiple torpedo hits to do fatal damage to a large warship, while an exploding mine could actually break a ship in two. Being immobile, mines basically had to wait for an unsuspecting victim to come to them; no commander would ever willingly take his ship into waters known to be mined. Torpedoes, on the other hand, though they carried smaller warheads than mines had the advantage of being capable of transport to where the targets could be found, whether by battleships, cruisers, destroyers—or submarines.

Surprisingly, since early in his career he had been a torpedo specialist, von Tirpitz was not terribly quick to grasp the potential of the submarine, but then, he was not alone, for the British had no better idea of how to employ their submarines than von Tirpitz did his; indeed, the scope of the possibilities for submarine warfare was demonstrated almost by accident. Von Tirpitz regarded the submarine, as did most senior naval officers, as an effective coast defense weapon, but hardly a worthy adjunct to a seagoing battle fleet. For von Tirpitz, the most effective method of delivering a torpedo attack was with flotillas of dedicated torpedo boats, small, fast, lightly armed vessels that eventually merged in design and function with the craft built specifically to combat them, the torpedo-boat destroyer, whose name was quickly shortened to simply "destroyer." Charging out of smoke screens or from behind the friendly battle fleet, the torpedo boats used their high speed to dash in toward the enemy battleships and fire off salvos of torpedoes, then turn away and retreat under cover of the friendly fleet's guns. The enemy fleet was compelled to alter course and speed and disrupt formations in order to avoid the onrushing torpedoes, and the ensuing confusion was almost guaranteed to ensure that some of them hit their targets; collisions and ramming among the enemy warships was also a likely possibility. In any event, an attack by enemy torpedo boats was a threat no battle fleet could afford to take lightly.

While the submarine was in effect just another form of torpedo boat, with the added advantage of being able to submerge and so attack invisibly, it was generally ignored by both the British and German navies. Perhaps "ignored" is too strong a word in the case of the Royal Navy, which was the first navy to form a separate submarine arm, but certainly they were never accorded a particularly high priority within the fleet or the Admiralty. The nickname the submarine force gave itself—"the Trade"—was in a way indicative of the less-than-high esteem in which the submarine service was held, the moniker being an oblique reference to the middle-class origins of most of its officers, surface ships being regarded as more socially acceptable postings by the titled and aristocratic.

For Germany, no such sobriquet existed for the High Seas Fleet's submarine force, as the German Navy actually acquired its first submarines almost as an afterthought. In early 1903, both Russia and France placed orders for nearly identical submarines to be built by Krupp's sprawling *Germaniawerft* shipyard at Kiel. The German Naval High Command thought it best to keep an eye on what its neighbors to the east and west were doing, and so ordered a few submarines of its own, built to a similar design, simply to learn what these new crafts could do. In October 1904, the first German submarine, unimaginatively christened the *Unterseeboot-1* (Undersea boat-1 or *U-1* for short) slid down the ways and joined the Kaiser's fleet. Looking for all the world like a mad scientist's mechanical shark, she was 110 feet in length, displacing just under 500 tons, and mounted a single 75 mm deck guns forward of her conning tower. Hidden behind sliding plates in the bow and stern of her rivet-covered hull were four torpedo tubes, two forward, two aft. She carried a crew of 37 enlisted men and 4 officers.

Admittedly, by getting into the game rather late, the Germans were able to avoid some of the technical mistakes of other nations' navies, such as gasoline engines, with all their attendant dangers from fires and fumes, or the folly of steam powered submarines, which continued in service in some navies until long after the First World War had ended, instead employing heavy oil, then later Diesel motors, in their submarines. And since the finest optical engineers in the world were found in Germany, the optics of the U-boats' periscopes, painstakingly crafted by Zeiss, were markedly superior to any other navy's.

The British, while never doubting the supremacy of the dreadnought battleship, had begun their own cautious development of a submarine force: with the French, Russians, and Germans all building them, the Royal Navy simply could not afford to ignore them. The result was the Royal Navy's first submarines, the A-1 class, larger and more powerful versions of the original American Holland boats on which they were based. British submarine development then proceeded apace: 1906 saw the introduction of the Diesel powered D-class, large boats of 500 tons. The E-class of 1914 displaced 700 tons, carried four 18-inch torpedo tubes, and was capable of speeds up to 16 knots on the surface and about 10 knots submerged. August 1914 saw plans in hand for an additional 60 boats to be added to the fleet within the next year.

On the other side of the North Sea, though, Germany was taking a tremendous technical lead. Her U-boats were generally larger than contemporary British classes, their Diesels more powerful, their optics better, and their torpedoes larger, faster, and more accurate. While the speeds of the German and British submarines were comparable, the U-boats' range was nearly twice the

1,500 mile range of Britain's newest submarines, the E-class. On the eve of war in 1914, Germany possessed nearly twice as many modern submarines as Great Britain.

It was not that the High Seas Fleet had any real idea of what to do with their submarines, any more than the Royal Navy did with theirs. In the light of the spectacular successes that accrued to the German submarine fleets in two World Wars, it is easy to believe that the German Navy had some long-gestating plan in place for exploiting the U-boats to their maximum advantage when war exploded in August 1914. Nothing could be further from the truth. As Edward Horton put it in his magnificent book *Submarine,*

> The Germans were not developing any sinister master plan, they were not consciously developing 'the ultimate weapon.' They were getting into the swim with everybody else and they built the type of submarine they did for the logical reason that it was the only one that could be of any use to them…. As Europe hurtled toward war, Germany was not looking to the submarine as her salvation any more than Britain was looking to it for her ruin.

The hesitation of both the British and German admiralties to place much reliance on the theoretical capabilities of their submarines was not due wholly to hidebound conservatism, bureaucratic inertia, or lack of imagination on the part of their officers. It was again a question of reliability. Submarine service was—and still is—the most hazardous duty in any navy. Before the war so many submarines had been lost through human error, mechanical malfunction, or accident that it seemed nothing short of fantasy to imagine any but supporting and ancillary missions for them in wartime. That they would be able to lunge out and strike at enemy ships hundreds, even thousands, of miles from their bases was inconceivable.

But they *did* carry torpedoes, and when operating within known waters from prearranged positions, submarines had the potential to stage deadly ambushes on enemy warships. A friendly fleet could easily draw a pursuing enemy across a line of submarines lying in wait, the submersibles suddenly popping up in the midst of the enemy force, firing torpedoes in all directions, creating chaos and confusion. This was one of the tactics von Tirpitz *did* envision for his U-boats, and, in the war that was about to break across Europe, it became a cornerstone of many of the operations conducted by the High Seas Fleet in its attempt to bring the Grand Fleet to battle.

The British Admiralty suspected that the Germans might employ just such a tactic. Admiral Fisher, writing to a friend in 1904—the year before the building of *Dreadnought*—declared, "I don't think it is even faintly realized —the immense impending revolution which the submarine will effect as offensive weapons of war." Long convinced of the value of torpedoes, Fisher understood that even more so than torpedo boats the submarine was the ideal method of delivering this potent weapon. Along with his near-evangelistic attitude toward naval gunnery, Fisher inculcated a profound awareness of the menace of submarines and torpedoes in the generation of officers who commanded the Royal Navy in the Great War.

Mines were another story altogether. Although a mine worked on the same principles as the torpedo in its effects, it was not a method of warfare that the Royal Navy readily adopted. Great Britain, in fact, had long made it a policy to oppose mining open waters, at one point having the prohibition of such practice written into one of the Hague Conventions. When the war began, one of the most vigorous opponents was the First Lord of the Admiralty, Winston Churchill, who rightly called mines "a pollution of the seas," threatening friend, foe, and neutral alike. That did not stop the Royal Navy, once war with Germany had come, from laying nearly 4,000 mines in the waters off Heligoland Bight, which dominated the entrance to Wilhlemshaven, Germany's principle naval base on the North Sea. The Germans in their turn mined the approaches to several of Britain's larger ports, but then went a step farther and laid a number of minefields in the shallower sections of the North Sea. These were supposedly international waters, where the use of mines were banned. The purpose of these minefields, both German and British, was, of course, to sink ships, warships, and merchantmen alike, and discourage neutral shipping from using British or German ports.

Long before the war began, though, the Royal Navy had recognized that torpedoes and mines would have a profound effect on how any blockade of an enemy coast would be conducted. By 1913, the Admiralty informed the Committee of Imperial Defense that the long-standing plan of keeping several squadrons of battleships cruising the North Sea just over the horizon from Heligoland Bight, where Royal Navy destroyers and light cruisers kept a watchful eye on the High Seas Fleet, was being abandoned in favor of a distant blockade. The risk to the capital ships of the fleet from minefields laid in secrecy, surprise torpedo-boat sorties by night or day, and submarines lying in ambush was simply too great. The light units continued to patrol off Heligoland, but the fleet was withdrawn to the north of the British Isles.

Heligoland Bight is a string of islands that stretch along the Dutch and German shores of the North Sea; it takes its name from the largest of these islands, Heligoland, which sits alone some 20 miles farther out. Once a Danish possession, the islands were seized in 1807 by Great Britain; they were home to a sparse population of fishermen and their families to whom the nominal change in nationality meant little. Another such change came in 1890, when Britain gave up the islands to Germany in exchange for the surrender of Germany's claims to the African island of Zanzibar. Once under the German flag, the islands quickly became a major naval base, fortified with heavy gun emplacements and concrete bunkers, while minefields guarded the approaches to the island and the waters behind them, which led to Wilhelmshaven.

It was these protective measures, along with the large number of torpedo boats and later submarines that were stationed at the island, which compelled the Royal Navy to rethink its strategy of close blockade. The report to the Imperial Defense Committee concluded that attempting to maintain such a blockade, while effective for a time, would result in "a steady and serious wastage of valuable ships," which would eventually jeopardize the Royal Navy's numerical advantage over the High Seas Fleet. The alternative was a "distant" blockade, which in the simplest terms meant closing off the entire North Sea, denying neutral merchant shipping access to German ports, and containing the German Navy in waters where it could do the least damage while simultaneously minimizing the risk to the Royal Navy. Great Britain's peculiar geographic advantage, sitting astride the only two exits from the North Sea—the Dover Straits in the English Channel and the northern passage up by the Orkney Islands off Scotland—made the task a fairly simple one. Mahan had predicted as much, remarking that "Great Britain cannot help commanding the approaches to Germany." A paper prepared by the Imperial Defense Committee in December 1912 described in some detail how such command could be carried out:

> Owing to recent developments on mines, torpedoes, torpedo craft and submarines, the passage of the Straits of Dover and the English Channel by ships of a power at war with Great Britain would be attended with such risks that, for practical purposes, the North Sea may be regarded as having only one exit, the northern one.

By positioning the dreadnoughts of the Royal Navy—grouped into what became known as the Grand Fleet—in ports along Scotland's North Sea coast, that exit, too, could be firmly and decisively shut. The cruisers that would have been patrolling off Heligoland were now watching the 200-mile wide gap between Scotland and Norway, with the battleships of the Grand Fleet only a few hours steaming away should the High Seas Fleet attempt to force its way into the North Atlantic. An Admiralty plan drawn up in response to the Committee paper demonstrated how the Royal Navy took advantage of this new deployment:

> As it is at present impracticable to maintain a perpetual close watch off the enemy's ports, the maritime domination of the North Sea…will be established as far as practicable by occasional driving or sweeping movements carried out by the Grand Fleet…in superior force. The movements should be sufficiently

frequent and sufficiently advanced to impress upon the enemy that he cannot at any time venture far from his home ports without such serious risk of encountering an overwhelming force that no enterprise is likely to reach its destination.

In short, if the High Seas Fleet chose to sortie into the North Sea, it would find the Grand Fleet waiting for it.

Now the board was set, the pieces were moving. All of the elements that combined to bring about the Battle of Jutland were in place: the two immense fleets of dreadnoughts and battlecruisers, the British blockade of the North Sea, the German plans for reducing Britain's naval superiority, and the Royal Navy's aggressive sweeps of the North Sea in search of the High Seas Fleet. All that remained to be accomplished before the great battle of annihilation for which both navies looked and at the same moment dreaded was for their admirals to bring the fleets into collision.

Chapter 4

The Price of Admiralty

In the clash of the Grand Fleet and the High Seas Fleet that inevitably came, the personalities, training, experiences, and professional competence of four men did more to determine the battle's outcome than any other factors. These men, two German and two British, were the admirals who commanded the fleets: *Vizeadmiral* (Vice Admiral) Reinhard Scheer, *Konteradmiral* (Rear Admiral) Franz Hipper, Vice Admiral David Beatty, and Admiral of the Fleet Sir John Rushworth Jellicoe.

A word here about naval rank and organization is necessary. The word "fleet" itself had come to possess more than one meaning. In some cases it was used to collectively refer to the navy as a whole—"the fleet"—but more properly it identified a specific administrative and tactical grouping of ships. Experience and experiment had led both the Royal Navy and the Imperial German Navy to conclude that for battleships the ideal tactical formation, combining flexibility and concentrating firepower, was a squadron of four ships, preferably of identical or similar characteristics. In some circumstances a squadron might consist of as many as eight ships, in which case it was divided into two equal divisions. Two or more squadrons made up a "fleet," which was then given a specific name, e.g., "the Atlantic Fleet" or "the First Battle Fleet." In extraordinary circumstances, two or more fleets could be combined into one massive body of ships, as when the Royal Navy's Channel Fleet, Home Fleet, and Atlantic Fleet were combined to form the Grand Fleet in 1914.

Squadrons and fleets were commanded by admirals. There were four levels or grades of "admiral" in both the Royal Navy and the Imperial Navy during the First World War—in ascending order of rank they were rear admiral, vice admiral, admiral, and admiral of the fleet (the Royal Navy) or grand admiral (the Imperial Navy). Originally the names were a description of the function attached to that rank in the early days of fighting sail. A rear admiral was given command of the rear portion, usually the after third, of a battle fleet and allowed the authority to act independently of the van (main body) of the fleet should the tactical situation change in a way to which the admiral in overall command could not respond. A vice admiral was originally intended to be a second-in-command, usually given charge of the van of the battle fleet, leaving the admiral-in-command free to oversee the fleet as a whole. An admiral was simply that—the officer in overall command of the battle fleet.

Time and the introduction of steam had blurred to some degree the practical distinctions among the ranks, so that by the early twentieth century they simply became grades of command responsibility, usually defining the size of the force placed under an individual officer's command. With weather and possession of the wind gage no longer critical factors in battle, for example, the need for a "rear admiral" to actually command the rear of a battle fleet had become moot. Now the rank was ordinarily given to the officer commanding a single squadron. Vice admirals, instead of being second-in-command to the admiral, commanded small, individual fleets, often in a semi-independent role. An admiral exercised command over larger fleets, while admiral of the fleet and grand admiral were relatively recent innovations in the command structure, created when the size and complexity of modern battle fleets grew to hitherto unimagined proportions, introducing a level of authority that coordinated and controlled the movements and actions of two or more fleets. In 1914, there were two such collections of ships, the greatest concentrations of naval power the world had ever seen. They were the Grand Fleet, which made its home port in the majestic but remote fastness of Scapa Flow at the mouth of the North Sea, and the High Seas Fleet, which was moored at the North Sea's base, in the Heligoland Bight.

Though Germany's geographic position gave her access to both the Baltic and North Seas, it was clear to even the most amateur armchair strategist well before the Great War that the North Sea was the critical area of operations for the High Seas Fleet. The Baltic was a strategic dead-end: it led nowhere, and engaging the Russian Navy offered no opportunity for any sort of decisive action that could influence the course of the war. While the port city of Kiel remained the Imperial Navy's largest navy base and the traditional home of the High Seas Fleet, the North Sea anchorage at Wilhelmshaven became the base for most of the Imperial Navy's operations during the Great War. A very young city, Wilhelmshaven was founded in 1869 by the Prussian King Wilhelm I—hence its name—on the site of an old pirate refuge on the west bank of the Jade River; the broad, deep anchorage at the river's mouth, known

The Price of Admiralty

75

as the Jade Roads, was ideal for mooring a fleet of warships. Just a few miles off the coast sat the long, relatively shallow bay known as Heligoland Bight. With only a handful of navigable deep-water channels leading through the island chain into the Bight and from there to Wilhelmshaven, and with those channels protected by minefields and covered by heavy guns that no sane enemy commander would dare to challenge, Heligoland offered a defensive position for the High Seas Fleet's main anchorage, which was the envy of many navies around the world. It was the perfect setting for staging swift, aggressive action against the Royal Navy in the North Sea.

Unfortunately for Germany, swift, aggressive action was sorely lacking in the opening months of the war, due in no small part to the character of the man given command of the High Seas Fleet, Admiral Friedrich von Ingenohl. By all accounts an able administrator and an excellent peacetime admiral, von Ingenohl was not a fighting admiral in anybody's opinion. Almost from the beginning of their training as cadets, naval officers have ingrained into them the belief that the worst offense any commanding officer can commit, be he a lieutenant in charge of a gunboat or a fleet admiral, is losing his ship or ships for any reason. Consequently, as a rule such men are apprehensive about losses, resulting in careful, conscientious seamanship in peacetime and cautious, conservative planning in wartime.

But in von Ingenohl such apprehension assumed the proportions of a phobia, and any action against the Royal Navy that offered the slightest threat of the loss of or damage to any of the High Seas Fleet's battleships or battle-cruisers was almost reflexively forbidden. As a consequence, for all of its apparent bustle and activity the High Seas Fleet accomplished very little in the first six months of the war, and when von Ingenohl was relieved of command of the High Seas Fleet on February 2, 1915, no one in the Admiralty was particularly sorry to see him go. Irresolute to the point of near immobility, von Ingenohl's timidity had allowed Great Britain to not only convoy the British Expeditionary Force to France in complete safety, but also to redeploy almost the entire British army between the months of August and December 1914 without the loss of a single Tommy to action by the High Seas Fleet. Repeatedly prodded by Berlin to do something, he reiterated time and again that he was merely following the instructions given to him personally by the Kaiser.

This was unfair to the Kaiser: Wilhelm II was no coward; rather it is more accurate to say that he was not a naturally brave man, and, while von Ingenohl's overarching fear of losing any of his capital ships was reinforced by Wilhelm's natural desire to avoid an all-out clash with the Royal Navy, the Kaiser had never intended his words of caution to be an excuse for complete prostration by the High Seas Fleet. What Wilhelm wanted to avoid at all cost was a confrontation with the Grand Fleet under circumstances that could easily send a sizable portion of his precious fleet to the bottom of the North Sea for little or no purpose. The High Seas Fleet had been built as an instrument of national policy, to expand Germany's power and influence beyond the continent of Europe, and the Kaiser had invested a tremendous sum of Germany's national treasure along with his personal prestige in seeing the fleet become a reality, so, of course, he was loathe to see any part of it risked for anything less than a decisive opportunity. Hence his instructions of August 29, 1914, for the fleet to "hold itself back and avoid actions which can lead to greater losses [than those of the enemy]," and requiring his personal authorization for any operations intended to produce a decisive action.

But in the aftermath of the Battle of Dogger Bank the Kaiser decided he had had enough of von Ingenohl. There the British and German battle cruiser squadrons had clashed on January 24, 1915, and the Germans had lost the heavy armored cruiser *Blücher* while they were being chased back into Heligoland Bight without, apparently, inflicting serious damage on any of the British ships. Despite firm intelligence that the dreadnoughts of the Grand Fleet were nowhere near the action, von Ingenohl refused to bring up the battleships of the High Seas Fleet to support the German battlecruisers, instead turning tail and running back into the protected waters of the Bight. Once again citing the Kaiser's instructions as justification for his fear of losing any of his precious battleships, von Ingenohl temporized, rationalized, and made excuses, but nothing he said could save his command. It was one thing to avoid engagements with superior forces; it was something else entirely to appear to meekly flee before a foe of equal strength. This was too much even for the highly cautious Wilhelm, who had bitterly upbraided his senior admiral barely a month before von Ingenohl's failure to properly support Hipper's battlecruisers during the attack that became known as the Scarborough Raid. "The effort to preserve the fleet," the Kaiser raged at the time, "must under no circumstances be carried so far that favorable prospects of a success are missed owing to the prospect of possible losses." Now von Ingenohl had done precisely the same thing, and it was too much even for Wilhelm's cautious nature. He ordered von Ingenohl to haul down his flag.

It was a popular decision within the fleet as well as with the Naval Staff, who had chafed under not only the Kaiser's restrictive orders, but also under von Ingenohl's less-than-inspired leadership. Unfortunately, his replacement, Admiral Hugo von Pohl, who had been chief of the Naval Staff, proved in the event to be cast much in the same mold. In giving command of the fleet to von Pohl, the Kaiser emphasized his restrictions on the High Seas Fleet's operations, and von Pohl, who had never advocated aggressive action as a staff officer, voiced no objections as commander in chief. Instead, von Pohl pushed for more freedom of action for the U-boats, being one of the first proponents of unrestricted submarine warfare against Great Britain's shipping lines, and formulated the idea of declaring a war zone around the British Isles as a reprisal for the British government's closure of the North Sea.

All through 1915 then the dreadnoughts and battlecruisers of the High Seas Fleet followed a very dull routine. Working in a squadron rotation, one week was spent patrolling inside Heligoland Bight, a pointless exercise as the minefields, torpedo-boat flotillas, and shore batteries ensured that the Royal Navy would never venture into those waters; the next week was spent anchored, with steam up and ready for action that never came, at Schillig Roads, another large anchorage in the Bight. A day was spent making the transit of the Kiel Canal into the Baltic Sea, where two weeks was spent on gunnery practice, then a return passage through the canal where the ships tied up at the docks of Wilhelmshaven; the crews were given shore leave and slept in barracks ashore while work parties did essential maintenance and repairs on the ships. It was a seemingly pointless routine, as numbing to the mind as it was corrosive to the spirit for officers and crew. The men of the High Seas Fleet were as keenly enthusiastic and anxious for action as their Royal Navy counterparts.

Von Pohl's tenure as commander in chief was destined to be short, though not as a consequence of his actions or lack of them. Von Pohl was dying of liver cancer, and on January 8, 1916, he had to be carried from his flagship, *Friedrich der Grösse*, to a hospital ashore. The next day, he resigned his command, and ten days later command of the High Seas Fleet was given to *Vize-Admiral* Reinhard Scheer.

Reinhard Scheer was immortalized for one supreme moment in his career: he was the man who led the High Seas Fleet into battle with the Grand Fleet at Jutland. Yet there was much more to the life and character of the man than a single battle, no matter how titanic. While not as dynamic or colorful—or controversial—a personality as Jackie Fisher (both men would have cringed at any such comparison), Scheer shared one significant personality trait with the British admiral: both men passionately believed in waging war with every means at their disposal. Fisher had once written in a memorandum about the Hague Convention of 1895, which was trying to bring some measure of civility to modern warfare, that "the essence of warfare is violence, and moderation in warfare is imbecility." Scheer, while not so eloquent as Fisher, certainly would have agreed.

Like almost all of his contemporaries on both sides of the North Sea, Scheer had chosen a seaman's life early on. Fifty-three years old at the time of his appointment to command of the High Seas Fleet, he had spent 38 of those years rising through the ranks of the German Navy's officer corps. Coming from a middle-class family as did so many of Germany's outstanding naval officers, Scheer was the son of a schoolmaster from Obernkirschen, near Frankfurt, on the River Main, born in 1863. At the age of 15 he became a naval cadet; again like Fisher, who described himself at the time of his entry into the Royal Navy as "penniless, friendless, and forlorn," Scheer could count on neither social standing nor family fortune to enhance or further his career: success in the Imperial German Navy would be his only by dint of talent and hard work.

Hard work was something of which he was not afraid: many years later, in retirement, Scheer recalled quite fondly the long months he spent aboard the frigate *Niobe,* the Imperial Navy's training ship. It was a physically demanding life, for *Niobe* was a full-rigged sailing ship, and the cadets could be turned out at any hour of the day in any weather to take in or make sail, repair spars or rigging, or tend to some other urgent need of the ship. Scheer discovered that he was a born seaman, and for the rest of his life he was never happier than when he had a moving deck under his feet.

It was early on in his career, too, that Scheer began taking an immense pride in being a part of the naval profession: he began taking a serious interest in the history of naval tactics and developed an appreciation for emerging technologies, particularly those with applications to naval weaponry. In this way he became one of the Imperial Navy's first torpedo experts and began developing methods by which this new weapon could be integrated into the tactics of the High Seas Fleet.

While he was never regarded as a spectacular officer—not always a bad thing, as sometimes those officers who shine brightly in their early careers find themselves promoted far beyond their abilities and consequently do more harm to their service than good—Scheer rose steadily in rank as his career progressed. He was promoted from *Kadet* to *Leutnant zur See* (the equivalent of an Ensign in the Royal Navy) in November 1882 and served on the armored frigate *Friedrich Karl,* then shifted to *Hertha,* an armored corvette, when he was promoted to *Oberleutnant zur See* (junior Lieutenant) in 1885. He spent two years in *Herta,* circling the world, a posting that perfected his skills as a seaman. Then came a posting to the German East Africa Squadron, followed by four years ashore as a student at various Imperial Navy technical schools. Returning to sea duty in April 1893 he was promoted to *Kapitanleutnant* (Lieutenant), serving as the torpedo officer aboard the light cruiser *Sophie,* which was part of the East Africa Squadron. Two years later he was back in Germany, assigned to the Torpedo Research Command in Kiel as an instructor.

The Price of Admiralty 79

It was during his tenure at the Research Command that Scheer met a pretty young schoolteacher named Emillie Mohr. They were married in 1899—Scheer was only 36, but Imperial Navy officers tended to marry younger than their Royal Navy counterparts. Although the marriage ended in tragedy 23 years later (Emillie was murdered by an intruder in the couple's Berlin home), it was a happy union; Scheer became the proud and doting father of two daughters and a son. At the same time, shore duty brought professional as well as personal benefits. His growing reputation as a torpedo specialist brought him to the attention of Admiral Alfred von Tirpitz, who soon took an active part in furthering Scheer's career, first by posting him to the Navy Office Torpedo Section, then in arranging for him to take command of a destroyer flotilla upon his promotion to *Korvettenkapitan* (Lieutenant Commander) in April 1900. So successful was Scheer at this posting that he subsequently wrote a textbook on destroyer tactics, which helped earn his promotion to *Fregattenkapitän* (Commander) in January 1904. He was promoted to *Kapitan zur See* (Captain) on March 21, 1905, and in 1907 took command of the battleship *Elsass,* one of the last predreadnoughts built for the Imperial German Navy. Because she was his first battleship command, Scheer was always fond of the predreadnought ships.

Scheer's optimism and lack of pretense made him widely admired by his colleagues and subordinates, although at times he could be an exasperating taskmaster. His chief of staff, Captain Adolf von Trotha, later recalled, with equal degrees of respect and annoyance, that:

> He never stood on ceremony with young officers. But he was impatient and always had to act quickly. He would expect his staff to have the plans and orders for an operation worked out exactly to the last detail, and then he would come on to the bridge and turn everything upside down. He was a commander of instinct and instant decision who liked to have all options presented to him and then as often as not chose a course of action no one had previously considered.

Not all of Scheer's officers were so admiring of him, however. Captain Ernst von Weizsäcker, who served as Scheer's Flag Lieutenant, that is, his senior signals officer, wrote a more balanced appraisal after Scheer's death:

> We knew Scheer was made up of different stuff from Pohl…. His old friends had given him the odd nickname of "Shooting Bob" on account…of his likeness to his fox terrier…. Scheer's success lay in his ability to make a decision, but he knew nothing of tactics, although he was against sitting in harbor and liked to get the fleet to sea when he could…. In other words, Scheer was much like any other admiral and by no means the tactical genius and superman that the present day historians try to make out.

One characteristic that set Scheer apart from the majority of his colleagues was his thoughtful approach to naval strategy. Instead of being merely a gifted technician like Franz Hipper or a first-class peacetime administrator like von Ingenohl, he approached naval warfare from a more cerebral perspective. In this Scheer once again resembled Jackie Fisher. At a time when the majority of officers on both sides of the North Sea were utterly enamored of and devoted to the big gun, Scheer was specializing in torpedo warfare. Much like Fisher, he developed an early appreciation for the potential of the torpedo, and with it the newfangled submarine. Though never advocating abandoning the battleship as the primary weapon of the High Seas Fleet, he began to work out a theory of "combined arms," employing guns, torpedoes, and mines, submarines and surface ships—and later airships—in combinations that exploited each system's greatest strengths. It was Scheer who developed the tactical doctrine of using dreadnoughts to draw an enemy's warships into a submarine or torpedo-boat ambush, which when it had run its course would leave the wounded enemy warships at the mercy of the German battle fleet.

In his ability to recognize that, powerful as it was, the dreadnought battleship had limitations and vulnerabilities, coupled with his expertise as one of Germany's first and foremost experts on torpedoes, Scheer openly and enthusiastically embraced the mine and the submarine as worthwhile means of prosecuting the war against the Royal Navy. Indeed, while he was not yet prepared to accept the idea that Germany's U-boats alone could win the naval war against Great Britain, he was one of the earliest and most articulate advocates of unrestricted submarine warfare as one of the most effective ways of cutting off Britain's supply lines and crippling her ability to wage war. In concepts like this, Scheer was far ahead of not only the majority of his colleagues, but also of most of the officers of the Royal Navy.

From all indications Scheer also appreciated that there was such a thing as a "philosophy" of sea power, a concept that would have come as no surprise to centuries of British captains and admirals, but that was lost on the majority of German naval officers. Scheer understood that a significant part of the prestige and authority of British sea power stemmed from the legend of the Royal Navy's invincibility. It then followed, he reasoned, that a significant defeat inflicted upon the Royal Navy—not a glorious exchange of ships in some thunderous, Trafalgar-like engagement between equal battle fleets, but rather an action that allowed an isolated squadron of the Grand Fleet to be overwhelmed and annihilated—would shatter that legend. In so doing, it would take with it much of the confidence, arrogance, and sense of superiority that gave the Royal Navy such near-omnipotent authority around the world. Likewise, the morale of the British people, which took the supremacy of the Royal Navy as more than being granted, almost as a God-given right,

The Price of Admiralty

would be gravely shaken. A victory against the Grand Fleet, then, would have consequences and repercussions all out of proportion to the actual losses suffered by the British. It was a concept that Scheer developed and refined, first as chief of staff of the High Seas Fleet, to which he had been appointed on December 1, 1909, then as *Konteradmiral* Scheer, his promotion coming in June 1910. He spent all of 1911 and 1912 ashore, working for von Tirpitz, then returned to the fleet as the commander of the Second Battle Squadron. At the end of 1914, in a sign of the professional respect the German Admiralty felt for Scheer's abilities, he was given command of the Third Battle Squadron, the newest and most powerful squadron in the High Seas Fleet. Finally, the opportunity for Scheer to put his theories and plans into action came when he succeeded Hugo von Pohl as commander in chief of Germany's entire assemblage of dreadnoughts.

The one man more than any other who was key to the successful execution of any plan of Scheer's was Rear Admiral Franz Hipper. Hipper was probably the best-known and most professionally competent admiral to serve in the Imperial German Navy. Even in photographs he projected an aura of authority: handsome and resplendent in his dress uniform, his balding pate and steady gaze projecting a sense of strong intellectual gifts, his moustache and goatee adding a dashing touch to his image, he looked every bit the charismatic naval hero he was.

Born on September 13, 1863, into a middle-class family as just plain Franz Hipper—the ennobling "von" only came to him many years later, after the Battle of Jutland—he grew up far from the sea, in Wielheim, a small town in Bavaria. A naval career seemed the least likely of futures for him, but by that strange, inexplicable process by which young men growing up in a landlocked existence become consummate sailors, young Franz Hipper found himself drawn to the sea.

Of course, there was most likely a good deal of pragmatism in his decision to join Imperial Germany's fledgling naval service—a well-founded pragmatism that never descended into cynicism was Hipper's overarching characteristic all of his life. In Wilhelmine Germany, the ranks of the Imperial Army's *offizierkorps,* while theoretically open to men of common birth, were still the virtually exclusive domain of the German nobility. For an ambitious and intelligent young man born into Germany's middle class who sought a career in uniform, the Imperial Navy presented far more scope and opportunity. Indeed, because of the technical and technological nature of the naval profession, it was regarded with disdain by most of the Teutonic aristocracy. Consequently, the navy's officer corps was predominantly middle class, both in composition and values. Hardworking, fiercely patriotic, driven to succeed by a sense of inferiority to the Royal Navy, which they almost slavishly imitated in traditions, customs, and practice, the officers of the Imperial German Navy formed a closely knit community, reminiscent of Nelson's "Band of Brothers," which the young Franz Hipper found irresistible.

He got a relatively late start in his naval career, joining the Imperial Navy in 1881 at the age of 18. Like Scheer, his rise throughout the ranks of the Imperial Navy was steady if not spectacular. His first seagoing posting as a *Kadet* was as in SMS *Leipzig,* a nondescript light cruiser, the following year. In 1884 he was promoted to *Leutnant zur See,* a rank he held for an extraordinarily long time, serving in several different ships, ranging in size from torpedo boats to cruisers, gaining experience at stations in Europe, Africa, and Asia. The rise to *Kapitan Leutnant* finally came in January 1895. From 1899 to 1902 he served as the *Navagationsoffizier* aboard the personal yacht of Kaiser Wilhelm II, *Hohenzollern,* a posting that earned Hipper a promotion to *Korvettenkapitan.* He reached the rank of *Fregattenkapitän* in 1905, and on April 6, 1907, was appointed *Kapitan zur See.* Five years later he was named a *Konteradmiral* and given command of the First Scouting Group, the Imperial Navy's battlecruiser squadron.

Unlike Scheer, or the two German admirals' British counterparts, Jellicoe and Beatty, Franz Hipper left behind no memoirs, nor has he been the subject of numerous biographies. Consequently, much of his character has been obscured by the passing of time and remains subject to conjecture, which is best left alone. It is indisputable that Hipper was a fighting admiral by anyone's definition; he never appeared to suffer from the professional phobia that is too often the hallmark of peacetime admirals: the fear of losing ships. His mission was to sink enemy warships; he accepted as part of that mission the risk that some of his own ships might be sunk in the process. He was also a realist in other ways: he held no regrets about the loss of life among British civilians when his battlecruisers raided the North Sea coastal towns of Scarborough and Hartlepool. With typical forthrightness he stated that "It is a regrettable but obvious fact that modern war is blind; it involves both combatants and non-combatants, slaying indiscriminately.... The first objective is to break a nation's morale; the collapse of physical resistance will follow." It is not difficult to imagine Hipper wholeheartedly endorsing *Kapitanleutnant* Schwieger's destruction of the *Lusitania* for just these reasons.

On more than one occasion Hipper was heard to refer to war and battle as "business"; it was a telling remark, for it revealed the pragmatism with which he approached his profession. Not for Hipper was any of the muddleheaded nonsense about the "romance of the sea": he was widely known for his "unruffled calm," as his chief of staff once described his demeanor during battle, his posture ramrod straight, his expression calm, and a cigar clenched in his teeth. To him the naval service was indeed a profession, as much as the practice of a medical doctor or a financier on land: war and battle the reasons for which he had trained. Like any good businessman, he believed that in order to be successful he had to become a master of his calling. Ships were assets, to be used and utilized to their fullest, and just as in the business world risks had to be taken in order to gain an advantage over the competition.

Inevitably, Hipper chafed under the Kaiser's excessive caution and the timidity of von Ingenohl and von Pohl. When Scheer replaced von Pohl, Hipper was convinced that there would be fundamental changes in the way the High Seas Fleet pursued its war against the Royal Navy. He was right, for Scheer was every bit as aggressive as Hipper, but he had no idea at the time that Scheer's plans did not include him.

The stress of the first 18 months of the war had taken their toll on Hipper, who began to experience sleepless nights, the discomfort of which was compounded by sciatica, excruciatingly painful under any conditions. Two months after Scheer replaced von Pohl, Hipper applied for sick leave, turning over command of the First Scouting Group to *Konteradmiral* Friedrich Bödecker. It was while he was taking his cure at Bad Neundorf that he unknowingly came close to being permanently replaced. Scheer had written to the chief of the German Naval Staff, Admiral Henning von Holtzendorff, requesting that Hipper be retired, claiming that he lacked "the qualities of robustness and elasticity" that command of the First Scouting Group required. Von Holtzendorff disagreed and told Scheer so in no uncertain terms. No more was said of the matter, and Scheer and Hipper worked together for another two years before Scheer was promoted to the chief of staff position and Hipper succeeded him as commander in chief of the High Seas Fleet; yet the suspicion remained that for some unknown reason, some enmity existed between the two men, which led to such an unseemly episode. Nevertheless, Hipper was the man who, at the head of his column of battlecruisers, was leading the High Seas Fleet toward the battle when the Grand Fleet sailed out from Scapa Flow.

Scapa Flow! To this day there are few names as evocative of the majesty and power of massed war fleets as that of the great anchorage in the Orkney Islands off Scotland's northern coast. Made up of some 70 islands, the majority of them hardly more than barren rocks, the Orkneys sit at the top of the North Sea, mostly clustered around the basin of the Flow itself, while the geographic position of the Orkneys allows them to dominate the North Sea. Barren, rocky, windy, and hardly hospitable, the Orkneys are islands of stark but majestic beauty, much like the warships of the Grand Fleet, which called Scapa Flow home during the years of the Great War.

Prior to 1914 Scapa was not even an Admiralty anchorage; it had served as an exercise area for the fleet for a number of years, but permanent installations were few, while the facilities for serving and maintaining a fleet were nonexistent. The Royal Navy's most important dockyards and bases had been built along the English Channel, mostly in the seventeenth and eighteenth centuries, when Britain's most likely foes were the French, Dutch, or Spanish, either singly or in some combination. The eventual ebb of Dutch and Spanish sea power, and ultimately the rapprochement with France in the first decade of the twentieth century, had shifted the focus of the Royal Navy, as the perceived naval threat from Imperial Germany grew from an unlikely possibility to a near-absolute certainty. In the decade before the war began, new major bases were built at Rosyth and Cromarty Firth along Scotland's North Sea coast, but while Scapa had been proposed as the site for a permanent base as early as 1909, it was essentially ignored and left undefended.

That changed in the closing days of July 1914. When Churchill ordered the dispersal of the Fleet halted following the summer maneuvers, the majority of the ships were redirected northward to Cromarty and Scapa Flow. By nightfall on August 1, more than 100 warships, including 21 dreadnoughts and 4 battlecruisers, along with their escorting cruisers and destroyers, were anchored in the Flow.

It was not an ideal anchorage—yet. What made it particularly attractive to the Admiralty was the command it gave of the North Sea: with a fleet permanently based at Scapa Flow, the Royal Navy could literally dictate who could enter and leave that body of water. Also, there were three widely separated exits from the basin of the Flow, which meant that the danger of the fleet being bottled up by a blocking force was all but nonexistent, while the waters around Scapa were expansive enough to allow for realistic maneuvers and gunnery training to be carried out. There were two major problems, which in August 1914 made Scapa less than ideal, one of which was insoluble, while the other could be resolved.

The former was that because Scapa Flow was sited in the Orkneys, it was detached from Britain's rail network, and literally everything the fleet required by way of supply had to come by ship. Coal, oil, replacement parts, replacement personnel, food, ammunition, mail—all had to be carried from the mainland to the islands. This limitation had to be accepted: building a railway across the Pentland Firth, which separated the Orkneys from Scotland, was simply impossible. The second obstacle was that there was little in the way of permanent defenses: the only artillery available at the start of the war was the few small batteries of Royal Artillery supplied to the local Territorial troops, while searchlights, spotting posts, and telephone and telegraph lines for communication simply did not exist. Nor were there any shore facilities, not even a single canteen, for the crews of the ships that were to be based there.

More critically, at least from the perspective of the new commander in chief of the Grand Fleet, Admiral Sir John Jellicoe, was that there were no defenses against torpedo-boat attacks or, worse yet, from submarine attack. In the early months of his command, which coincided with the beginning of the war, Jellicoe's chief concern, and it was not unrealistic, was that the High Seas Fleet might stage a massed-torpedo-boat attack against his dreadnoughts as they were sitting motionless at their moorings. Being well-versed in the technical capabilities of the German Navy, he was also legitimately worried that a strike by U-boats might be contemplated as well.

The geography of Scapa Flow and the Orkneys as a whole did provide some considerable measure of defense against such an eventuality, particularly against U-boats. With its wildly uneven bottom, racing currents, and rushing tidal races, the waters around the islands were extraordinarily tricky to navigate for those who were unfamiliar with them and particularly hazardous to submarines, which were small and susceptible to being thrown far off course and position by currents and tides. But for Jellicoe, relying on the partiality of Mother Nature to protect his fleet was not sufficiently reassuring, so he pressed the Admiralty to make the defenses of the Flow a priority, which they did. By late spring 1915, minefields had been laid (some of them capable of being remotely detonated from the shore), electrical detection devices installed, booms drawn across stretches of the entry channels into the Flow, and blockships and huge concrete barriers carefully sunk and emplaced in others, while the numbers of patrolling destroyers and trawlers increased dramatically. During the whole of the Great War, only two U-boats were known to have dared try to penetrate the defenses of Scapa Flow: one was rammed and sunk by a patrol boat, the other was blown up by one of the electrically controlled mines. (It was not until 1940, in the *Second* World War, that the U-boat defenses of Scapa Flow were penetrated; *Kapitanleutnant* Gunther Prien, with an extraordinary measure of good luck, took *U-47* through a gap in one of blocked channels and torpedoed the battleship *Royal Oak.*)

In 1916, the eyes of the Grand Fleet—indeed of the whole British Empire —were focused on two British admirals, one charismatic but tragically flawed, the other a self-effacing nautical genius. They were Vice Admiral Sir David Beatty and Admiral of the Fleet Sir John Rushworth Jellicoe. Together they were an amazing study in contrasts.

In 1916, the most popular officer in the Royal Navy—at least with the British public—was not the First Sea Lord, Admiral Jackie Fisher, nor the commander-in-chief of the Grand Fleet, Admiral John Jellicoe. Instead, it was one of Jellicoe's subordinates, the commander of his battlecruiser squadron, Vice Admiral David Beatty.

David Beatty was a vain, aggressive, thrusting, ambitious officer, self-confident to the point of being cocksure, and charismatic, always seeming to be in the thick of the action, wherever and whatever it might be. Beatty possessed that indefinable yet unmistakable gift called "leadership," although his tactical and strategic talents proved to be inferior to his ability to persuade men to follow him into battle.

When he worked, he worked hard; when he played, he played hard. His driving nature led him to do everything in life at top speed, whether he was engaging an enemy fleet or playing a set of tennis. He made it clear to the captains commanding the ships of his squadron that he expected them to execute their maneuvers at the highest speed possible. Likewise his officers and crew soon became accustomed to his habit, whenever his command was scheduled to leave port, of returning from shore at the precise moment that the ship was scheduled to raise anchor: he expected everything to be in readiness for an immediate departure.

Yet the adjective that best describes David Beatty is "opportunistic," in both its best and its worst meanings. While he was always on the alert for a chance to thrust himself into the thick of any action, he was equally adept at seizing any opportunity to thrust himself into the public spotlight. He was spectacular, but hardly brilliant. Like Nelson, he was audacious, unquestionably a fighting admiral, yet he was more inclined to impulsiveness than to taking calculated risks. This was a characteristic that extended into his private life as well, ultimately much to Beatty's dismay.

Born in Cheshire in January 1871, the second of five children, Beatty was haunted for decades by the knowledge that his father and mother were not legally married at the time of his birth; bastardy was a devastating social stigma in Victorian England, and much of Beatty's subsequent ambition seems to stem from a drive to prove himself superior to the circumstances of his birth. The entire Beatty family was famous for its horsemanship, the eldest son, Charles, becoming a well-known jockey and steeplechase rider; riding and athletics remained passions of David Beatty's for the whole of his life. His father was a retired Army officer, and all three of David's brothers followed their father's footsteps: he was the only sailor in the family.

He became a naval cadet in 1884, at the then-usual age of 13. Ranking in the middle of his class, Beatty had his first sea posting aboard the battleship *Alexandra*, in the Mediterranean Fleet. It was the beginning of seven years of rather undistinguished service: Beatty was not a poor officer; rather he was the sort who languished in the routine of peacetime. In 1896, that began to change when he was given command of one of the gunboats that accompanied Major General H.H. Kitchener's expedition up the Nile to retake Khartoum and reassert British authority over the Sudan. In one of the first skirmishes with the Arabs, a shell struck Beatty's gunboat without exploding, and Beatty, exhibiting extraordinary coolness, simply picked it up and threw it overboard. Later, during Kitchener's famous victory at the Battle of Omdurman, Beatty brought his gunboat close inshore where its guns could provide direct support to Kitchener's soldiers. This earned him an invitation to accompany Kitchener even further up the Nile, to the mud fort of Fashoda, where a French expedition had staked a claim for France's sovereignty over the upper Nile Valley. Roundly impressed by the young lieutenant's conduct, Kitchener was instrumental in arranging for Beatty to be awarded the Distinguished Service Order, an accomplishment that led to Beatty being promoted to the rank of commander ahead of more than 400 officers senior to him.

Returning to England at the conclusion of Kitchener's Nile adventure, Beatty got his first taste of public adulation and at the same time fell in love. The object of his affection was an American, Ethel Tree, a woman of striking beauty and remarkable background. She was the only child of Marshall Field, owner of the Chicago department store and possessor of an immense fortune. The attraction for Beatty was both physical and financial, for his naval pay amounted to only a few hundred pounds a year, hardly sufficient to continue Beatty in the lifestyle to which he had been accustomed during his youth and had grown to take for granted. There was one obstacle to the two of them becoming a couple: Ethel Tree was a married woman.

To David Beatty, an obstacle was simply something meant to be overcome; he promptly set about doing so in Ethel's case. His forceful nature and dashing style, which did so much to further his naval career, here brought about the source of some of his greatest personal happiness and deepest misery: his choice of a wife. It is a mistake to discount the effect his marriage had upon his career, although it is an equal mistake to presume that it affected his command decisions.

Before Beatty could properly pursue Ethel, however, he was posted to the battleship *Barfleur* and sent to the Far East. Arriving there just as the Boxer Rebellion was bursting into flame across China, Beatty took a party of 150 sailors and Royal Marines to the port of Tientsin, which was under heavy attack by the Boxers. For nine days he was in almost constant combat, much of it hand-to-hand. Inevitably, he was wounded, twice within 20 minutes, both times in the left arm; he was invalided back to Great Britain, and once there he began his suit of Ethel Tree in earnest. She, in turn, was thoroughly smitten with the handsome, dashing young officer (he had recently been promoted at the age of 29 to captain in recognition of his service in China) and soon divorced her husband, leaving him with sole custody of their only child. On May 22, 1901, David Beatty and Ethel Tree were married.

The years that followed were turbulent, to say the least. When Edward VII succeeded his mother Victoria the same year the Beattys were married, the social standards became somewhat more relaxed, but Ethel's thrusting social ambition, which matched David's professional ambition in intensity, began to become a source of embarrassment for Beatty. At times his wife sought to influence which appointments he was given, with an eye to the social advantages particular offices and commands might offer. At other times she tried to persuade him to leave the Royal Navy altogether.

Beatty, meanwhile, was becoming a competent naval officer, strict, efficient, respected by his crews if not always well-liked. Given command of a succession of cruisers, he drove them hard but turned them into prizewinning ships that were envied throughout the fleet. By the end of 1908, Beatty's name was atop the seniority list of the Royal Navy's captains. But a technicality prevented him from taking the next step: he lacked sufficient time at sea to qualify for promotion to admiral. At this point Admiral Fisher personally intervened and orchestrated an exception to this regulation. Thus on January 1, 1910, David Beatty was appointed a rear admiral, at the age of 38 the youngest flag officer in the Royal Navy since Nelson.

Beatty himself was envied by many of his fellow officers—his rapid promotion, his stunning wife, their vast fortune, all provoked a degree of jealousy that was more than just professional. (When Beatty was once accused of driving HMS *Suffolk* too hard and disciplinary action was considered, Ethel was heard to declare, "What? Court martial my David? I'll buy them a new ship!") In 1911 he was offered the post of second-in-command of the Atlantic Fleet, an assignment that usually marked the holder for one of the Royal Navy's fleet commands. Beatty declined—the fleet was based at Gibraltar, and Ethel simply refused to relocate to what was a social backwater. Tongues wagged, and heads shook: refusing such an assignment was unheard of, and it was rumored that Beatty would never again be offered another seagoing assignment.

Yet fate intervened for him once again, this time in the shape of the new First Lord of the Admiralty, Winston Churchill. Appointed in October 1911 when H.H. Asquith reshuffled his Cabinet, Churchill needed a private secretary, and Beatty's unconventional lifestyle and career appealed to Churchill's unconventional personality, and the newly minted rear admiral was summoned to Whitehall for an interview. Upon their first meeting (the story may be apocryphal) Churchill supposedly looked Beatty up and down, then announced, "You're rather young to be an admiral!" to which Beatty shot back, "You're rather young to be a First Lord!"

The Price of Admiralty

The truth was that Beatty never held a high opinion of Churchill's talents, although typically he was careful to conceal this from the First Lord himself. Churchill, in turn, was utterly charmed by Beatty and believed that he possessed a first-class strategic mind. He was also unaware that Beatty was maneuvering himself into position to take command of the Battlecruiser Squadron, which became available in the spring of 1913. Churchill wholeheartedly recommended Beatty for the post, naming him to it over the heads of several admirals much senior to Beatty. On March 1, 1913, Rear Admiral David Beatty hoisted his flag aboard HMS *Lion,* which was his flagship for the next four years.

Again he was at the center of a storm of controversy: it was said by his critics, as well as a number of thoughtful observers, that he was too young, he was too inexperienced, he lacked dedication, and he lacked the professional competence necessary for such a major command. Beatty seemed to take it all, good and bad, in stride, with an apparent self-confidence that bordered on out-and-out arrogance, and the persona with which the British public became so familiar began to develop.

And yet the public persona of David Beatty does not bear close examination: the key to understanding it can be found in, of all places, the photographs taken of him while in command of the Battlecruiser Squadron and later the Grand Fleet. The admiral's hat tilted at a rakish angle over the right eye, the nonregulation six-button coat—his hands thrust into the pockets—the erect posture, and the square-jawed, glint-eyed expression, all combined to project a confident, cocksure, even arrogant, aura. But the expression never changes, and the pose never varies, ultimately revealing that it is exactly that, a pose. Scheer, who never openly sought public, as opposed to professional, recognition, had few photographs taken of him, formal or candid; likewise Hipper. Candid pictures of Jellicoe abound, some so casual that he can be seen with a cigarette in his hand. Yet casual or candid photos of Beatty are rare to the point of being almost nonexistent.

Beatty became a victim of his own success, trapped by the very public image he had striven so hard to cultivate. With his vitality, unquestionable courage, and knack for being at the center of any action, he had come to embody the British public's ideal of the Royal Navy—fearless, aggressive, keen for action, and supremely self-confident. But because he had neglected the service schools and colleges that allowed his colleagues to develop their expertise and specialties, he lacked technical skills; more critically, he lacked a sound understanding of the capabilities and limitations of the ships he commanded. Because he had spent too much time in shore duty instead of at sea, he was a seaman of only average ability. In short he was deficient in the tools required to do the job asked of him. Yet Beatty's misfortune was that having created for himself the image of the quintessential British naval officer, once war came, he had to do his best to live up to it.

The overriding impression made by Admiral Sir John Rushworth Jellicoe, even seven decades after his death, is that of a man possessed of a quiet but extraordinary intelligence. In this sense Jellicoe was the complete antithesis of Beatty: while Beatty was often spectacular, he could never be considered brilliant; Jellicoe, on the other hand, was brilliant but never spectacular.

He was a small man, standing five feet, five inches tall (Beatty stood only two inches taller), although he had a presence that seemed to impart to him a more impressive stature. Born into a middle-class family in the seafaring town of Southampton, in 1859, John Jellicoe was almost preordained for a life at sea. His father was the marine superintendent and commodore of the Royal Mail Steam Packet Service, and "Jack," as the future Admiral of the Fleet was nicknamed, was surrounded by the sights and sounds of ships, shipyards, and docks from his earliest days. He was a clever boy, not gifted with a soaring, abstract intellect like Fisher, but rather with a keen and penetrating practical intelligence: he always wanted to know why and how things worked. If he had not joined the Royal Navy, he almost certainly would have joined one of the great British steamship companies. His natural gifts of quiet leadership made taking the path to command equally inevitable; had he not done so, he would have made a brilliant engineer. One of his most astonishing characteristics was that he was never known to raise his voice: such was the respect and authority which he naturally commanded that he never needed to.

The summer of 1872 saw the 13-year-old Jellicoe join the Royal Navy as a cadet at the training school *Britannia*. Two years later, when his class graduated as midshipmen, he stood at the top of its 38 members. Even then he had high ambitions: in the flyleaf of one of his textbooks he had neatly written in a 13-year-old hand, "Property of Admiral Sir John Jellicoe." *Britannia* was just the first of a succession of schools to which Jellicoe was posted in between his seagoing assignments: eventually he became recognized as an expert in torpedoes, navigation, and seamanship, but above all, gunnery. By the time Jellicoe was promoted to commander, in 1891, he had acquired the complete technical education that Beatty so sorely lacked and that was mirrored in his counterparts across the North Sea, Scheer and Hipper.

By that time he had also begun the collection of adventures and incidents that marked his life. It was aboard HMS *Colossus,* when a seaman fell overboard and was swept away, that Jellicoe, then a lieutenant, first demonstrated his not inconsiderable personal courage, diving in after the man, and, swimming strongly, reaching the sailor and keeping him afloat until a boat from *Colossus* could reach them. In 1884 he came to the attention of Jackie

The Price of Admiralty

91

Fisher, while serving on the staff of HMS *Excellent,* the Royal Navy's Gunnery School, which Fisher commanded. Fisher recognized Jellicoe's outstanding personality and intellect, and immediately took him under his wing, grooming him for future promotion and eventual high command.

In 1891 Jellicoe was given the post of commander (that is, executive officer) of HMS *Victoria,* the flagship of the Mediterranean Fleet under Vice Admiral Sir Thomas Tryon. Jellicoe was aboard *Victoria* on June 22, 1893, when through a combination of faulty signals and maneuvers, the flagship was fatally rammed by HMS *Camperdown.* Jellicoe, who had been fighting a severe fever, was able to make his way out onto the open deck and into the water, and so survived. Three hundred fifty-eight of the 649 aboard *Victoria* did not, including Tryon. Because Jellicoe had been on the sick list when the accident occurred, no stigma by association was attached to him, and he continued his progress through the ranks of the Royal Navy, being promoted to captain the following year.

His technical expertise took him back to England, where he specialized in developing naval ordnance. In 1897, he met Gwendoline Cayzer, the 19-year-old daughter of a wealthy shipowner, Sir Charles Cayzer. Romance blossomed, but before the couple could act, Jellicoe was posted to the Far East Squadron. It was a routine assignment until the summer of 1900, when the Boxer Rebellion flared across China and laid siege to the European Legation in Peking.

A hastily assembled relief column of half a dozen European nationalities was assembled under the command of Vice Admiral Sir Edward Seymour; Jellicoe was named his chief of staff. The column's advance was halted 70 miles short of Peking, and in a furious firefight Jellicoe was hit in the left lung by a Chinese bullet. Told that the wound was mortal, he made out his will (he left all he had to his mother) and then calmly prepared to die.

Instead, he began to recover. While the relief column was retreating back to Tientsin, Jellicoe began to regain his strength. Surgeons later declared that the location of the bullet made it inoperable, so he carried it inside his body the rest of his life, but it never gave him the slightest problem. His return to England to convalesce was his opportunity to make his relationship with Gwendoline Cayzer permanent, and they married in July 1902. Altogether they had six children, five daughters and a son, the latter being born when Jellicoe was 59 and retired from the Royal Navy.

His next major task began in the fall of 1904, when Admiral Fisher asked Jellicoe to sit on the design board for HMS *Dreadnought,* followed by an assignment as the director of Naval Ordnance, responsible for the design of all guns and ammunition used by the Royal Navy. In 1907, when he was promoted to rear admiral and given the knighthood he had anticipated as a cadet, he was appointed second-in-command of the Atlantic Fleet, the same position Beatty declined four years later. He then became Third Sea Lord, charged with the design, fitting out, and repair of all the ships of the fleet. These postings made him intimately aware of the capabilities of the ships of the Royal Navy, as well as their weaknesses, and he began comparative studies of German designs to learn the same about Great Britain's most likely future naval opponent. Further technical postings followed, and then in December 1910 he was given command of the Atlantic Fleet. It was shortly after this that his five-year-old daughter, Betty, died of a mastoid infection.

A year later Jellicoe was posted as second-in-command of the Home Fleet, a post that usually designated its holder as a future First Sea Lord or Admiral of the Fleet. Promotion to Vice Admiral came in 1912, and he returned to Whitehall as Second Sea Lord. By this time even foreign observers were forced to take notice of his competence: the German naval attaché to London, Captain Wilhelm Widemann, filed a report with von Tirpitz in which he stated:

> If one asks English naval officers which admiral would have the best chances for a brilliant career on the basis of his capability, one almost always receives the same answer: beside Prince Louis of Battenberg, unquestionably Sir John Jellicoe.

By contrast, Beatty never received mention in any of Captain Widemann's reports.

The heavy emphasis that Jellicoe placed on technical education throughout his career, as well as the specialized technical posts he held at various times, should never give the impression that he was nothing more than a glorified engineer or technician. Jellicoe was very much a leader in his quiet and unassuming way as was the flamboyant Beatty in his; Jellicoe perceived very early in his career that no matter how technologically advanced a warship might be, a mediocre crew could render it essentially ineffective. For Jellicoe, then, the well-being of the sailors under his command and care became every bit as important as the maintenance and upkeep of the ships they served. When the Grand Fleet moved to Scapa Flow in August 1914, Jellicoe almost immediately began a program of improvement on the limited facilities of the anchorage. Canteens were set up, postal delivery improved; he had a golf course built, a cricket pitch constructed, and a football (soccer) field laid out. He encouraged athletic competitions between ships' crews, whether rowing, tug-of-war, or cross country runs, all in the effort to sustain the men's all-important morale. It was an utter contrast to the life of the sailors of the High Seas Fleet, who, though they lived ashore in barracks in comfortable

Wilhelmshaven, had less to do in their spare time than their British counterparts on the windswept Orkneys.

When war began to overshadow Europe in July 1914, Jellicoe was traveling north in a railway car, bound for Scotland and Scapa Flow, preparing to assume the position of commander in chief of the Grand Fleet. On August 14, the transfer of command took place. Once settled into his new command, Jellicoe set to work with a will. His first responsibility was the defense of the British Isles and the sea-lanes that supplied it; it was up to him to determine how that would best be done. Jellicoe's position as commander in chief of the Grand Fleet carried with it greater responsibility for the outcome of the war than any similar post in any of the warring nations. Of Jellicoe, Winston Churchill wrote that he was "the only man who could lose the war in an afternoon." This was nothing less than the truth, although the implication that if Jellicoe could lose the war in a matter of hours he could also win it in that same amount of time, an assumption many of the Admiral's critics made in the years to come, is patently false. Jellicoe understood as few others did, and this is the true measure of the depth of his intellect, that his first duty, which overrode any and all other considerations, was the preservation of the Grand Fleet as a fighting entity. With it, Britain was the greatest of the Great Powers; without it she was nothing more than a minor island nation off the northwest coast of Europe. Again, Churchill's words, dramatic as they are, offer the most precise articulation of Great Britain's dependence on her fleet:

> …consider these ships, so vast in themselves, yet so easily lost to sight on the surface of the waters. Sufficient at the moment, we trusted, for their task, but yet only a score or so. They were all we had. On them, we conceived, floated the might, majesty, dominion and power of the British Empire. All our long history built up century after century, all our great affairs in every part of the globe, all the means of livelihood and safety of our faithful, industrious, active population depended on them. Open the seacocks and let them sink beneath the surface…and in a few minutes—half an hour at the most— the whole outlook of the world would be changed. The British Empire would dissolve like a dream; each isolated community struggling forward by itself; the central power of union broken; mighty provinces, whole empires in themselves, drifting hopelessly out of control, and falling prey to strangers; and Europe after one sudden convulsion passing into the iron grip and rule of the Teuton and of all that Teutonic system meant. There would only be left far off across the Atlantic unarmed, unready, and as yet uninstructed America to maintain, singlehanded, law and freedom among men….

Jellicoe was, on many levels, all too well aware of this. While on paper the supremacy of the Royal Navy over its German opponent appeared overwhelming, Jellicoe knew better. Accidents, repairs, and ships detached for specific assignment away from the Grand Fleet all eroded some measure of the Royal Navy's strength, at times leaving the margin of superiority narrowly thin. Jellicoe knew that losing even a single squadron in action against the High Seas Fleet, without corresponding losses by the Germans, could prove crippling. The Germans had the opportunity to choose if, when, and where they would attack the Grand Fleet, giving them the initiative to strike when the British fleet was numerically at its weakest.

Jellicoe had no similar luxury: while he could lose the war in an afternoon, he could not win it. Defeat of the Royal Navy proved fatal to Great Britain, defeat of the High Seas Fleet was an inconvenience to Germany. No corresponding strategic benefit would accrue to Great Britain should the German Navy suffer a crippling defeat as would occur should the Grand Fleet suffer a serious setback. No strategic opportunities for intervening along the German coast existed, nor could access to Russia through the Baltic be ensured, or even assumed, as Germany could close off the straights between her Baltic shore and Sweden. Attacking the High Seas Fleet held too many risks for the Royal Navy: simply by remaining in Scapa Flow and barring the German Navy access to the North Atlantic, Jellicoe understood, the Grand Fleet was doing the job for which it had been built—protecting the British Isles and the Empire.

It was in translating this understanding into operational reality that Jellicoe's particular genius manifested itself. Perhaps it was his fascination with machines that gave Jellicoe the ability to envision the Grand Fleet as a mechanism, its parts moving in intricate, interrelated patterns. Whatever it was, Jellicoe had an uncanny ability to predict enemy movements and intentions, and then place his ships in positions that gave them the best advantage over the enemy. He had first demonstrated this in fleet maneuvers in 1913, when, given command of an invasion force tasked with landing on Britain's North Sea shore, he handled his forces so adroitly and outmaneuvered his opponents so completely that Churchill, who was observing, called off the exercise, lest foreign observers learn too much from it. He next demonstrated this ability in the action that became known as the Battle of Heligoland Bight, on his own initiative reinforcing the British raiding force, an action that probably saved a British squadron from annihilation. Another example came a few months later, during the Scarborough Raid, when Jellicoe wanted to take the whole of the Grand Fleet to sea, based on his concern that the High Seas Fleet might be laying an ambush for Beatty's battlecruisers. The Admiralty overruled him, but events proved him right, for that was exactly what the German Naval High Command had planned, and only the timidity of the German commander, Admiral von Ingenohl, saved Beatty from being utterly crushed. By the early spring of 1915, Jellicoe was routinely taking the Grand Fleet into the North Sea on "sweeps" designed to catch any German forces unaware and annihilate them. For Jellicoe, the best method of effecting the defense of the realm was clear: if the High Seas Fleet were to ever sortie into the North Sea in strength, it would find the Grand Fleet there, waiting for it.

Chapter 5

Twisting the Lion's Tail

When Britain and Germany went to war on August 3, 1914, the staff, officers, and ratings of the Royal Navy, from the greenest midshipman in the smallest destroyer in Scapa Flow to the First Lord in Whitehall, were eager for action against the High Seas Fleet. Likewise in Germany, most of the officers and certainly all of the ratings were prepared for, even anticipating, facing off against the British. But in Berlin, at the highest levels of the Naval High Command, prevarication and timorousness bordering on cowardice, rather than the bold action for which the German dreadnoughts and battlecruisers had been built, were the order of the day. Consequently, for all of its repetitions in toasts in High Seas Fleet war rooms, when it finally had arrived, "Der Tag" was not welcomed with cries of "Death or Glory" and thunderous broadsides ranging out toward the British foe. Instead, it was met with the cries of gulls overhead in the rigging, the slap of harbor chop against ships' gunwales, and the quiet puttering of motor launches making their way between ship and shore.

The timidity began at the very top with the Kaiser. Wilhelm, for all of his uniformed bombast and militaristic fantasies, shied away from conflict and confrontation in real life. He was also suddenly faced with a harsh reality that he had apparently never previously recognized: as the existence of the High Seas Fleet had been insufficient to intimidate the British, it now had to prove its worth by actually fighting—and in doing so risking all of the national treasure and prestige poured into its creation. Having agreed to the construction of a fleet whose entire strategy was founded on risk, Wilhelm suddenly realized he had no desire to carry that risk through to its conclusion. Having built these magnificent warships, he was loathe to gamble with their existence, despite the fact that this was their very purpose.

98 Distant Victory

His senior admirals, Alfred von Tirpitz excepted, were of a similar mind, none more so than the commander in chief of the High Seas Fleet, Admiral Friedrich von Ingenohl. Like military history on land, naval history is replete with examples of commanding officers who are excellent, even outstanding, administrators in peacetime, but who are hopeless and hapless as leaders in war. Von Ingenohl was one such officer. It is difficult to say at this remove whether his reluctance to engage the British fleet was due to a simple lack of an aggressive nature or instead to an overdeveloped sense of awe of the Royal Navy. Whatever the specific cause of von Ingenohl's reluctance to risk a battle with the British fleet, it effectively immobilized the High Seas Fleet.

The British, in particular, chafed at this inaction, and when by the third week of the war the High Seas Fleet gave no indication that it was prepared to leave the protection of Heligoland Bight and try conclusions with the Royal Navy, a handful of the more aggressive British officers began to cast about for ways of goading the Germans into action. British submarines had been keeping watch on Heligoland since the early days of August 1914. It did not take long for them to recognize a pattern in the movements of the German torpedo boats and light cruisers that patrolled the area: each evening at dusk a group of German torpedo boats, supported by light cruisers, steamed 20 miles out into the North Sea. There the cruisers took up station while the torpedo boats continued northwest for another 10 to 12 miles, setting up a patrol screen that guarded the approaches to Heligoland during the night. Commodore Roger Keyes, eager and aggressive, in overall command of the British submarine force, concocted a plan for attacking these patrols using his submarines acting in concert with a force of light cruisers and destroyers that was based at Harwich under the command of the another fire-eating commodore, Reginald Tyrwhitt.

The plan, which was perhaps a bit more complex than it truly needed to be, called for the Harwich flotilla to attack at dawn, just as the German patrols were withdrawing and were at their weariest. Tyrwhitt's light cruisers and destroyers would drive the German ships away from the Heligoland coast toward a waiting line of British submarines. A second line of subs would be positioned to intercept any reinforcements that might be sent out to the beleaguered German light units. The *coup de grace* to the German torpedo boats and cruisers would be delivered by the Harwich Force, supported by armored cruisers or even a pair of battlecruisers. In Commodore Keyes' ideal scenario, the Grand Fleet would be standing out in the North Sea in distant support of the operation, on the off chance that the High Seas Fleet might sortie. In addition to the damage done to the German Navy's light forces, Keyes hoped to inflict a psychological blow on the Germans as well, convincing them that, as he put it, "when we go out, those damned Englanders will fall on us and smash us!"

When the War Staff ignored Keyes' plan, the Commodore approached the First Lord of the Admiralty, Winston Churchill, on August 23, 1914. Churchill, who was as fond of aggressive action as Wilhelm was shy of it, was immediately impressed with the plan. The next day convened a meeting with the Admiralty's senior operational officers, who studied the plan and made changes to the deployments and forces, refining it for maximum effect. It was decided that the support of the Grand Fleet was unnecessary: the five armored cruisers and two battlecruisers already committed to the operation were more than sufficient to deal with any likely German response. If the German battle fleet should sail after all, the British forces should be fast enough to outrun it. Keyes and Tyrwhitt were instructed to be prepared to take their commands to sea as early as August 26, with the actual operation scheduled for August 28.

In a lapse of communications that unfortunately characterized much of the Admiralty's conduct of the war, it was not until August 26 that the commander in chief of the Grand Fleet, Admiral John Jellicoe, was informed of the pending action. Even then he was told only that "a destroyer sweep of the First and Third Flotillas with submarines suitably placed is in orders for Friday from East to West, commencing between Horns Reef and Heligoland, with battlecruisers in support." Jellicoe's keen intellect soon perceived that there was more to the pending action than he was told and was rightly concerned by the apparent lack of support for an operation so close to the German coast. Nearly 50 of the Royal Navy's warships would be concentrated just a few miles from the German coast: if something went wrong and the German battle fleet were to somehow suddenly appear, the wolves would well and truly be among the chickens, for the British forces would be utterly inadequate to face the German dreadnoughts.

Instead, Jellicoe, who appears to have deduced the spirit if not the details of Keyes' plan, wanted to bring the Grand Fleet out into the North Sea in support, ready to intervene should the High Seas Fleet sortie. The Admiralty disagreed, citing a key provision of the plan—that the timing of the attack was calculated so that it would take place while the tides were too low to allow the battleships and battlecruisers to sail from Wilhelmshaven. Whitehall did give Jellicoe permission to send additional battlecruisers to join up with Tyrwhitt's Harwich Force, and Jellicoe promptly seized the opportunity to send David Beatty's First Battlecruiser Squadron and Commodore William Goodenough's First Light Cruiser Squadron to reinforce the two battlecruisers— *Invincible* and *New Zealand*—and five armored cruisers of the covering force.

Still, because the Admiralty refused to make Jellicoe privy to the entire operation, the orders he gave Beatty and Goodenough were vague and incomplete. When Beatty signaled to his battlecruisers, "We are to rendezvous with *Invincible* and *New Zealand* at 0500 to support destroyers and submarines…. Operation consisting of a sweep…. Heligoland to westward…. Know very little, shall hope to learn more as we go along," he was telling the literal truth, for he did not even have the position where Tyrwhitt's force would begin its westward sweep or what course it would follow. That information did not reach him until four hours after the battlecruisers had left Rosyth; neither Beatty nor Goodenough were ever informed of the positions of the lurking British submarines.

By this time Keyes and Tyrwhitt had already sailed as well, but, though the Admiralty tried to inform them of Beatty's and Goodenough's pending rendezvous with them, instead of being forwarded to the two commodores' flagships, the messages languished on their respective desks in port. Consequently, neither had any idea that other British forces were at sea—the captains of the submarines and destroyers had been told before sailing that the biggest British ship in the immediate waters surrounding the Bight would be a light cruiser: if they saw anything larger, they could assume that it was German—fair game for the destroyers' and submarines' torpedoes.

This situation led to some tense moments just before dawn on August 27 when the Harwich force encountered a trio of four-funneled light cruisers. In the darkness their silhouettes were shadowy and their nationality uncertain. The British crews were already at action stations and began training their guns and torpedo tubes at the unidentified warships. Cautiously, Tyrwhitt had the lights on his flagship, HMS *Arethusa*, flash out a recognition signal, to which the unknown ships promptly replied with the correct response, then identified themselves as part of the First Cruiser Squadron, one of them Goodenough's flagship, HMS *Southampton*.

Relieved, Tyrwhitt quickly flashed an inquiry, "Are you taking part in the operation?" Goodenough replied, "Yes. I know your course, and Beatty is behind us." This was the first news Tyrwhitt had that the British battlecruisers were out in full strength, and he quickly informed his command to be on the lookout for the new arrivals. For Keyes, the situation was still dangerous, for there was no way to communicate this latest news to the submerged submarines. All anyone could do was wait and hope that none of the British warships fell afoul of one of their own submersibles.

First contact between the British and German forces came just as dawn was breaking at 0526. *E-9*, one of three British submarines designated as the "bait" to lure the German torpedo boats and cruisers into the waiting ambush, spotted the German torpedo boat *G-194* and fired one torpedo at her. As *G-194* was turning in an attempt to ram *E-9*, she sent an alert signal to Wilhelmshaven, and, just as Keyes and Tyrwhitt had hoped, the V Torpedo Boat Flotilla was ordered out from Heligoland to hunt for British subs.

A little more than an hour later, destroyers from Tyrwhitt's First Destroyer Flotilla sighted *G-194* and opened fire on her. When the German torpedo boat signaled that it was now engaged with British destroyers, Rear Admiral Franz Hipper, who was in overall command of the Heligoland defenses in Wilhelmshaven, assumed reasonably enough that the British were launching nothing more than a "hit-and-run" raid with their destroyers and submarines, and so ordered the light cruisers SMS *Stettin* and *Frauenlob* to support the German torpedo boats, but saw no reason to send out any larger ships.

For some reason, *G-194's* signal failed to reach the V Torpedo Boat Flotilla: expecting nothing more demanding than hunting submarines, the ten little ships had only partially raised steam before sailing, and now faced a squadron of larger, more heavily armed British destroyers while they could only muster barely half their top speed. Tyrwhitt sent HMS *Laurel* and three other destroyers to intercept the German torpedo boats, which attempted to withdraw as the British ships came dashing in.

Seeing the German ships turn away, Tyrwhitt tried to recall his four destroyers, but the rapidly changing visibility caused his signal to go unseen. The commodore then decided to lead *Arethusa* and the rest of the First Flotilla after them: a sharp exchange of fire quickly developed, with *D-8*, *G-9*, *S-13*, *T-33*, and *V-1* all taking heavy damage. The torpedo boats attempted to run under the cover of the 8-inch shore batteries on Heligoland, but the shifting morning mist prevented the guns from intervening. For Tyrwhitt it was just as well, for as he was chasing the escaping German ships the 200-foot high cliffs suddenly appeared out of the fog, and he hastily turned his squadron away before the German gunners could find the range.

All the while First Destroyer Flotilla, led by the light cruiser *Fearless*, was keeping a parallel course to the north but taking no part in the action. This was in keeping with Keyes' original plan, where the First Flotilla would be held back to sweep down on the German torpedo boats once they were engaged by the Third Flotilla and were safely out of range of the shore batteries. Tyrwhitt's ships were now beginning to overtake the second line of German ships: suddenly, just a few minutes before 8 o'clock, the light cruisers *Frauenlob* and *Stettin*, steaming hard, came into range. Now it was the British destroyers who were outgunned, and it was their turn to withdraw. *Fearless* quickly turned toward *Stettin* and opened up such a flurry of shellfire that a German officer aboard *Frauenlob* thought *Stettin* looked as if she "were in boiling water." When one of her forward guns was knocked out, *Stettin* turned back toward Heligoland, her mission accomplished: the German torpedo boats were able to successfully escape the British destroyers. Despite the damage she had inflicted, *Fearless* did not follow, but continued the sweep of Heligoland Bight: pursuing *Stettin* would have brought *Fearless* within range of the Bight's guns.

Meanwhile *Arethusa* and *Frauenlob* were locked in a fierce gunnery duel. Tyrwhitt's flagship was newly built and had been in commission for just over two weeks: now, at the worst possible time, some of *Arethusa's* teething problems began to make themselves known. Within minutes of the beginning of the engagement, two of her six 4-inch guns had jammed, while her after 6-inch gun stopped working as well. Her wireless set was inoperable, and a hit down along her waterline was flooding the engine room. *Frauenlob's* gunnery was remarkable: Tyrwhitt later counted 15 hits on Arethusa's port side alone. But despite her damage, the British cruiser was still a fighting concern, and ten hits from the forward 6-inch gun had torn into *Frauenlob,* including one on her bridge that killed or wounded every officer and rating stationed there, including her captain. Reeling, *Frauenlob* turned away, seeking the protection of the Heligoland guns. Wisely, Tyrwhitt chose not to try and pursue the stricken German cruiser, and instead at 0830 turned *Arethusa,* her condenser holed and her speed dropping, back toward the main action.

Meanwhile, as Tyrwhitt's destroyers were engaging the German torpedo boats, Commodore Keyes aboard HMS *Lurcher* had taken station to the northwest, and just as *Arethusa* and *Frauenlob* were breaking off their action, Keyes sighted several cruisers looming out of the mist to the north of him. Never having received the message that Goodenough's First Light Cruiser Squadron and Beatty's battlecruisers would be reinforcing him, Keyes flashed a report to *Invincible* and *New Zealand,* which were standing off to the west where they were expecting to finish off the German torpedo boats: he had spotted, he said, two enemy light cruisers and had begun shadowing them. In reality they were HMS *Lowestoft* and HMS *Nottingham:* Goodenough had detached them from his squadron and sent them ahead to aid the beleaguered *Arethusa.* When Goodenough received Keyes message, he did not realize that the unidentified ships were, in fact, his own cruisers, and he altered course toward *Lurcher.*

Upon seeing four more unidentified ships where none were expected to be, Keyes assumed this quartet was German as well, and believing himself hopelessly outgunned, began racing toward *Invincible* and *New Zealand,* signaling them that he was trying to draw the four unknown warships into range of the battlecruisers. The farce was compounded when Tyrwhitt signaled to Goodenough: "Please chase westward.... Commodore Keyes is being chased by four light cruisers"—in other words, asking Goodenough to chase after himself. The whole ludicrous situation was not ended until sometime after

9:00 AM, when the morning sun burnt off enough of the mist to allow Keyes to positively identify the silhouette of *Southampton,* Goodenough's flagship. Keyes then signaled to Tyrwhitt and the two battlecruisers, with a rather understandable peevishness, that "Cruisers are our cruisers [of] whose presence in the area I was not informed."

The danger that the mislaid Admiralty signals of the previous night had created was not over yet, however. Goodenough formed up his squadron with Tyrwhitt's with the intention of continuing the planned sweep westward—carrying them right across Keyes' lines of waiting submarines. It was not long before the inevitable happened: *E-6,* sighting a light cruiser where no British ship larger than a destroyer was supposed to be, fired a pair of torpedoes at the unknown ship. The target was in reality Goodenough's own flagship, *Southampton,* which turned toward the torpedo tracks, evading both of them, intent on running down and ramming the submarine. A tragedy was avoided only when *E-6* crash-dived and *Southampton* narrowly missed her.

While *Southampton* and *E-6* were dodging one another, farther to the northwest *Nottingham* and *Lowestoft* had overtaken the torpedo boat *V-187,* already being pursued by a quartet of British destroyers. At a range of 4000 yards the two light cruisers opened fire on the hapless German ship and quickly left it dead in the water and sinking. The British destroyers then stood by, and when *V-187* finally went down at 0910, they put boats into the water to rescue survivors.

It was just then that *Stettin* returned to the battle, and her reappearance interrupted the rescue operation. Not wanting to face *Stettin's* powerful guns (the German 4.1-inch gun had remarkable hitting power for its size), the British destroyers were forced to recover their boats as quickly as possible—two were set adrift, empty and abandoned. Two others, belonging to HMS *Defender,* were too far away to be picked up and so were left behind, with one British officer and nine British seamen between them, along with 28 German prisoners.

Suddenly a torpedo track appeared out of nowhere, and *Stettin* put her helm hard over to avoid it, then, when a lookout spotted the periscope of the submarine responsible, turned toward it at high speed, intending to ram. The submarine, the British *E-4,* crash-dived, then surfaced 20 minutes later, after *Stettin* had left the area. The British sailors, believing themselves abandoned in the middle of Heligoland Bight, cheered their deliverance, while the stunned Germans resigned themselves to their captivity. As it turned out, the *E-4* had room to spare only for the British officer and seaman, along with three selected German prisoners. The remainder were left in the boats, after being given water, biscuits, and the correct course for Wilhelmshaven.

104   Distant Victory

HMS *Fearless* had joined up with the limping *Arethusa* at 1017, and both ships stopped while the engineering crews of both ships worked frantically on the *Arethusa's* engines. In less than 45 minutes, feed lines had been repaired, the condenser patched, the worst of the holes in the hull plugged, and all but two of her guns restored to working order. It was not a moment too soon, for a quartet of German light cruisers was rapidly approaching from the east, and the two British ships were out of range of support from the battlecruisers and armored cruisers on station to the west.

They were *Stettin,* which was still lurking about in the lingering haze, along with *Köln, Strassburg,* and *Ariadne.* A fifth, *Mainz,* was on its way. In Wilhelmshaven Hipper seethed with frustration, for it was clear that the British raid had been carefully timed to coincide with the low tide that prohibited the German battlecruisers and dreadnoughts from leaving port. Nonetheless, the German capital ships were raising steam in the hope that they could put to sea before the action was over. Von Ingenohl had summoned enough courage to permit a limited sortie: the only British ships reported were destroyers and light cruisers, none of which represented a serious threat to the German battleships and battlecruisers. So if there was an opportunity to clean up what was left of the British light forces, then it was to be quickly seized.

This was precisely the circumstances that Jellicoe had envisioned: the action against the German torpedo boat patrols was taking far longer than had originally been planned, and the longer the British forces lingered so close to the German shore, the greater the danger of the High Seas Fleet making an appearance. Even with the reinforcement of Beatty's battlecruisers, the British could suddenly find themselves badly outnumbered and outgunned: this was the concern behind Jellicoe's initial request to take the Grand Fleet to sea in support of the operation.

Meanwhile the four German cruisers arrived piecemeal, their commander, Rear Admiral Leberecht Maass, not taking the time to concentrate his forces. It was a mistake for which he, his ships, and his men paid dearly. The first to appear was *Strassburg,* which loomed out of the mist and began firing on *Arethusa.* Straddling the British cruiser repeatedly, *Strassburg* was unable to obtain a single hit before a torpedo attack by the destroyers of the Third Flotilla forced her to turn away, giving *Arethusa* a chance to turn to the west, putting as much distance between herself and the Germans as possible.

No sooner had he done so than *Köln* appeared, steaming up from the southwest. Thinking her to be a much larger armored cruiser, Tyrwhitt frantically signaled to Beatty at 1100: "Am attacked by a large cruiser.... Respectfully suggest that I may be supported. Am hard pressed." Beatty sent the whole of the First Cruiser Squadron to Tyrwhitt's aid; Tyrwhitt ordered his destroyers to launch another torpedo attack, and just as *Strassburg* had done, *Köln* turned away.

For the next 30 minutes *Arethusa* was able to make her way west, having worked up to a speed of 20 knots. At 1130 another German light cruiser appeared, this one SMS *Mainz,* which immediately opened fire on the destroyers screening *Arethusa.* None of the German shells struck home, nor did any of the torpedoes fired by the British ships. Though she appeared to be undamaged, *Mainz* abruptly broke off the action and turned southeastward: her lookouts had sighted Goodenough's four cruisers bearing down hard on her. These four ships began a furious shelling, hitting *Mainz* at least twice before she was able to slip into the shifting mists. It did not save her, though, for just moments later she passed across the bows of *Arethusa* and the destroyers of Tyrwhitt's Harwich Force. The destroyers charged in, some as close as 1,000 yards, and launched torpedoes.

Mainz dodged furiously, and her guns kept up an astonishingly accurate fire, hitting four of the attackers, one of them, *Laertes,* taking four hits and temporarily losing all power. But it was a hopeless fight: her rudder jammed by her frantic maneuvering and her port engine knocked out by a shell hit, Mainz found herself turning back toward Goodenough's four cruisers, now less than 6,000 yards away. Suddenly she staggered as one of the destroyers' torpedoes struck her. One of her officers described what happened next: "The ship reared, bent perceptibly from end to end, and continued to pitch for some time. The emergency lights went out." By now almost every salvo from the four British cruisers was hitting home. Her upperworks aflame, fires burning out of control below decks, *Mainz* began sinking by the bow. Her mainmast slowly bent forward, then toppled across what was left of her superstructure. At 1220, her captain ordered the ship scuttled: a moment later he was killed when a shell burst on the remains of the bridge. Five minutes later Goodenough ordered "Cease Fire" and instructed HMS *Liverpool* to launch her boats to pick up survivors. Commodore Keyes' flagship, HMS *Lurcher,* arrived on the scene just at this moment. Keyes took her alongside the sinking German cruiser, urging as many of the *Mainz's* crewmen to jump aboard as could make it; a total of 220 were rescued this way. A few moments later, *Mainz* rolled over onto her starboard side, then at 1305 turned bottomup and sank.

Tyrwhitt, having broken off the action with *Mainz* and leaving her to Goodenough's four cruisers some 20 minutes before she went under, was not out of the woods yet. Five more enemy cruisers were on their way to the battle, and *Arethusa* had effected some rough-and-ready repairs, it was clear to everyone aboard that she was in no condition to put up any kind of fight; neither were many of her escorting destroyers, in particular *Laurel*, *Liberty*, and *Laertes*.

It was just at this moment that *Strassburg* and *Köln* returned to the battle, much to Tyrwhitt's dismay. He felt that he had already used up a lifetime's worth of luck in one morning, and now it seemed that it was about to run out: Goodenough's four cruisers were nowhere in sight, and Tyrwhitt's destroyers had exhausted their torpedoes. Just as the first shells from the two German cruisers began to fall about *Arethusa*, Tyrwhitt looked to the west and spotted the dark shape of a huge warship looming out of the mist, belching smoke from its three great funnels, four massive gun turrets swinging in his direction. Four more equally huge dark shapes followed. It took only seconds for the commodore to recognize them: British battlecruisers. Beatty had arrived.

When Tyrwhitt's signal asking for Beatty's help had reached HMS *Lion* at 1100, the five British battlecruisers had taken up a position some 40 miles northwest of Heligoland, where Beatty paced the bridge of his flagship, HMS *Lion*. As he later put it, the signals sent by Keyes, Tyrwhitt, and Goodenough throughout most of the morning "contained no information on which I could act." Beatty had reason for concern, even worry: the operation off the Bight was taking far longer than had originally been planned, and the German response was far more vigorous than had been anticipated. Tyrwhitt's destroyers had been in German waters for nearly four hours, and as the hands on the bridge clock approached 1200, Beatty became concerned that the High Seas Fleet might begin to sortie out from Wilhelmshaven: theoretically the tide would be high enough at 1300 to allow the German dreadnoughts to begin crossing the Jade Bar: they could reach the scene of the action by 1400. There was a danger that Tyrwhitt's Harwich Force, even reinforced by Goodenough's squadron of light cruisers, could be overwhelmed without Beatty's support.

Yet there was an equally real threat to Beatty's battlecruisers, should he take them into the action. There was the not inconsiderable danger of enemy minefields, and there was the threat of the British submarines that had no idea there would be British battlecruisers in the operational area. Not only that, but should the High Seas Fleet make it over the Jade Bar, there was the real chance that Beatty's five ships could face the combined strength of the German battle fleet. In his mind, Beatty felt that the submarines were the least likely threat, but still he hesitated. His aggressive nature made him want to dash in, but the weight of responsibility for five of the Royal Navy's most powerful warships held him back. Turning to his flag captain, *Lion's* commanding officer, Captain Ernle Chatfield, he asked rhetorically, "What do you think we should do? I ought to go forward and support Tyrwhitt, but if I lose one of these valuable ships, the country will not forgive me." Chatfield, bearing none of Beatty's burden of command, replied, "Surely we must go!" Something in his flag captain's demeanor seemed to make up Beatty's mind, and at 1135 he ordered his five battlecruisers into line and turned toward the Bight.

It took just over 60 minutes for *Lion* and her consorts to reach the battle, but when they did, their presence was decisive. In the space of barely 20 minutes they turned what had been an indecisive skirmish into Great Britain's first naval victory of the war.

Either by a stroke of luck or extraordinary seamanship, the five battlecruisers had steamed almost directly for Tyrwhitt's little flagship, and as they passed *Arethusa* they quickly ranged in the German light cruisers. *Stettin* was once again lucky enough to escape into the mist; *Köln* was not so fortunate. For seven minutes she was the sole target of the five battlecruisers: *Lion, Queen Mary, Princess Royal, Invincible,* and *New Zealand.* No one was able to count the number of times *Köln* was hit, but within minutes she was ablaze from bow to stern. The sudden appearance of the old two-funneled light cruiser *Ariadne,* the first such ship ever built for the German Navy, gave *Köln* a respite, but only briefly. Charging in on the British battlecruisers at high speed, she appeared to be preparing to launch torpedoes. Captain Chatfield took no chances, shifting his ship's gunfire from *Köln* to *Ariadne.* Three quick salvos were all that were needed to tear the gallant but doomed little ship apart. Though she remained afloat for another two hours and was taken in tow by the cruiser *Straslund, Ariadne* had suffered too much, and at 1510 rolled over and sank.

Meanwhile Beatty's five ships had thundered past *Köln,* covering the withdrawal of *Arethusa* and Tyrwhitt's destroyers. Turning about the northwest, he sent out a general signal to all British ships: "Retire." Once again passing by *Köln, Lion* put two salvos into her, and she quickly sank stern first. Beatty instructed four of his escorting destroyers to launch boats to pick up survivors, but when a (false) report of a submarine was received, the boats were recovered and the destroyers fled. Two days later, a single survivor, a stoker, was discovered among a mass of floating corpses. Rear Admiral Maass had gone down with his ship.

The Battle of Heligoland Bight was over. The most heavily damaged British ship, *Arethusa,* was able to reach Harwich after being towed most of the way there by HMS *Hogue.* The damaged British destroyers all reached port under their own power. Not a single British ship had been sunk, while British casualties were remarkably low, given how hot the action had been—35 killed and 40 wounded. Beatty was roundly cheered by the fleet when the First Battlecruiser Squadron returned to Scapa Flow; Tyrwhitt became something of a

108 Distant Victory

national hero when the details of *Arethusa's* action were made public. The Royal Navy had steamed into the enemy's "front yard" and inflicted a serious defeat; the boost to national morale was immeasurable.

At the same time, though, the battle threw a harsh and unflattering light on some aspects of the Royal Navy in action, particularly the Admiralty's handling of signals. The quality of British signaling before and during the battle was deplored by many senior officers. Sighting and situation reports were almost always incomplete, usually consisting only of the number and type of enemy ships sighted, but lacking such essentials as course, speed, and even the most rudimentary positions. While these were considered routine duties during peacetime maneuvers, the stress and strain of actual combat made them far more difficult; it was a problem that was overcome only with experience.

The most egregious errors, however, were three committed by the Admiralty. The first was Whitehall's failure to adequately brief Jellicoe as to the size, scope, and objectives of the operation: had he not on his own initiative sent Beatty and Goodenough to join the attacking force, Tyrwhitt's and Keyes' pair of light cruisers and two destroyer flotillas might well have been overwhelmed by the German forces. The second error was the mishandled signals informing the two commodores of the pending reinforcement by the battlecruisers and armored cruisers, which came perilously close to causing tragic "friendly fire" incidents. And third, the Admiralty never advised Beatty and Goodenough of the positions of the British submarines, which led to *E-6's* mistaken torpedo attack on *Southampton* and could have led Beatty to bring his battlecruisers into positions where they would be in danger of similar attacks. Equally absurd was the Admiralty's reaction after the battle when it was learned that the ships had fired significantly more rounds of ammunition than peacetime projections had forecast. Rather than adopt naval doctrine to conform to reality, Whitehall issued a memorandum urging commanding officers to attempt to bring their ammunition expenditures in line with Admiralty expectations. Unfortunately for the Royal Navy, such petty bungling remained a hallmark of the Admiralty's administration until the end of the war.

Still, Heligoland Bight *was* a victory for the Royal Navy: the Germans for their part had showed themselves to be courageous, dedicated, and professional. For the rest of the war there was never any suggestion anywhere within the Royal Navy that the Germans were anything but a first-class opponent. Yet, for all that, they had been bested, and that sense of confidence which transcended arrogance that had sustained the Royal Navy since the days of Trafalgar was given a new validation.

The Germans, for their part, had very little with which to console themselves after the battle. Three light cruisers—*Mainz, Ariadne,* and *Köln*—and a torpedo boat—*V-187*—had been sunk, three other cruisers had been damaged, *Frauenlob* severely, and casualties totaled 712 killed (including Rear Admiral Maass), 530 wounded, and 336 taken prisoner. While the various British commanders had kept their squadrons relatively well in hand, the tactics of Maass, his gallant death notwithstanding, were poor: the coordination of his forces was nonexistent, he never concentrated all of his light cruisers into an effective squadron, and his reports to his superiors were vague and misleading. Nor had the staff work in Wilhelmshaven been much better: many of their responses and reactions to the unfolding situation in the Bight were based on assumptions rather than hard information, a mistake that almost certainly led to the loss of *Ariadne* and *Köln.* More than any of that, however, the confidence of the German naval high command had suffered a serious blow: the Royal Navy had challenged the High Seas Fleet on its very doorstep and left the German Navy with a bloody nose.

Some senior officers, such as Hipper, understood that the battle had driven home the lesson that the German Navy still had much to learn about the realities of naval warfare. At the same time, the individual performance of the ships and their crews was more than credible: they had stood toe-to-toe with the Royal Navy and fought tenaciously. The Battle of Heligoland Bight revealed that the real failure within the German Navy lay in its High Command, which, rather than contesting control of the North Sea with the Royal Navy, tacitly conceded it to the Grand Fleet by meekly hiding the High Seas Fleet behind the minefields, shore batteries, and sheltered waters of the Bight.

Eventually the German Admiralty was stung into action, as all through the autumn months British destroyers and cruisers patrolled the North Sea seemingly at will, with occasional sweeps eastward from Scapa Flow and down the Danish coast by the Grand Fleet. Even after the disastrous loss of *Hogue, Aboukir,* and *Cressy,* this pattern was not seriously disrupted for more than a few weeks. By the end of October 1914, plans had been drawn up for a raid on the coast of Norfolk by Hipper's battlecruisers that, it was hoped, would put an end to this complacency. The result was an incident that became known as the Yarmouth Raid.

The reasoning behind the raid was relatively simple; at heart it was just revenge for Heligoland Bight. The Norfolk coast was chosen as the site of the raid because it was within 24 hours' steaming distance from Wilhelmshaven, and the approach was virtually risk-free. The German squadron had to pass through two well-charted German minefields, shell the coastal towns within its range, then make good its escape before the British battlecruisers could descend upon it from Cromarty and Rosyth on the Scottish coast—

Scapa was too far away for the Grand Fleet to arrive in time before the German warships were back in the safety of the waters of the Bight.

This was the second reason for the raid: the German Naval High Command was confident that, when the alarm was raised that German warships were shelling the British shore, the British Admiralty would respond by immediately sending Admiral Beatty's battlecruiser squadron to intercept the Germans. Hipper's plan was then to draw the advancing British warships across multiple German minefields and lines of waiting U-boats. All in all, it seemed an elegant plan.

The result of the Yarmouth Raid was, however, an unmitigated fiasco. At 0630 on November 3, Hipper brought *Seydlitz* (Hipper's flagship), *von der Tann,* and *Moltke,* along with the armored cruiser *Blücher* and four light cruisers, into Yarmouth Bay, prepared to bombard the town. However, a single British destroyer patrolling the bay, HMS *Halcyon,* drew the attention of the German warships, which opened a furious fire on the little ship, obscuring her in a flurry of shell splashes. Amazingly, *Halcyon* was not hit, although splinters damaged her wireless and wounded three crewmen. Equally untouched was the destroyer *Lively,* which came rushing to *Halcyon's* aid as soon as the sound of the German guns was heard. A trio of British submarines, *E-10, D-5,* and *D-6,* were lying in Yarmouth Bay and immediately put to sea—the *D-5* soon ran into a German mine and sank with the loss of all hands but four.

It took some time for Hipper to get his forces in hand—it appears that at first he believed the destroyers were part of a screen for a larger force, but, when no more British warships appeared, he realized he was wasting valuable time sparring with them. It was now time to turn back to Wilhelmshaven, so, after firing a handful of shells in the direction of Yarmouth, the German battlecruisers put about and set a course for Germany. They arrived off Schillig Roads late that night in a thick fog that prevented them from entering Wilhelmshaven.

The next morning, though the fog had not yet lifted, the cruiser *Yorck* tried to make her way into the harbor; instead, she drifted off course and ran into one of the defensive minefields protecting the Roads. Striking two mines within two minutes, *Yorck* rolled over and sank in the shallow water, the upturned bilge of her keel providing a tenuous refuge for most of her crew; some 235 of them drowned or died of exposure before they were rescued.

The Imperial Navy's second action in the North Sea, and its first attempt at taking the offensive, had been an appalling failure. True, the British lost one submarine to a German mine, but the loss of the cruiser *Yorck* was far more damaging. The "bombardment" had achieved nothing except the disturbance of a few cubic yards of sand on a British beach. Worst of all, Hipper's powerful force appeared to flee from just two British destroyers and a handful of submarines.

But why had the Royal Navy not come out to confront Hipper? The answer was simple: the Germans had overplayed their hand. There was nothing at Yarmouth of a particularly strategic importance, certainly nothing to justify risking three battlecruisers and an armored cruiser to destroy. The Admiralty suspected that the raid was a ruse, designed to divert the Royal Navy's attention from activity elsewhere, possibly an attempt by the High Seas Fleet to break out into the North Atlantic. Consequently, the Admiralty did little other than to raise the state of readiness among the forces positioned along the North Sea coast. Once it became clear that the German squadron was steaming back toward Heligoland and Wilhelmshaven, they were already too far away to be overtaken by Beatty's battlecruisers or Jellicoe's battleships. It was as if the Germans had played a gigantic bluff and the British, however unwittingly, called it.

The Imperial Navy's next foray into the North Sea came six weeks later, in mid-December, after some of the embarrassment of the Yarmouth Raid had faded and the lessons taught by it were adequately learned. This time, a sortie by at least part of the Grand Fleet—hopefully Beatty's battlecruisers—was virtually ensured by the nature of the target and the ferocity of the attack. Three British coastal towns felt the fury of a German naval bombardment: Scarborough, Whitby, and Hartlepool.

Again, a factor in the choice of targets was their relative closeness to Heligoland, less than 24 hours steaming time away; again, the German plan was to lure British warships into minefields and U-boats lying in ambush. There was more at stake for the Germans this time around, however: a successful action would go far toward restoring the morale of the High Seas Fleet, which had suffered badly with news of the destruction of Admiral von Spee's Far East Squadron in the Battle of the Falkland Islands earlier that month. It would also awaken the British public to the fact that the British Isles were not immune from attack; it was hoped the resulting public clamor would keep the Lord Kitchener's newly raised army of volunteers committed to the defense of Great Britain rather than sent to France.

The curtain went up on what history remembers as the Scarborough Raid just after 8 o'clock on the morning of December 16, 1914. Hipper's First Scouting Group, having sailed from Wilhelmshaven the night before, had encountered heavy weather on its way across the North Sea, and Hipper chose to leave behind the light cruisers and destroyers screening his big ships some 50 miles out to sea. The First Scouting Group then split into two smaller groups as they approached the British coastline. The Southern Group, the battlecruisers *von der Tann* and the newly commissioned *Derfflinger*, emerged

112   Distant Victory

from the morning fog off the seaside resort of Scarborough, swung their gun turrets around, and opened fire on the defenseless city.

There was a calculated brutality to the bombardment that to this day defies rational explanation. The world has become accustomed—one could even say numb—to atrocities, perhaps inevitably given the horrors that humanity has inflicted on itself in the last century. But in late 1914, most of those horrors were yet to come, and the death and destruction caused by Hipper's bombardment created a fury of outrage, not only in Britain but around the world. Scarborough had been famous as a seaside resort for more than half a century: it was known for little more than that, as there was no industry nor any military or naval installations in the town; as a military target its value was nil. Yet for nearly 30 minutes, *Defflinger* and *von der Tann* rained more than three hundred 11-inch shells on the town, leaving behind a cratered landscape of roofless houses, splintered trees, broken bricks, and shattered glass. Nearly every window in the town had been blown out, three churches suffered direct hits, and the Grand Hotel, perched on a cliff overlooking the North Sea, had been singled out as a target. When the gunfire ceased, 17 people were dead and 97 had been wounded. All of them were civilians.

Twenty miles up the coast from Scarborough sits the little fishing village of Whitby. Perched on the River Esk, it is overlooked by a twelfth-century abbey sited on a cliff; on December 16, 1914, its single claim to any significance was the coast guard signal station. That apparently was enough to make it a legitimate military target in German eyes; certainly Hipper, who had conceived and developed the operation, never expressed any objections. At 0900 that morning the two battlecruisers of the Southern Group shelled the village for ten minutes, leaving behind two dead and considerable wreckage.

Hartlepool, 40 miles farther north along the coast, was an altogether different proposition than Whitby or Scarborough. The harbor there contained six docks, two tidal basins, and several foundries and engineering works, and, because much of the cargo that made its way into and out of the port had some military significance, the town was, under the terms of international law, a legitimate target. It was also defended: a battalion of the Durham Light Infantry was garrisoned there, and a small squadron of two light cruisers and four elderly destroyers was stationed in the harbor. The shore defenses consisted of three well-sited 6-inch guns.

Hipper, aboard *Seydlitz* and leading *Moltke* and *Blücher* in line ahead, loomed out of the morning fog less than four miles from the shore and opened fire. For the next hour more than eight hundred 11-inch and 8-inch shells tore into Hartlepool. The German guns ranged in on the shipyard, the foundries, the railyard, and the gasworks. Then, inexcusably, they turned on the residential sections of the city: ten churches, a dozen public buildings, a library, five hotels, and more than 300 private homes were demolished. Entire families were slaughtered: in one house struck by a German shell, the mother, father, and six children were killed in the explosion; miraculously, a six-month-old infant survived. Dead bodies lay in the streets, some covered with broken masonry and shattered glass.

The four elderly British destroyers tried to close with the German ships, hoping to launch torpedoes, but only one, HMS *Doon,* got close enough to launch—the single torpedo she got off missed, and a shell burst close by killed one of her crewmen and wounded 11 others. The three shore guns put up a fight far out of all proportion to their size or numbers: the pair known as the Heugh Battery hit *Seydlitz* three times and *Moltke* once, while the single gun sited near the lighthouse at the entrance to Hartlepool Harbour scored four hits on *Blücher,* causing serious damage, knocking out one of her main turrets, putting two of her 5.9-inch guns out of action, and damaging her bridge.

After nearly an hour of nonstop firing, the three German ships put about and headed back out into the North Sea to rendezvous with *von der Tann* and *Derfflinger.* Behind him, in the wreckage of Hartlepool, Hipper left 86 dead and 424 wounded, all of them civilians. The only naval casualties suffered by the British were those aboard *Doon.* Eight German seamen were killed and 12 wounded, all in the action off Hartlepool.

As he made his way back across the North Sea, Hipper anticipated overtaking his screen of light cruisers and destroyers, as he expected that the Royal Navy might well appear in strength at any moment. He was well prepared for this, and, in fact, he was looking forward to it: the whole purpose of raiding defenseless seacoast towns was to draw out that part of the Grand Fleet that was closest to the raid and mostly likely to respond precipitately. Waiting off Dogger Bank in the North Sea for just such an eventuality, Hipper knew, were two squadrons of the High Seas Fleet's battleships.

In fact, the British were already responding to the German attack on the coastal towns, though not in quite as hasty a manner as the Germans expected. At the time of the Yarmouth Raid, Room 40 had yet to come into being, but by mid-December 1914 it was very much a going proposition, and communications between the German Naval High Command and Wilhelmshaven, as well as those between German warships at sea, were closely monitored. Well before Hipper had left the Jade, the Admiralty knew something was in the air. Piecing together the various signals allowed the analysts in Room 40 to follow, and to some degree predict, the movements of Hipper's ships, and this information was relayed to Jellicoe at Scapa Flow. The crucial message was sent at 2130 on December 14—*before* the German ships even sailed:

114   Distant Victory

...German First [Battle] Cruiser Squadron with destroyers [will] leave Jade River on Tuesday morning early and return Wednesday night. It is apparent from information that battleships are unlikely to come out. The enemy force will have time to reach our coast. Send at once, leave tonight, the Battlecruiser Squadron and Light Cruiser Squadron supported by a Battle Squadron, preferably the Second. At daylight on Wednesday they should be at some point where they can make sure of intercepting the enemy during his return.

Jellicoe, who believed in always concentrating his forces, was unhappy with the Admiralty's decision to split his fleet, preferring to take it out *en masse;* nevertheless, he reacted promptly. The Second Battle Squadron, under the command of Vice Admiral Sir George Warrender, made up of six of the Royal Navy's newest and most powerful dreadnoughts—*King George V, Conqueror, Orion, Monarch, Ajax, and Centurion*—was ordered to get underway immediately, accompanied by Commodore Goodenough's four cruisers. A cable went down to Cromarty, where Beatty was waiting with four battlecruisers, sending him on his way as well. Still, the commander in chief felt that force was inadequate, just as he had—and as events proved, justifiably so—before Heligoland Bight, fearing that it would present the Germans with exactly the opportunity they were seeking, a chance to overwhelm and destroy an isolated squadron of the Grand Fleet. The Admiralty, with the knowledge provided by Room 40 causing it to feel far more sanguine about German capabilities and intentions, overrode Jellicoe's concerns, and the squadrons sailed as originally instructed.

But Jellicoe's fears were as well-founded as the Admiralty's confidence was not. Unknown to Churchill and Admiralty staff, Room 40 was unable to provide them with one crucial piece of information: von Ingenohl had sailed from Wilhelmshaven with two squadrons of battleships and was waiting to rendezvous with Hipper on his return from bombarding the British coast. Consequently, Admiral Warrender believed that he was sailing to intercept a German squadron made up solely of battlecruisers and armored cruisers.

What played out over the next 48 hours was part drama, part comic opera. While Jellicoe was unable to overrule the Admiralty on the composition of the British forces, he was still in operational control, and so he instructed Warrender and Beatty to rendezvous at a point roughly 100 miles east of Scarborough and 185 miles west-northwest of Heligoland. He believed that this position would place the British ships where they could most easily intercept the German battlecruisers on their return from their raid. Such was Jellicoe's genius that he had intuitively chosen a position less than 30 miles south of the spot Admiral von Ingenohl had chosen to rendezvous with Hipper.

Yet chance intervened in a strange way, and the clash of battle squadrons that might have occurred never took place. In the early morning hours of

December 16—before Hipper began bombarding Scarborough and Hartlepool—Warrender's Second Battle Squadron and Beatty's Battlecruiser Squadron were just making contact when Beatty's destroyer screen caught sight of von Ingenohl's fleet. As the destroyer and torpedo boats skirmished, in the poor light and visibility the British lookouts mistook the Germans for a small raiding force of light cruisers. At the same time, lookouts on von Ingenohl's ships spotted Warrender's battleships and identified them for what they were. Von Ingenohl, his natural timidity reappearing, suddenly thought that the whole of the Grand Fleet was out and preparing to descend upon him. Transmitting an order to Hipper (which was immediately picked up by Room 40) to press home the attack on the British towns, von Ingenohl then turned his battleships around and made for the safety of Wilhelmshaven at top speed. He did not bother, however, to inform Hipper that he was returning to base, nor did he make mention of sighting the British battleships.

Meanwhile, Warrender, who had assumed tactical command of the British forces, was preparing to attack what he believed was a much smaller force when a message arrived advising him of the attack on Hartlepool. Both he and Beatty immediately turned their squadrons to the west, Warrender signaling his intention to steam toward Hull for some inexplicable reason. Beatty made it known that he believed the British warships should make for Scarborough, where they stood a much better chance of intercepting Hipper's retreating battlecruisers. Signals from Jellicoe soon followed that confirmed Beatty's judgment: by 1100 both Beatty and Warrender were in a position to bring Hipper to battle no matter which way he turned, Beatty to the north of the Germans' intended course and Warrender to the south, with either able to fall upon the enemy as soon as he engaged the opposite force. Commodore Tyrwhitt, ordered up from Harwich with his cruisers and eight predreadnought battleships, was steaming hard to reach a position behind Hipper's squadron: the British would have the Germans effectively surrounded.

Hipper, believing that von Ingenohl was waiting for him at Dogger Bank, steamed confidently through a gap between two minefields just after 1100, approaching the rendezvous point designated by Admiral von Ingenohl, ready for any encounter with the Royal Navy. The sun was shining, the sky was clear, and the early afternoon held the prospect of the long-anticipated action with the Royal Navy. Signals from von Ingenohl himself, as well as the torpedo boats and light cruisers screening the German battle squadrons, made it clear that the British were, indeed, out in some force.

Then, in less than 15 minutes, the notoriously fickle weather of the North Sea closed down completely. What had been a clear blue sky turned to a cloud-laden leaden grey; a fresh breeze suddenly rose to a near-gale force; visibility, which had been as much as 15 miles, was cut to a fifth that distance. Worst of all, as conditions deteriorated, not wanting to pass by the waiting German battleships, Hipper attempted to confirm von Ingenohl's position, only to be informed that the German battleships had fled toward Wilhelmshaven some hours before. Upon learning this, Hipper gave out with what his Flag Captain, Hugo von Waldeyer-Hartz, described as "an old-fashioned Bavarian oath." Now Hipper's squadron was no longer the lure to draw the British into an ambush—instead, circumstances gave every indication that he was the one being drawn into a trap.

Bickering between Goodenough's light cruisers and Hipper's cruiser screens had begun as the German battlecruisers and their escorts drew close to Beatty's position, although neither side was able to obtain any hits. Because Goodenough reported that he was engaged with only a single German cruiser, Beatty did not realize just how close Hipper's ships were. An ambiguous signal caused Goodenough to break off the action and then lose contact with the Germans, just as Beatty came to realize that Hipper was passing to the south of him: Beatty was attempting to reposition one of the unengaged cruisers, but because his flag lieutenant failed to clarify to which ship the order was directed, the effect was to draw Goodenough away from the German cruisers. When Goodenough tried to find them again, they had vanished in the rain and mist.

All was not lost for the British, though, and Hipper was not yet out of the woods, for by sheering away southward from Goodenough, the German ships were drawing toward Warrender's Second Battle Squadron. The six dreadnoughts would have made short work of Hipper's battlecruisers, for not only did they massively outgun the German ships, they were far more heavily armored, essentially invulnerable to the Germans' 11-inch guns. At 1225 Warrender signaled Beatty, "Enemy cruisers and destroyers in sight. Enemy's course east. No battle cruisers seen yet."

Now the comic-opera element came into play. Beatty, believing that Hipper's battlecruisers would be following the light cruisers and attempting to slip past Warrender's slower battleships, turned his four battlecruisers eastward in an attempt to take up a position ahead of Hipper's projected course. Unknown to Beatty, just 15 minutes before he made his turn to the east, the German light cruiser SMS *Straslund,* which had earlier reported sighting the British battlecruisers, now passed on a reported sighting of Warrender's battleships. From the distance between the two sightings Hipper instantly realized that *two* powerful British squadrons were positioned ahead of him, and so ordered his five ships to alter course to the north-east, intending to pass to the north of the British trap.

The foul weather aided the Germans as well, allowing the light cruisers and torpedo boats to vanish in the murky visibility and slip past Warrender and Beatty. Warrender continued to take his six battleships westward to the edge of the minefield through which Hipper had so recently passed, while Beatty spent the next two hours wandering around the south and west of Dogger Bank, utterly unaware that Hipper had taken a long detour to the north of the Bank, and would approach the Jade Roads and Wilhelmshaven the following morning. By 1547 both British admirals realized that their quarry had eluded them, and Warrender signaled, "Relinquish chase. Rejoin me tomorrow."

Once the British and German ships had returned to their home ports, recriminations and finger-pointing began on both sides of the North Sea. Beatty felt that he had been let down by both the Admiralty and Goodenough, the Admiralty for not providing accurate information on German strengths and positions, especially when they knew that the High Seas Fleet was out in strength, and Goodenough for failing to read Beatty's mind when the Admiral sent a confusing signal to one of his cruisers that resulted in Goodenough losing contact with the Germans. The real culprit was Beatty's flag lieutenant, Ralph Seymour, who seemed to spend most of his naval career making a hash of critical signals and in this case was responsible for the ambiguous signal that caused Goodenough to break off his action with Hipper's cruiser screen. But Beatty—who was well-known and widely liked for his personal loyalty to his staff—could not bring himself to punish his subordinate, and so Seymour remained.

Once safely in Wilhelmshaven, Hipper made his fury at von Ingenohl known. While the admiral could be justified in his decision to return to the safety of the Jade when he believed that the whole of the Grand Fleet was bearing down on him, nothing could excuse his failure to let Hipper know that the High Seas Fleet was no longer in a position to support the First Scouting Group. The German battlecruisers had been left alone and exposed to a vastly superior British force, and had Hipper not specifically asked for von Ingenohl's position, there was no way of telling how many more hours would have passed before he became aware of what he bluntly termed was von Ingenohl's "betrayal."

Von Ingenohl tried to temporize and explain away his actions by claiming that he had been following an Imperial directive instructing him to avoid risking the ships of the High Seas Fleet, but no one took his rationalizations very seriously. Even the cautious Wilhelm upbraided the admiral for missing such a golden opportunity to alter the balance of naval power in the North Sea in Germany's favor. Rather than fly at the first sighting of a British battleship, he thundered, "The effort to preserve the fleet must under no circumstances be carried so far that favorable prospects of a success are missed owing to the prospect of possible losses." The admiral remained in his post, but it was clear to everyone that as a consequence of his conduct during the Scarborough Raid his days in it were numbered.

That the basic plan for the Scarborough Raid was sound and had nearly worked to perfection left Admiral Franz Hipper feeling unsettled. As December 1914 passed into January 1915, he continued to brood over how close he had come to success, as well as has how many times he had failed to bring the British to battle. It occurred to him that the British must have some source of foreknowledge of German operations, for they always seemed to appear at the most inconvenient times. But rather than suspect that German naval signals had been compromised—and to be fair there was very little evidence to suggest to the Germans that this was the case—Hipper believed the culprits to be British spies hidden among the trawlers and fishing smacks that plied the rich fishing grounds of the Dogger Bank. Once he was convinced this was so, he became determined to do something about it, drawing up a plan for clearing the Bank of all civilian craft, no matter what nationality. The operation would directly involve the ships of the First Scouting Group, while the High Seas Fleet would once again be positioned to cover the German battlecruisers' withdrawal. While its primary objective was to eliminate the suspected spy ships, it had the added attraction of once more possibly luring the British battlecruisers out of Cromarty, where they could be met by the combined weight of the High Seas Fleet.

Hipper pressed the plan on von Ingenohl, who gave it only tepid support, but because he feared offering evidence to support the claims of his critics who questioned his fighting spirit, he allowed Hipper to continue to develop the project. When in the third week of January 1915 the weather forecasts called for clear skies over the North Sea, Hipper suggested that it was the perfect opportunity for his sweep of the Dogger Bank. Von Ingenohl at first resisted, but when Hipper pointed out the limited nature of his plans and that the battlecruisers would not be going as far west as they had in December, von Ingenohl relented—with one provision. The High Seas Fleet would not be supporting him, so if there was the slightest chance that the British would intercept the German battlecruisers, the operation would be called off. Hipper bridled at this, but conceded.

At 1745 on January 23, the First Scouting Group left the Jade: it consisted of the battlecruisers *Seydlitz, Moltke,* and *Derfflinger* (*von der Tann* was in dry dock), the armored cruiser *Blücher,* four light cruisers, and 19 torpedo boats. The inclusion of *Blücher* was a mistake. A curious hybrid, almost but not quite a battlecruiser, she had been built during that period of transition from traditional battleships and cruisers to dreadnoughts and battlecruisers.

Although she carried twelve 8.2-inch guns mounted in six turrets, *Blücher* was not fast enough to keep up with the 26-knot battlecruisers, nor were her guns powerful or long-ranged enough to take on a British battlecruiser on anything like equal terms. In short, *Blücher* was a liability, although Hipper did not see her as one.

As had happened in December, in Whitehall Room 40 had already been monitoring the German wireless and knew most of the details of the operation. Most importantly, the British Admiralty knew that the High Seas Fleet was *not* coming out this time. Perhaps the trap that went awry the previous December could be successfully sprung. Vice Admiral Beatty was immediately instructed to take his battlecruisers out of Rosyth, and Commodore Tyrwhitt was to bring the light cruisers and destroyers of his Harwich Force north: the two squadrons would rendezvous at Dogger Bank at 0700 on January 24.

Just before daybreak, at 0714 on January 24, the German light cruiser *Kölberg* sighted the light cruiser *Aurora,* part of Tyrwhitt's Harwich Force. When *Aurora* challenged the German ship, *Kölberg* opened fire on her, quickly scoring two hits; *Aurora* immediately returned fire, scoring two hits of her own. Both ships began transmitting sighting reports to their respective squadrons. The Battle of Dogger Bank had begun.

The Germans were handicapped throughout the war by poor, incomplete, or faulty intelligence, and rarely more so than at Dogger Bank. When Hipper heard *Kölberg's* guns, even before receiving her report, he ordered his ships to turn toward her, that is to port, to the south, as according to Naval Intelligence in Berlin the only British warships in the vicinity were light cruisers or destroyers. No sooner had the cruiser *Stralsund* made her turn than her lookouts spotted heavy funnel smoke to the north-north-west. It was Beatty's five battlecruisers. For a few moments Hipper debated whether to stand and fight, but, mistaking the British ships for dreadnoughts, he decided to turn back for Wilhelmshaven: he could not outfight British battleships, but he could certainly outrun them. At 0735 he gave the order to turn to the south-west and head for Heligoland Bight, intending to run behind its protection and so reach the Jade and Wilhelmshaven. After nearly half an hour had passed and the British ships had not fallen behind but instead had actually further closed the range to his squadron, Hipper realized that he was confronting Beatty's Battlecruiser Squadron. By that time the range had already dropped to 25,000 yards, just out of range for the "Big Cats'" 13.5-inch guns, and impossibly far for the Germans' 11-inch weapons.

The Germans were steaming in a straight line-ahead formation, with the flagship *Seydlitz* in the lead, followed by *Moltke* and *Derfflinger,* with *Blücher* bringing up the rear. Beatty was leading his ships in a line-ahead echeloned to port, leading the way in HMS *Lion,* with *Tiger* and *Princess Royal* immediately following, the slower *New Zealand* and *Indomitable* having fallen slightly behind. As soon as he saw the Germans alter course to the southwest, Beatty began signaling for more speed. Running along a parallel course to the Germans, Beatty had the advantage of being downwind of Hipper, so freeing his ships of the clouds of coal and gun smoke that were being created, making ranging and spotting the fall of shot much easier for the British.

The first ships to attack Hipper's battlecruisers were seven of Tyrwhitt's destroyers. Latching on to *Blücher* at the rear of the German line, they tried to close to within torpedo distance, but the German cruiser responded with such a furious hail of 8.2- and 5.9-inch shells that the destroyers sheered off without firing a single torpedo. Seeing that the little ships could get nowhere near the Germans, Beatty told them to stand clear. He would push his battlecruisers as hard as possible and settle the affair with gunfire.

Beginning at 0810, a succession of flag hoists went up *Lion's* signal halyards as Beatty demanded more and more speed. The first signal raised read: "*Lion* to Battle Cruisers: Speed 24 knots." Over the next 45 minutes, at intervals between 7 and 11 minutes, each successive hoist raised the squadron speed by a full knot, until at 0854, Beatty ordered 29 knots, a full knot faster than the design speed of the "Big Cats" and three knots faster than the highest speed of which *New Zealand* and *Indomitable* were capable.

But the relentless pressure began to pay off, as the British squadron began to overhaul the German. It was at this point that *Blücher* became a critical liability to Hipper. The armored cruiser's best speed was 23 knots, and soon she began to lag behind the rest of the First Scouting Group. Hipper now faced a terrible choice, for within moments *Blücher* would be within range of the leading British ships: he could either abandon *Blücher* to certain destruction, or he could slow his squadron and try to defend the cruiser, and risk having his three battlecruisers torn apart by the heavier British guns.

At 0905, *Lion* opened fire on *Blücher* and scored her first hit four minutes later. Within ten minutes *Tiger* and *Princess Royal* had opened fire, and *Lion* shifted her guns to the battlecruiser *Moltke*. Hipper had chosen to try to save Blücher and fight it out with Beatty. At 0915 *Moltke* began firing back at *Lion,* and within minutes the waters around both squadrons were boiling with shell splashes.

Blücher, though, was bearing the brunt of the British fire, the third salvo to strike her ripping her hull open and reducing her speed to less than 20 knots. Two of her gun turrets were smashed, and her after superstructure was demolished. Desperately firing back at her tormentors, aside from a single hit on *Lion* she could make no effective reply as the British ships were still out of range. As the British battle line overtook her, each battlecruiser in succession began firing on *Blücher,* while Beatty began engaging the rest of

Hipper's ships. Sensing that the German armored cruiser was done for, he tried to bring some order to his ships' distribution of fire, and at 0935 ordered the signal hoisted, "Engage the corresponding ship in the enemy's line." This way, Beatty reasoned, each of Hipper's battlecruisers would be engaged with one of his "Big Cats," while *Indomitable* and *New Zealand* could deal with *Blücher*. Instead, the result was confusion and near chaos.

Captain Thomas Pelly of HMS *Tiger,* the second ship in line, understood the order but not how it would be applied, and so instead of turning his guns on *Moltke,* the second ship in the German line, he opened fire on *Seydlitz. Tiger* was a new ship, and as a result her gunnery was rather poor—she was overshooting the German flagship by as much as 3,000 yards. To make matters worse, her spotters were mistaking the shell splashes from *Lion's* guns as their own and correcting for them rather than their own falling shots. Consequently, *Moltke* was allowed to range in on *Lion* completely undisturbed. It was about this time that Hipper began to realize that he faced an agonizing choice. The superior speed of the British battlecruisers meant that it was not possible for him to break off the action whenever he chose: he was committed to this battle.

At 0945 a devastating blow fell upon his own flagship: a 13.5-inch shell from *Lion* struck aftermost 11-inch turret, penetrated the armor, and exploded in the turret trunk. Powder charges caught fire, and flames shot up into the turret, igniting the charges there and burning it out, incinerating the guns crews. At the same time, flames passed down the turret trunk, into the handling rooms, and forward through a service tunnel to the magazine of Dora, the next turret forward. Two great columns of flame shot out of the turret roofs 200 feet into the air; the entire ship shook from the force of the explosions.

Deep inside what was left of the turret trunks, a handful of badly burned survivors were able to open the emergency valves that flooded both magazines, sparing *Seydlitz* a catastrophic detonation. But the loss of two of the battlecruiser's five main turrets left her crippled and outgunned. There was now no way for Hipper to outfight Beatty: he had begun the battle outnumbered five to four; with the now-inevitable loss of *Blücher* that margin would fall to five to three, and with the loss of almost half of *Seydlitz'* main guns, the real margin was closer to five to two and one-half. Sending out an urgent plea for help from the High Seas Fleet, Hipper ordered a course to the southward, toward Heligoland and the protection of its minefields and shore batteries. He would do his best to save his three battlecruisers. *Blücher* was on her own.

When observers on *Lion* saw towering flames shoot up from *Seydlitz'* two after turrets, what had happened was obvious. The time had come, Beatty believed, to press home the attack. But before he could issue any instructions for his ships, *Seydlitz* replied with two near-crippling blows of her own. The first was an 11-inch shell that struck *Lion's* port side at the waterline, penetrating her armor and detonating inside the ship. Electrical power to several critical systems, including fire control, was knocked out, and the ship took on a list to port. Just moments later two shells together struck her port bow, buckling plates and letting hundreds of tons of seawater into the ship. *Lion's* speed dropped to 24 knots, and five minutes after Beatty ordered all of his ships to close with the German battlecruisers, all power failed throughout the ship as her last dynamo gave way under the load. The list increased to ten degrees, and her speed fell even further, to 15 knots.

Tiger was quickly overtaking the flagship when she, too, felt the fury of German fire. A hit on the roof of the Q turret took it out of action, although there was no fire or internal explosion. Other hits were scattered up and down her length until it seemed the ship itself was on fire. *Princess Royal* was relatively untouched, as was *Indomitable; New Zealand* was still concentrating her gunfire on the hapless *Blücher.* It was at this moment that a critical error in British signaling was made: at 1054, Beatty himself spotted what he believed was a periscope and, believing that Hipper was drawing him into a U-boat ambush, ordered his entire squadron to alter course 90 degrees to port, cutting across the wake of the German squadron. As soon as he believed that his ships were clear of the possible danger, he ordered the squadron back onto its original course to the north-east. Unfortunately, because *Lion's* wireless was inoperable, this signal had to be made by flag hoist; at the same time Beatty wanted his ships to press home their attack, so he ordered a second signal to be made: "Attack the rear of the enemy."

It was at this moment the insufferable Lt. Ralph Seymour reappears. The primary responsibility of a flag (or signals) lieutenant is to assure that the signals hoisted (or sent) are correct in content and *in their proper order.* Here Seymour failed at his duty miserably, for instead of hoisting the two signals in succession, which would have indicated that they were separate instructions, he had them hoisted together. The result was that the rest of the squadron read the signal as "Attack the rear of the enemy, course northeast." To Rear Admiral Sir Archibald Moore, who was now acting as squadron commander with *Lion* out of the battle, only *Blücher* fit this description, and so he ordered the battlecruisers to swing about and return to the beleaguered German cruiser. Beatty, who was transferring his flag to the destroyer *Attack,* was beside himself with frustration, for Moore was allowing Hipper's three remaining ships to get away, but there was nothing he could do.

Blücher did not last long under the concentrated fire of four battlecruisers and Tyrwhitt's destroyers and light cruisers. Torpedoes and heavy shells tore the armored cruiser apart, and at 1207 she heeled over sharply to port, floated for a few minutes, then went under. Boats from the British destroyers and light cruisers were quickly lowered and began picking up survivors, but only 234 of *Blücher's* 1,200-man crew were saved. More might have been rescued but for the untimely arrival of the Zeppelin L5 and a German seaplane. The low clouds prevented the Zeppelin from bombing the British ships, but the seaplane, her crew mistaking the sinking *Blücher* for a British cruiser, swooped in low and began dropping bombs. Although none hit, Commodore Goodenough decided that it was too dangerous for his small ships and so ordered a withdrawal. By this time Hipper's battlecruisers were just a smudge of smoke on the eastern horizon, and the British squadron, a battered *Lion* in tow, turned back for Cromarty.

Dogger Bank, like the Battle of the Bight, was a British victory: *Blücher* had been sunk, *Seydlitz* heavily, possibly critically, damaged, without the loss of a single British ship; *Lion's* damage, while serious, was nowhere near as severe as that done to Hipper's flagship. Its moral impact was just as significant: the image of *Blücher,* torn and rolling onto her side, was all the visual evidence the British public required to maintain its faith in the invincibility of the Royal Navy. For the Germans, it was a sobering affair. It did, indeed, seem, as Commodore Keyes had predicted, that "when we go out, those damned Englanders will fall on us and smash us!" How the British seemed to know in advance of every major operation by the High Seas Fleet in the North Sea remained a mystery, but as far as the Naval High Command was concerned, there would be no more such opportunities presented to the Royal Navy.

The battle contained warnings and lessons for both sides, though not all of them were heeded or learned. The dreadful confusion caused by Lt. Seymour's mishandled signals was never properly addressed, nor was the misunderstanding over the British ships' distribution of fire: both of these problems returned to haunt the Battlecruiser Squadron. For the Germans, the critical lesson of the battle came from the near disaster to *Seydlitz.* Improved methods of handling powder charges and better flash protection in the turret trunks was the result; the British, who had not experienced a similar catastrophe, made no changes in how shells or powder was handled in the magazines.

Finally, for the Germans the last lesson drawn from Dogger Bank was that sending the First Scouting Group out without the support of the High Seas Fleet was an invitation for the British to do what the Germans had been attempting to do to the Grand Fleet—catch the isolated squadron unawares with overwhelming numbers and destroy it in detail. Had it not been for Lt. Seymour's bungled signals, Rear Admiral Moore might well have sent all three German battlecruisers to the bottom. That was a risk that no one in the Imperial German Navy wanted to run again. Though more than 16 months passed before it sortied once more into the North Sea, when it came out again, the High Seas Fleet came out in strength. The stage was being set for a clash of titans.

Chapter 6

Gambit

The 16 months between the High Seas Fleet's defeat at Dogger Bank and the Battle of Jutland was a pivotal period for Germany, dramatically changing her role in the Great War in both scope and shape. For the High Seas Fleet itself, two pieces of drama followed hard on the heels of the return of the First Scouting Group to Wilhelmshaven, both of which had consequences leading directly to the clash of battle fleets at Jutland.

The first was the dismissal of Admiral Friedrich von Ingenohl. Nine days after Dogger Bank, he was ordered to haul down his flag, was dismissed by Kaiser Wilhelm, and was sent into retirement; with him went his chief of staff, *Vizeadmiral* Richard Eckermann. Von Ingenohl's place was taken by the chief of the Naval Staff, Admiral Hugo von Pohl. Reputed to be a good seaman, von Pohl was supposedly a better naval tactician than his predecessor; certainly he was a better politician: there are some indications that von Pohl engineered von Ingenohl's dismissal with an eye to becoming his replacement. Certainly von Pohl was ambitious, as demonstrated by the next major event involving the German Navy, one that had grave consequences, both politically and militarily, for Germany.

When the declaration of unrestricted submarine warfare in the "war zone" around Great Britain was made by Germany on February 15, 1915, it was as much the result of frantic political maneuvering on the part of von Pohl, with very little reference to his fellow admirals, the naval staff, or anyone else in the German government save for the Chancellor, Theobald von Bethmann-Hollweg, as it was a product of sober political and military consideration. From late autumn 1914 von Pohl had been a strong advocate for abandoning the Cruiser Rules and allowing the U-boats a free hand to sink on sight, without any warning, any merchantman of any nationality they encountered.

Von Bethmann-Hollweg, analyzing such a course of action from a purely legalistic perspective, wrote to von Pohl:

> Viewed from the standpoint of international law, U-boat warfare is a reprisal against England's hunger blockade. When we consider the purely utilitarian rules by which the enemy regulate their conduct...we may conclude that we are entitled to adopt whatever measure of war is most likely to bring them to surrender.

This was all the endorsement the little admiral needed, and he began working out a plan for a U-boat campaign against Great Britain. He conveniently forgot that the Chancellor had gone on to remind him that, while unrestricted submarine warfare might be permissible in theory, in fact it would be so provocative to the neutral powers, particularly the United States, as to be counterproductive. Only once Germany's strategic position on both the Eastern and Western Fronts was secure could such a course of action be contemplated.

Not that von Pohl appeared to lack support among the German admirals: Reinhard Scheer for one was very outspoken in his advocacy of submarine warfare. Addressing the growing severity of the British blockade of Germany, Scheer declared, "The gravity of the situation demands that we should free ourselves from all scruples which certainly no longer have any justification." Von Tirpitz himself had told an American reporter, "England is endeavoring to starve us. We can do the same, cut off England and sink every vessel that attempts to break the blockade." But Scheer was a vocal advocate of submarine warfare coupled with surface action by the High Seas Fleet: he did not regard the U-boats alone as being capable of defeating British sea power. For his part von Tirpitz knew he was speaking only in terms of purely military considerations and not addressing political realities.

Von Tirpitz also agreed with von Bethmann-Hollweg that unrestricted submarine warfare could only be instituted once Germany's strategic position on land was incontestible. The Kaiser himself was well aware of the political as well as military perils of an unrestricted submarine campaign, particularly the risk of an open rupture or even declared hostilities between Germany and the United States. Great Britain, despite the often high-handed nature of her conduct of the blockade of Germany, had never gone quite far enough to provoke the Americans into retaliation. Germany must at all costs avoid being goaded into doing just that.

Von Pohl first presented his plans for a submarine blockade of Great Britain in late November 1914, and again mid-December, but was rebuffed both times by the Chancellor and the Kaiser on political grounds. When he broached the subject yet again a month later, their response was still the same.

But this time, von Pohl was playing a craftier game than merely advocating a new strategic policy: sensing even before Dogger Bank that von Ingenohl's days as commander in chief of the High Seas Fleet were numbered, he began scheming to succeed him. When the appointment actually came, effective February 4, 1915, von Pohl played his hand. On February 1 he met once more with von Bethmann-Hollweg, again pressing his arguments for an unrestricted U-boat campaign. Once more the Chancellor reiterated his fears of provoking neutrals, particularly the United States; going further this time, von Bethmann-Hollweg flatly stated that should a U-boat mistakenly sink an American ship or American citizens lost their lives on a neutral ship, the result might be war with America. Von Pohl deftly countered this by pointing out that if the effect of announcing unrestricted submarine warfare in a war zone around Great Britain was to frighten neutral shipping away from the British Isles, which was one of the primary assumptions of all the senior German naval officers, then the chances of such an incident would automatically be drastically reduced. It was a specious argument, since it was based purely in assumption, but the Chancellor did not know that. Then von Pohl went even further and flatly lied to von Bethmann-Hollweg: though he had no practical experience in submarines whatsoever, the little admiral blithely assured the Chancellor that U-boat skippers could readily distinguish between enemy and neutral vessels, and so would attack only those belonging to the Allies. So glibly did von Pohl make his case this time that von Bethmann-Hollweg was convinced, and so withdrew his objections.

The admiral next lied to his successor, Admiral Gustav Bachmann, assuring him that the unrestricted U-boat campaign had already been approved by the Kaiser and was now the Imperial Navy's strategic policy. No such imperial approval had yet been given, but with the Chancellor's opposition out of the way, von Pohl knew exactly how to get it. Playing on Wilhelm's love of military pomp and pageantry, the admiral staged an elaborate change of command ceremony on February 4 in Wilhelmshaven. There, with the Kaiser besotted with naval ardor, von Pohl presented the order for beginning the U-boat campaign to Wilhelm, who signed it virtually unseen.

Once the deed was done and became public knowledge, the other admirals of the Imperial Navy were aghast, as much at how it was accomplished as what was done. Von Tirpitz, while embracing the concept, considered von Pohl's actual plan for blockading Great Britain poorly conceived and impossible to execute. Admiral Georg von Müller, chief of the Naval Cabinet, roundly condemned von Pohl on all counts: his methods were devious, the declaration was poorly worded, the timing of its release was ill-advised, and its objectives were beyond the means of the German Navy. It seemed remarkable to no one at the time that one of von Pohl's arguments for unrestricted

128　　　　　　　　　　　　　　　　Distant Victory

submarine warfare was the Kaiser's prohibition on fleet engagements that might result in serious losses among the High Seas Fleet's battle squadrons. Turning over to the U-boats the primary responsibility for carrying the naval war to the British would, von Pohl rationalized, protect the German dreadnoughts. That it also meant von Pohl would never have to personally lead the fleet into battle was something no one appears to have noticed.

Precisely the sort of incident that von Bethmann-Hollweg feared came to pass with the destruction of the *Lusitania* on May 7, 1915: American outrage was so great that the Imperial German Government feared a rupture in diplomatic relations would occur, with war between America and Germany soon to follow. While it was clear that President Wilson preferred a diplomatic settlement to the crisis, it was impossible to be certain that Congress or the American people—or both—might not force his hand. While von Bethmann-Hollweg and his ambassador in Washington, DC, Johann von Bernstorff, kept that dangerously simmering pot from boiling over, at the same time the German Navy was compelled to reimpose restrictions on the U-boats in August 1915. It was an action that Wilhelm, though recognizing its political necessity, found particularly onerous, as to him it smacked of humiliation. Von Bethmann-Hollweg had been right all along: as long as the issue was "if" not "when" Germany would win the war, alienating the United States was too dangerous a proposition.

That knowledge kept the Kaiser nursing his grudge all that autumn and into the early winter, and it made him receptive to the strategic designs of his Minister of War, who was also chief of staff of the Imperial German Army, Field Marshall Erich von Falkenhayn. Of all the men in Germany, civilian or uniformed, von Falkenhayn probably knew Germany's strategic position best. At a conference in December 1915 attended by Germany's senior generals and admirals, von Falkenhayn bluntly laid out the facts. Food and raw materials could no longer be imported; Germany's merchant marine had ceased to exist; nearly all of her overseas colonies were already lost; the High Seas Fleet was helplessly shackled by Imperial restrictions and timorous leadership; the German Army had yet to inflict a decisive defeat on any of the Allies; and Austria-Hungary was reeling from a series of defeats by the Russian Army and was still capable of fighting only because she had Germany's support. That was the bad news. The good news was that the German Army occupied all but a tiny corner of Belgium along with most of industrialized France; in the east the defeats inflicted on the Russians were even more severe than those handed to the Austrians. But while victory was still possible, it was far from inevitable.

To change that, von Falkenhayn proposed two solutions, one on land and one at sea. The first was to be a "limited operation" around the French fortress city of Verdun, where the German Army could take full advantage of its massive superiority in artillery and bleed the French Army white as it sought to defend the city. As von Falkenhayn calculated it, the casualties would become unbearable for France by the end of 1916: with the French Army—"England's best sword" was how von Falkenhayn described it—defeated, the British would have to sue for peace. To make doubly sure of that, the seagoing solution he recommended was simple: a resumption of unrestricted submarine warfare.

The German admirals embraced von Falkenhayn's proposal wholeheartedly. The number of oceangoing U-boats had doubled since February 1915, and the admirals now calculated that their submarines could sink British merchant ships almost twice as fast as British shipyards could replace them, a rate that would, they believed, compel Great Britain to make peace within six months. The effect on neutral opinion was irrelevant: even if the United States were sufficiently outraged as to declare war on Germany, the war in Europe would be over before the Americans could effectively intervene. The new chief of the Naval General Staff, Admiral Henning von Holtzendorff, made his recommendation to the Chancellor in just such terms.

Von Bethmann-Hollweg, determined to settle the U-boat question, convened a conference of his own in the second week of January 1916, which included the Kaiser, the Ministers of War and the Navy, and the Army and Navy chiefs of staff. The Chancellor was adamant in his opposition to any resumption of unrestricted U-boat warfare: the risk of antagonizing the United States was always too great, and there was no way of guaranteeing that the Americans could not intervene before Great Britain collapsed. It would be foolish to stake the future of the German Empire on such an assumption. He rejected von Holtzendorff's arguments outright: if Germany had learned nothing else from the start of the war, the one unmistakable lesson was that warfare was not simply an exercise in mathematics—how long the British would hold out was a question of British endurance, not a numerical equation. Germany's strategic position, though not perilous, was in a balance: for the time being she was strong enough to hold off her enemies, but not powerful enough to overwhelm them. Provoking America into becoming an active belligerent rather than merely a source of supply for the Allies would irretrievably tip that balance against Germany. Let von Falkenhayn have his offensive at Verdun, the Chancellor argued, but do not unleash the U-boats again.

It was the Kaiser, of course, who had the final word. Wavering between ruthlessness and humanity—a never-ending conflict in that monarch's troubled soul—he tried to choose between the two opposing arguments. Finally, he produced what he regarded as a Solomonic compromise: the submarines were once more allowed to prey on enemy merchant shipping, but with limitations. Within the existing "war zone" Allied merchant ships, whether armed or unarmed, could be attacked without warning, while only those ships carrying defensive armament could be attacked without warning outside the zone—unarmed ships would be warned according to the Cruiser Rules. Attacks on passenger ships of any description were strictly forbidden— Wilhelm was determined that there would never be another *Lusitania* incident.

Weighing the political considerations, Wilhelm originally wanted the new U-boat campaign to begin after the fall of Verdun. Von Falkenhayn launched his offensive, named Operation *Gerricht* (an Old German word that translates as "Place of Punishment" or "Execution Ground"), on February 21, 1916, and after ten days of amazing success, the advance of the German Army slowly ground to a halt as the French resisted far more tenaciously than the general staff had believed possible, and the German assault troops began to run into logistical problems. It soon became obvious that there would be no swift victory here, but that von Falkenhayn's projection that the operation would require at least six months was a valid one, however gloomy. On March 13 Wilhelm finally gave permission for the U-boats to resume their campaign against Allied shipping.

One unexpected consequence of the debate over the new U-boat offensive was the sudden resignation of Admiral von Tirpitz as state secretary for the Navy. Thoroughly disgusted at the limitations placed on the U-boats, he believed that the new campaign would be ineffective at best and result in the loss of too many precious submarines and their equally valuable crews —or else some serious blunder by an overzealous U-boat skipper would result in disaster. Von Tirpitz had used the threat of resignation in the past to coerce Wilhelm into acquiescing to the admiral's will, but this time, heeding the political advice of his Chancellor, who had long had a stormy relationship with the admiral, the Kaiser chose to call von Tirpitz's bluff and accept his resignation. His replacement was Admiral Eduard von Capelle, a competent man who had long been von Tirpitz's assistant, but who lacked his former superior's drive and vision.

It took only a week before von Tirpitz's fears were realized. On March 24, the commander of *UB-29*, which was patrolling the English Channel along the Normandy coast, spotted a cross-channel steamer that he believed was carrying British troops to France. He fired two torpedoes at her, both of which struck home, blowing off the forward end of the ship; the vessel did not sink immediately, but only because it was close to its destination, the port of Dieppe. The captain of *UB-29* had made a dreadful mistake, however, for the stricken vessel was not a troopship at all, but rather the civilian cross-channel ferry *Sussex,* carrying 325 passengers. Eighty-eight people died in the attack, including four Americans.

President Wilson was furious. Not once, but twice since the *Lusitania* disaster German U-boats had broken the Kaiser's solemn pledge that passenger ships would be spared from submarine attack. No matter how loudly the Imperial government might protest that this latest incident was a genuine case of mistaken identity, the suspicion grew both within and without the American government that such pledges were merely being made in order to placate American public opinion rather than as actual statements of German policy. Wilson, taking a far harsher stance with Germany than ever before, addressed Congress on April 19, informing the assembled senators and representatives of the content of the diplomatic protest sent to Berlin:

> If it is still the purpose of the Imperial Government to prosecute relentless and indiscriminate warfare against vessels of commerce by the use of U-boats without regard to what the Government of the United States must consider the sacred and indisputable rules of international law and universally recognized dictates of humanity, the Government of the United States is at last forced to the conclusion that there is but one course it can pursue. Unless the Imperial Government should now immediately declare and effect an abandonment of its present methods of U-boat warfare against passenger and freight carrying vessels, the Government of the United States can have no other choice but to sever diplomatic relations with the German empire altogether.

This was a far cry from the earlier, vaguely worded declaration that Germany would be held "strictly accountable" for any losses suffered by American citizens as a result of a U-boat attack. Now Germany was being told the price it would have to pay—as well as how high the new stakes were being raised—if the U-boat campaign against civilian shipping was to continue.

It was an extremely large step for one major power to break off relations with another; it was a very small step from there to a declaration of war. The opening years of the twentieth century were the twilight and swan song of the classic, formal diplomacy that had been the hallmark of European international relations for nearly three centuries: after the Great War it was hijacked by thugs like Adolf Hitler, Benito Mussolini, and Joseph Stalin, or buffoonish amateurs like Neville Chamberlain. But the days before and during the First World War, the corps of trained, professional diplomats—the Foreign Ministers, ambassadors, and attachés—played a vital role in the way that nations communicated and miscommunicated with each other.

Collectively they shared a background of similar education and values, moved in the same social circles, knew many of the same friends and acquaintances, and often were related in some distant way by blood or marriage. They spoke common languages—usually French or English, or both—and because they had so much in common, they could interpret one another's inflections and nuances, both spoken and written, when communicating on behalf of their countries. Consequently, there was little place for bombast or meaningless posturing; likewise threats were rarely made idly.

It was a system that had been perfected over the course of three centuries and broke down only when someone openly defied the system, or when a nation, for example, Germany in July 1914, deliberately ignored it. A severance of diplomatic relations was not an act of mild protest, but rather a slap in the face of the nation with whom the break had occurred; it implied that nothing that nation had to say was worth hearing, that further communication was pointless. It was not a step taken to distance one nation from another in order to effect a "cooling-off" period in time of tension; rather it was the lull before the storm when one country began steeling itself for war with another. Consequently, the threat in Wilson's note to Berlin was not taken lightly by anyone in the German government.

For Bethmann-Hollweg, this was all the proof he required to support his view that the submarine campaign, however successful it might appear in the short term, was far too perilous a strategy in the long term. Germany simply lacked the strength to defeat the Allies *and* the United States. Even the Kaiser saw this: in a moment of particularly lucid insight, he was heard to murmur, "One must never utter it nor shall I admit it…but this war will not end with a great victory." Even though at one point he fumed against what he termed Wilson's "impertinence," Wilhelm saw the writing on the wall: the U-boats unchecked would spell Germany's doom. On April 24 the orders went out: all German U-boats were to observe the Cruiser Rules in all details whenever encountering a merchant ship, whether enemy or neutral. Going one step further, the new commander in chief of the High Seas Fleet, *Vizeadmiral* Reinhard Scheer, believing that such restrictions eliminated the U-boats' effectiveness, recalled the entire German submarine fleet to Wilhelmshaven. Germany's second, abortive U-boat offensive had been a dismal failure.

For the Royal Navy the months between the battles of Dogger Bank and Jutland were just as dramatic as they had been for the Imperial German Navy. The single most spectacular development was the Gallipoli campaign, an ambitious attempt to, in a single stroke, force open the Straits of the Bosporus and the Dardanelles between the Aegean Sea and the Black Sea, allowing Allied supplies to reach Russia, while at the same time knocking Turkey out of the war. In 1915 Russia was showing no sign of weakening yet, despite the heavy defeats she suffered at the hands of the Germans; in many ways those defeats were compensated by the maulings the Russians were repeatedly giving the armies of Austria-Hungary. But despite prodigious efforts, Russia's small but growing industrial base was unequal to the task of properly supplying her armies, and with each passing month her dependence on France and Great Britain for ammunition, artillery, and the rest of the tools of war grew.

The Gallipoli campaign could have been the one great masterstroke of strategy for the whole of the Great War had it succeeded. The brainchild of Winston Churchill, it was dependent on speed, ferocity, and sheer audacity in its execution: in the opening phases all three were abundant, as the initial naval bombardment of the Turkish forts protecting the Dardanelles below Constantinople on March 18, 1915, left the Turkish defenders battered, dazed, confused, as well as out of ammunition. But the follow-on amphibious landings on the Gallipoli peninsula in the Dardanelles Straits collapsed in failure. Failure to communicate and coordinate the efforts of the Royal Navy and the Army, as well as the War Ministry, resulted in almost five weeks passing before the landings began, time that the Turks put to good use, rushing fresh troops and supplies to the threatened peninsula, quickly hemming in the attacking Australian troops on their landing beaches.

Casualties mounted—40,000 by the end of August—with little to show for the effort as Gallipoli degenerated into a miniature of the Western Front, as Allied and Turkish trenches paralleled each other, sometimes scant feet apart, and as attack after bloody attack failed to drive the Turks back. The campaign was brought to an end in January 1916, when the Allied beachheads were quietly evacuated, having accomplished none of its objectives, the price of failure being almost 150,000 dead, wounded, and missing soldiers.

There were political casualties as well: General Sir Ian Hamilton was sacked, as was his naval counterpart, Rear Admiral Sir John De Roebeck; neither man ever held a command again. Churchill, the politician most closely identified with the campaign, came under harsh, sometimes openly vindictive criticism for the failure to achieve swift, decisive victory. Ironically, his most vocal and vociferous critics were the very men within the Cabinet who had given their approval to the operation as early as February 1915. But as often happens when a collection of mediocrities—which described most of Prime Minister H.H. Asquith's Cabinet—meets a figure of true genius, they banded together for self-protection and forced Churchill out of the office of First Lord of the Admiralty, his resignation coming on May 8. His successor, Arthur Balfour, was an accomplished political hack but lacked both experience and imagination involving naval affairs. Almost simultaneously, Admiral Sir John Fisher resigned as First Sea Lord, although his resignation had been long in coming, as Fisher and Churchill had lost the capacity to work together in harmony.

In practical terms Churchill's departure had little effect on the day-to-day affairs of the Royal Navy; instead, what was missed was the relentless drive, the never-ending search for new ways to "get at" the Germans, to carry the war to the Imperial Navy. Not that there was any sudden diminution of aggressive spirit within the Royal Navy: John Jellicoe and David Beatty both had their own ideas of how the High Seas Fleet might be brought to battle. But while Beatty was all for dashing into Heligoland at full speed, all guns blazing, in one tremendous "death or glory" rush, Jellicoe was willing to play a more patient game. Both men, along with every other officer and rating in the Royal Navy, expected that there would be one tremendous, Trafalgar-like confrontation between the British and German battle fleets, but Jellicoe understood perhaps better than anyone else that simply waiting, holding the threat of such a battle over the head of the German Navy like some great Damoclean sword, had its own corrosive and debilitating effect on the Germans. After all, though Trafalgar had essentially annihilated French and Spanish sea power for decades in a single afternoon, it had come about through two years' worth of patiently exercised British sea power, manifested in its blockade of the Continent. Similarly, Jellicoe knew, the British blockade of Germany was having its own insidious consequences.

That did not mean that Jellicoe refused to take advantage of any opportunities presented to him. Carefully he studied the Imperial German Navy's operations through the battle at Dogger Bank and noticed a few interesting and possibly useful details. Five times the High Seas Fleet or a major portion of it had sortied from Wilhelmshaven, but only once had it gone farther than 200 miles from port, during the Scarborough Raid, and then only Hipper's battlecruisers had gone that far. The German fleet never ventured farther north than the Horns Reef, some 120 miles up the Danish coast, while the German battleships had never gone west of Dogger Bank. It was in this predictability that Jellicoe eventually saw an opportunity.

In the months immediately following Dogger Bank, however, he devoted himself to more basic matters. The fleet was reorganized, with the Battle Cruiser Squadron renamed the Battle Cruiser Fleet, with all but one of the Royal Navy's battlecruisers being placed under Beatty's command. Communications systems and signals were overhauled and revised as a consequence of the Dogger Bank fiasco. The accuracy of the British battlecruisers' gunnery at Dogger Bank had been deplorable: only 2 percent of the shells fired by all five battlecruisers had hit their targets (German gunnery, legends to the contrary notwithstanding, was hardly better at 3.5 percent), and so gunnery training and practice firings began to occupy more and more time for the battleships and battlecruisers alike. When the opportunity for which Jellicoe was searching presented itself, he was determined that the Grand Fleet would be prepared.

He had to be careful. When in early 1916 the Admiralty began suggesting a series of seaplane raids on German naval installations to goad the High Seas Fleet to put to sea in pursuit of the aircraft's supporting ships, which in turn would lead the Germans in an ambush by the Grand Fleet, Jellicoe was adamant in his rejection of the idea. Writing to Beatty he put forward his reasons in typically logical and irrefutable manner, and Beatty, for all his aggressive nature, had to agree.

> I am being pressed into another [air raid], the idea being that it will bring the German fleet out. But if carried out at daylight and the German heavy ships do move, they won't be clear of the minefields and in a position where we could engage them before about four p.m. This is no time to start a fight in those waters. It also involves our hanging about for a whole day in a bad locality, using up fuel, especially of our destroyers....

Beatty responded by writing,

> I think the German fleet will only come out on its own initiative when the right time arrives.... Your arguments regarding the fuel questions are unanswerable (and measure the situation absolutely). We cannot amble about the North Sea for two or three days and at the end be in a condition to fight the most decisive battle of the war....

Beatty, though, articulated something that Jellicoe seemed to sense—that the High Seas Fleet *would* be putting to sea looking for a scrap: Scheer was cut from entirely different cloth than was von Ingenohl or von Pohl. As if he were reading Scheer's mind, Jellicoe described what he foresaw as the German's strategy:

> I imagine the Germans will try to entrap you by using their battle cruisers as a decoy. They know that the odds are you will be 100 miles away from me, and can draw you down to the Heligoland Bight without my being in effective support. This is all right if you keep your speed, but if some of your ships have their speed badly reduced in a fight with their battle cruisers, or by submarines, their loss seems inevitable if you are drawn into the High Seas Fleet with me too far off to extricate them before dark....

Jellicoe's prescience is amazing, for this was precisely what Scheer was planning for the High Seas Fleet. When the U-boats were recalled on April 24, 1916, Scheer felt humiliated that the German government had succumbed to American pressure. While never maintaining that unrestricted submarine warfare alone could prove decisive against Great Britain, he believed that,

Distant Victory

when employed in concert with operations by the High Seas Fleet, the stranglehold of the British blockade could be broken, and a counterblockade of Great Britain deployed in its place. Now, deprived of the submarine menace, Scheer felt that the moment had come for decisive action by the battleships of the Imperial Navy.

German naval strategy had always relied heavily on attrition to reduce the Royal Navy's numerical superiority—there was never any doubt in the minds of the German Naval High Command of the superiority of German ships and sailors. The means by which the strength of the Grand Fleet could be whittled away was through mines and submarine attacks. At first there were too few U-boats to make such a strategy possible, but in the spring of 1916, Scheer had nearly two dozen oceangoing submarines at his disposal.

Scheer's plan was to use these U-boats to set up ambushes at the entrances to the Grand Fleet's anchorages to attack the British battleships as they sailed: three lines of submarines, one each off Cromarty, off the Firth of Forth, and across Pentland Firth at Scapa Flow. With *Seydlitz* scheduled to come out of dry dock on May 17—she had struck a mine on April 23 during an abortive bombardment raid on Lowestoft—and the addition of the new *Lützow,* sistership to *Derfflinger* and Hipper's new flagship, the First Scouting Group would be able to put five battlecruisers to sea, acting as bait for the ten battlecruisers of Beatty's command. To lure Beatty out, Hipper would once again bombard British coastal towns and, once Beatty made his appearance, lure the British battlecruisers across yet another line of U-boats. Scheer was optimistic that between the submarines lying in wait off the Firth of Forth and the second ambush, two or three British battlecruisers could be effectively eliminated from Beatty's fleet, if not actually sunk outright. Hipper would then lure the surviving British ships into the waiting maw of the High Seas Fleet, which Scheer would position off Dogger Bank. Scheer was confident that even if Jellicoe took the Grand Fleet to sea in support of Beatty, it would be at least six hours before the British battleships arrived on the scene, by which time the German dreadnoughts would have disposed of Beatty's battlecruisers.

Planning was well underway for the operation when it had to be postponed: condenser problems with the new *König*-class battleships meant that it could not get underway before May 23. The day before the High Seas Fleet was to depart Wilhelmshaven, yet another postponement took place, as this time *Seydlitz* was not yet declared seaworthy. Time now became a critical factor, as the fuel supplies of the U-boats assigned to the ambush lines off the Grand Fleet's anchorages was limited. Already in place, they could not remain in position beyond May 31. On May 28, when weather conditions did not allow the German Navy's zeppelins to fly, thus depriving Scheer of the long-range reconnaissance that he deemed essential to the success of the coastal bombardment, Scheer substituted another plan, where the German battlecruisers would sail up the Danish coast, within full view of the British spies known to be stationed there, hoping they would prove an irresistible lure to Beatty. At midnight the whole of the High Seas Fleet was ordered to raise steam, preparatory to sailing. *Seydlitz* left dry dock the next day, and at 1540 on May 30, Scheer's flagship, the battleship *Friedrich der Grösse,* sent out the signal "31 G.G. 2490." It was the order to put to sea.

Nine hours later the majestic procession of light grey ships began. First came *Lützow,* with Hipper on her bridge, leading the First Scouting Group —4 more battlecruisers, 5 light cruisers, and 30 destroyers. Once they had cleared the Jade Roads, the main battle fleet followed: 16 of Germany's 18 dreadnoughts (*Konig Albert* remained behind because of condenser problems, while *Bayern* had only just been commissioned and was not ready to be taken into battle), 6 old predreadnought battleships, 6 light cruisers, and 31 destroyers. The old predreadnoughts really had no place in a modern battle line, as their armor and guns were no match for British dreadnoughts, but the commander of the Second Battle Squadron, *Konteradmiral* Franz Mauve, pleaded with Scheer to be allowed to accompany the fleet. Scheer, whose first battleship command had been part of this squadron, gave way to sentiment and agreed. It was a grave tactical error, however, as the top speed of these aging ships was fully two knots slower than that of the German dreadnoughts and four knots slower than the dreadnoughts of the Grand Fleet.

But as the sun came up on the morning of May 29, and the majestic sight of 99 German warships, resplendent in their light grey paint with clouds of black coal smoke pouring from their funnels, could be seen by everyone aboard them. This was it—this was *Der Tag.*

Unknown to Scheer, when *Friedrich der Grösse's* signal "31 G.G. 2490" was flashed to the German fleet, it was also flashed to Room 40. There, the cryptographers and cipher clerks quickly interpreted "G.G." to mean *Geheim geraten*—"secret advisory"—while the 31 was taken to mean May 31, and word was quickly sent to Scapa Flow. It had been suspected since mid-May that the High Seas Fleet had some sort of major operation laid on: the complete absence of U-boat attacks of any kind in the North Sea and the assembly of a large number of German warships in the Jade Roads had been regarded ominously. Jellicoe had been preparing a plan of his own, designed to lure Scheer farther from Wilhelmshaven than any German admiral had taken the High Seas Fleet. A squadron of British light cruisers would sweep into the Kattegat, the strait between Denmark and Sweden, covered by a single squadron of battlecruisers. The whole of the Grand Fleet, however, would be lurking far offshore, away from the prying eyes of German

138 Distant Victory

agents, waiting for the High Seas Fleet to take the bait and pounce on what it believed was an isolated British force. The proposed date for this operation was June 2.

But when the signals from Room 40 began arriving in Scapa Flow on May 29, Jellicoe put his plans on hold. An Admiralty signal arrived at 1716 on May 30, instructing both Jellicoe and Beatty to raise steam. At 1740, the long awaited signal was received aboard *Iron Duke,* Jellicoe's flagship: "Germans intend some operations commencing tomorrow morning leaving via Horns Reef. You should concentrate eastward of Long Forties [a shoal in the North Sea roughly 100 miles north of Dogger Bank] ready for eventualities." At 1800 in Scapa Flow, the Firth of Forth, and Cromarty, the signal went up "Raise steam for 22 knots and report when ready."

At 2130 the Grand Fleet began its own majestic procession, this one even more impressive than that of the High Seas Fleet. From Scapa Flow sailed 16 dreadnought battleships, 3 battlecruisers, 3 older armored cruisers, 11 light cruisers, and 36 destroyers; at Cromarty 8 more dreadnoughts, 4 more armoured cruisers, and 11 destroyers put to sea; from the Firth of Forth came Beatty's Battlecruiser Fleet of 6 battlecruisers, 12 light cruisers, and 27 destroyers. With them went the four awesome *Queen Elizabeth*-class battleships of the Fifth Battle Squadron. All in all 151 British warships had set out to do battle with the High Seas Fleet. Thanks to the efforts of Room 40, the Grand Fleet was sailing, ready to do battle, even before the High Seas Fleet had left Wilhelmshaven.

Scheer had no inkling of what was happening on the other side of the North Sea. The U-boats in which he had placed so much faith failed him miserably: not only did they not sink or damage a single British warship, they failed to get off even a single torpedo. Worse still for Scheer, none of them was able to make a report that the Grand Fleet had sailed in strength; apparently none of them even saw the massive processions of British warships leaving their anchorages. Scheer, already deprived of his zeppelins, was steaming into the North Sea in total ignorance of the threat coming out to meet him.

The separate squadrons of the Grand Fleet rendezvoused at dawn on May 31, twenty-four dreadnoughts and their escorts. The battleships steamed in a formation of six columns abreast, each column made up of four ships. Their escorts formed a loose ring around them, lookouts scanning the horizon, searching for the telltale smudge of smoke that would be the first warning of the enemy's presence. The battleships were steaming at 15 knots toward a point 100 miles west of Horns Reef, where Beatty's battlecruisers would meet them at 1400. As the morning passed into early afternoon, drills were held, routine maintenance work was done, the crews took their midday

Gambit

139

meals, and no one, save for Jellicoe and his senior officers and staff, expected to actually face the Germans that day.

Even Jellicoe began to have his doubts. A signal from the Admiralty had arrived at 1248 which informed him that Scheer's flagship, *Friedrich der Grösse,* was still in the Jade Roads. If that was true, then the planned German operation had been cancelled, or else there had never been an operation laid on at all. What Jellicoe did not know was that this was yet another blunder involving signals.

What had happened was that the Director of the Admiralty's Operations Division, Captain Thomas Jackson, had visited Room 40 that morning and asked for the location of Scheer's call sign, "DK." When he was told it was in the Jade Roads, he left without further comment or inquiry, assuming that this meant that Scheer had not sailed after all. A signal was sent to Jellicoe indicating that the High Seas Fleet had not left Wilhelmshaven; Jellicoe then concluded that the German operation was nothing more than another raid by Hipper's First Scouting Group.

Unfortunately, none of this was true. Captain Jackson, who has been charitably described as a "ridiculous, blustering, insufferable buffoon," had little regard for the men, many of them civilians, who worked in Room 40, and who therefore, he believed, could have little if any understanding of operational naval matters. He was regarded by the staff of Room 40 with an equal level of contempt and, on the rare occasions when he asked questions, was given only the barest possible answers. Consequently, when Jackson asked where Scheer's call sign "DK" was located, he was told, truthfully, that it was in the Jade Roads. What he was not told, because he did not ask and no one in the Room 40 staff was inclined to volunteer any information to him, was that whenever Scheer put to sea, his call sign automatically transferred to a shore station. The cryptographers and analysts could have told this to Jackson, had he been inclined to listen to them, but his dismissive attitude precluded that possibility. Scheer *was* at sea, the High Seas Fleet was with him, and petty bureaucratic squabbling and a naval nincompoop kept that knowledge from Jellicoe. In less than six hours this latest example of Admiralty bungling had serious repercussions for the Grand Fleet.

Beatty's Battlecruiser Fleet was steaming some 65 miles to the southeast of Jellicoe, drawn up in two columns of three ships, with the four battleships of the Fifth Battle Squadron steaming in line ahead 5 miles astern and to the northwest. Since dawn the fleet had been zigzagging to reduce the chances of a submarine attack, making 22 degree course alterations to port and starboard on the instructions of the flagship, HMS *Lion.* Commodore William Goodenough had his screen of light cruisers and destroyers spread out in a semicircle ahead of the battlecruisers, at a distance of 10 to 12 miles, the maximum visible range of signal flags. At 1400, there was nothing in sight but the 49 ships under Beatty's command. At 1410, Beatty gave the order to hoist the signal for all ships to turn north, anticipating the rendezvous with the Grand Fleet. Five minutes later, the hoist was hauled down, the signal to execute the order.

The light cruiser HMS *Galatea* had taken up station on the far port wing of the advance screen for Beatty's ships, and it was some moments before it became clear that the signal hoist aboard *Lion* had, indeed, been hauled down. Just as *Galatea's* helmsmen put her wheel over to port, a lookout on her starboard bridge sang out, "Ship ahead blowing off steam!" His sharp eyes had spotted a white plume of steam 8 miles away, the sign of a stationary ship. *Galatea's* captain, suspecting that perhaps the steam was coming from a merchant ship that had been stopped by a U-boat, ordered an increase in speed and steamed directly for the white cloud. Soon he could see the hull of a small Danish tramp steamer, which was eventually identified as the *N. V. Fjord*. But what caught *Galatea's* captain's eye was not the Danish steamer, but the pale grey silhouettes of a pair of German destroyers just beyond her. The ship's bugler sounded "Action Stations," and the lookout then spotted two German light cruisers. The signal went to the top of *Galatea's* mast, "Enemy in sight!" at the same time her wireless began frantically signaling the news to *Lion*. At 1428 *Galatea's* forward 6-inch gun bellowed, firing the first shot of the Battle of Jutland.

The morning had been just as uneventful for Hipper and Scheer as it had been for Beatty and Jellicoe. There was, however, a different air aboard the German ships: while most of the British crews believed that they would not be encountering the Germans this day, the German crews sensed almost to a man that a battle with the British was in the offing. The routine drill was to give the guns their daily cleaning at 1300, and once that was complete the officers and men rested uneasily. At 1428 the signal to "Clear for Action" was sounded throughout the First Scouting Group: the light cruiser *Elbing* had stopped a small Danish steamer, suspecting that it was, in fact, a British spy ship. While the officers of one of the destroyers accompanying *Elbing* boarded the Danish ship and inspected her papers and cargo, a British light cruiser suddenly appeared and opened fire.

When *Galatea's* report reached *Lion*, Beatty had been preparing for the rendezvous with Jellicoe—now that was the furthest thing from his mind. Almost instinctively he ordered the squadron to increase speed to 22 knots and turn southeast. He fully intended to get between the enemy and Wilhelmshaven, leaving the Germans no choice but to fight. In a muddle reminiscent of Dogger Bank, both signals were obscured by funnel smoke from the four ships of the Fifth Battle Squadron, which held its original course; inexplicably

Tiger, detailed to pass along *Lion's* signals by searchlight, failed to do so, and the four battleships, under the command of Rear Admiral Hugh Evan-Thomas, continued to steam away from Beatty's battlecruisers. Aboard *Lion* more than ten minutes passed before anyone realized that the battleships had not followed. At first, though, this seemed like a minor detail, as Beatty believed he was confronted by nothing more than a handful of German light cruisers and destroyers.

The rest of the battlecruisers followed *Lion's* lead, officers and men rushing about to get their ships ready for battle. Aboard most of them, afternoon tea had just been laid out, but the tea grew cold and the sandwiches stale before anyone had a chance to touch them. Watertight doors slammed shut, hatches were closed, scuttles were secured, all of them carefully dogged down; surgeons and their assistants began laying out bandages and surgical instruments; gun captains made certain that their turrets were secured and prepared, from the stacks of sandwiches and biscuits, to canteens filled with fresh water, to waste buckets for the gun crews' relief. On board HMS *New Zealand,* her captain, John Green, was carefully hanging a green stone tiki pendant around his neck, then wrapping himself in a black-and-white Maori war kilt, a gift from that fierce warrior people given during the ship's visit to her namesake dominion in 1913. As long as Green wore the stone and the kilt, he was assured, no serious harm would ever come to the ship: Green took no chances and donned the native garb with all due solemnity. When the word was passed throughout *New Zealand* that he had done so, the crew roared their approval.

At 1447 *Galatea* sent another signal to *Lion,* this one reading, "Smoke seems to be seven vessels besides cruisers and destroyers." Beatty took it to mean that Hipper's battlecruisers were just over the horizon. Seventy miles to the north, *Iron Duke's* wireless picked up the same signal, and Jellicoe came to the same conclusion. He ordered the fleet's speed increased to 19 knots, hoping to reach Beatty's position by 1800.

Hipper spotted the British battlecruisers first, dark grey, massive behemoths belching great clouds of dense, black coal smoke. At first he mistook them for the van of the Grand Fleet, and so signaled to Scheer, but a few moments later he corrected his mistake, recognizing the distinctive silhouettes of the four "Big Cats"—*Lion, Tiger, Princess Royal,* and *Queen Mary.* Standing on *Lützow's* bridge, calmly smoking a cigar, he was the very model of the calm professional naval officer. Sensing a unique opportunity, at 1538 he gave the order for the entire First Scouting Group to reverse course and begin steaming south. Slowing temporarily to 18 knots, he allowed his light cruisers and destroyers to resume their positions ahead of the battlecruisers, at the same time further enticing Beatty to follow him.

Beatty was all too willing to do so: apparently the Germans did not know how badly they were outgunned as well as outnumbered. With his six battlecruisers as well as the four battleships of the Fifth Battle Squadron, it was only a question of when, not if, the British would crush their German opponent.

Chapter 7

"There's Something Wrong with Our Bloody Ships Today!"

As he stood on the bridge of HMS *Lion,* gazing resolutely through his glasses at the approaching German battlecruisers, David Beatty could hardly believe his luck. This was Dogger Bank all over again, but this time he possessed two distinct advantages that he had lacked in the earlier battle: the Germans were much farther from the safety of the Heligoland, and Beatty had the advantage of numbers. With Hugh Evan-Thomas's Fifth Battleship Squadron added to his fleet, he had twice as many ships as the German battlecruiser squadron, and with the addition of the four *Queen Elizabeth's* 15-inch guns, he had almost three times the weight of shell as the Germans. And while the German battlecruisers were swift, their British counterparts were faster still: they would become anvil to the four *Queen Elizabeth's* hammer; the enemy ships would be pounded to pieces. There would be no escape for Franz Hipper this time.

As he stood on the bridge of SMS *Lützow,* gazing resolutely through his glasses at the approaching British battlecruisers, Hipper could hardly believe his luck. This was Dogger Bank all over again, but this time he possessed one distinct advantage that he had lacked in the earlier battle: he knew for certain that this time the main German battle fleet was coming up behind him in support. Soon he would have the advantage of overwhelming numbers and weight of shell, and even the presence of the four fearsome *Queen Elizabeths* of the Fifth Battleship Squadron would not be enough to save the British battlecruisers from being methodically pounded to pieces. His battlecruisers would be the anvil to the High Seas Fleet's hammer. There would be no escape for Beatty this time.

Almost simultaneously Beatty and Hipper each gave the order "Action Stations" and "Clear for Action"; bugles began sounding and drums beating, sending officers and ratings alike scurrying to their posts. Deep within the ships the "Black Gangs" of the boiler rooms began stoking the fire grates to increase speed. High above the decks of the battlecruisers, in the fire-control positions, gunnery officers were busy manipulating rangefinders and plotting tables, calculating ranges and bearing in order to work out the bearing and elevation figures passed down to the gun turrets.

Inside the gun turrets of both British and German ships, an intricate ballet was taking place. To an outside observer it would have seemed a chaotic amalgamation of shouts, moving men and machinery, mechanical clanks, clangs and rattles, and the intermittent ringing of bells. However, each movement of man and machine was carefully choreographed, practiced over and over again in countless drills, until the men worked as smoothly and methodically as the machines they served.

In their excitement, the magazine crews of some of the British battlecruisers were sowing the seeds of their own destruction: knowing that reducing the time between salvos improved the chances of their ship's guns getting hits on the enemy, they resolved to do their best to reduce that time to a minimum. In order to speed up the movement of propellant charges to the guns, cordite bags were stacked in the shell handling rooms and the magazine lobbies, while the flash doors were left open, eliminating the vital seconds necessary to repeatedly close them and open them again each time a shell or powder charge was passed through. Though they had no way of knowing, thousands of them would pay for their enthusiasm with their lives.

For some reason, though the British battlecruisers actually sighted their enemy counterparts first, almost ten minutes passed before they opened fire on the German ships. While this was far from the only tactical mistake Beatty made that afternoon, it was one of the worst, for he gave up the advantage the superior range his 13.5-inch guns gave him. The maximum range of the 12-inch guns mounted on *Lützow* and *Derfflinger* was only slightly more than 17,000 yards, 5,000 yards short of the maximum range of the 13.5-inch guns carried on Beatty's four "Big Cats"; the maximum range of the German 11-inch gun was shorter still. In other words, there was a 2.5 mile difference between the maximum range of the German guns and those on the British ships. In his haste to close with the enemy, Beatty surrendered this potentially devastating tactical advantage, for with the combination of superior speed and range, he could have dictated the conditions of the battle, keeping well outside of the reach of the German guns while pummeling the German battlecruisers almost at will.

It was a tactical lapse that Beatty could never fully explain, then or later. It was not a question of ignorance: even in the days of fighting sail, the captain of a more heavily armed ship often sought the "zone of immunity," ranges

"There's Something Wrong with Our Bloody Ships Today!"   **145**

where his guns could strike his opponent without fear of being struck by the enemy's smaller, lighter, and shorter-ranged guns. However, because the smaller ship was almost invariably the faster, a commander who found himself outgunned could choose to sail out of range entirely, use his speed to shorten the range until his own guns could reply effectively, or maneuver into positions where the enemy's heavier guns could not be brought to bear. But in Beatty's case, he not only had the advantage of larger, longer-ranged guns, he also had superior speed, which by careful maneuvering should have allowed him to keep Hipper in a position where the German battlecruisers were under constant bombardment without ever being able to make any sort of effective reply.

The most likely explanation is that Beatty's natural aggressiveness—never a fault in the eyes of the Royal Navy—blinded him to this opportunity. Having twice watched the German battlecruisers escape, he was determined to close with Hipper and at the same time place his own ships between the Germans and their home port, compelling the German battlecruisers to fight. Beatty chose a course for his squadron that converged upon the Germans, rather than merely paralleling them, giving up the range advantage in order to ensure a battle.

This suited Hipper perfectly, for he well knew the difference in range between the British 13.5-inch guns and his own 11-inch and 12-inch weapons, so closing the range between the battlecruiser squadrons actually worked in his favor. At 1545, when the range had dropped to 16,000 yards, he calmly gave the order to open fire. *Lützow's* first salvo roared out, followed an instant later by the guns of *Defflinger, Seydlitz, Moltke,* and *von der Tann.*

On the bridge of *Lion,* Beatty's officers waited anxiously for the order to begin firing to be given, but Beatty was busy dictating a signal to John Jellicoe. Captain Ernle Chatfield sent word to the admiral that the range was closing rapidly but received no reply. After a few more moments passed, Chatfield decided he could wait no longer and told his gunnery officer to open fire. A four-gun salvo crashed out, almost at the same instant that a ripple of fire ran down the German battle line.

The opening German salvoes were impressive, accurate, and tightly grouped. The first shots fell short by a mere 200 yards; the second salvo straddled *Tiger,* two of the four shells hitting her, the crash of tearing metal being clearly heard on the other British ships over the sound of the exploding shells. Beatty held his course for another five minutes, until the range was down to 13,000 yards, and then ordered the squadron to turn one point to starboard, bringing the British ships onto a parallel course with the German battlecruisers.

146   Distant Victory

Now the two squadrons began to slug it out in earnest as they steamed southward at a speed of nearly 26 knots. On the bridge of each warship the captain and his staff were watching the enemy fleet, observing the fall of their own shells as well as the enemy's. A signal officer, usually a junior lieutenant, was standing by, ready to carry any messages that his captain might wish to send to the flagship or other ships in the squadron; he was equally prepared to pass along any messages received. A signaler, either a senior seaman or a midshipman known for his keen eyesight, was posted with a telescope continually trained on the flagship, watching for signals to be hoisted. Range and bearing information was continually passed down from the spotting officers in the fighting tops, along with reports from various parts of the ship concerning casualties or damage. Blast and smoke from the guns washed across the deck, spray from the sea blew in the officers' faces, while often mugs of tea or coffee, sometimes laced with rum, were passed out among them. It was a scene of masterful calm and organization, yet underneath it all was the constant awareness that at any given moment, oblivion could overtake it all in a blinding flash of flame and crash of thunder as an enemy shell obliterated their position.

Broadsides bellowed out between the German and British squadrons, as Hipper's ships quickly found the range and began straddling Beatty's battlecruisers almost immediately. British gunnery left a lot to be desired in the opening salvos, some groupings passing more than two miles beyond their targets. HMS *Tiger's* gunnery was particularly appalling, a fact that Beatty later attributed, not without some justification, to the fact that a disproportionate number of her crew was made up of defaulters and apprehended deserters.

Further aggravating the problem was that at the outset of the action Beatty was denied the guns of the Fifth Battle Squadron, commanded by Rear Admiral Hugh Evan-Thomas, one of the best-shooting squadrons in the whole of the Grand Fleet. Here a signaling error was to blame, though for once Beatty's flag lieutenant, Ralph Seymour, was not responsible. Evan-Thomas's squadron was positioned five miles off Lion's port bow, a long distance for signaling by flag hoists; because of this *Tiger* was detailed with the responsibility of passing any signals made by *Lion* to Evan-Thomas's flagship *Barham* by searchlight. When Beatty gave the order for the Battlecruiser Squadron to turn to the southeast, *Tiger* failed to pass the signal along, and the Fifth Battle Squadron continued along its northerly course. *Barham's* captain, A.W. Craig, urged Evan-Thomas to follow *Lion's* lead, but the admiral declined, believing that Beatty would have specifically signaled if he wanted the battleships to follow. Nearly seven minutes passed before Beatty noticed that the four battleships had not followed the battlecruisers and instructed a recall

"There's Something Wrong with Our Bloody Ships Today!" **147**

signal to be sent by searchlight to Evan-Thomas. By then the Fifth Battle Squadron had drawn off nearly ten miles from the British battlecruisers and was hard-pressed to catch up.

Though *Tiger* was the first British ship to be hit, the most serious of the early blows struck by either side was a shell that burst on the top of the left gun of the *Lion's* Q turret, the blast peeling back the roof and front as though it were a sardine tin, killing most of the gun crew outright. A fire sprang up among the red-hot wreckage, and soon propellant charges began to burn as the wind, whipped up by the ship's speed, blew through the devastated turret. Flames began reaching out toward the turret trunk, which led to the shell handling rooms below decks and from there to the magazine, where some 400 tons of 13.5-inch shells were stored. Should the fire reach it, the magazine would explode, destroying the ship. Q turret had been manned by the Royal Marines under Major Francis Harvey, and it was in this moment that the Major added another page to the "Bootnecks" legacy of heroism. In shock, bleeding profusely from the stumps of both legs—they had been blown off in the explosion—Harvey dragged himself over to the speaking tube that led down to lower decks and with his dying breath shouted for the magazine to be flooded. It was just in time: when the magazines were reopened after the battle, the crews were found with their hands on the door clips—they had died in the act of securing them. The fire continued to burn for some time, but the magazines were safe and the ship was saved; *Lion* never left her place in the battle line. Major Harvey was honored with a posthumous Victoria Cross.

Yet such was the fury of the bombardment the two squadrons of battle-cruisers were unleashing upon each other that the destruction of Q turret went unnoticed on *Lion's* bridge until the marine sergeant, bloody, his uni-form singed, a stunned expression still on his face, appeared. Approaching Lt. William Chalmers, he announced in the curiously calm tones of those still in the grip of shock, "Q-turret has gone, sir. All the men were killed and we've flooded the magazines." At this, every head on *Lion's* bridge swiveled toward the young man, then turned to look aft. "No further confirmation was needed," Chalmers later wrote, "the yellow smoke was rolling up in clouds from the gaping hole, and the guns were cocked awkwardly. All this had hap-pened within a few yards of where Beatty was standing and none of us on the bridge had heard the detonation."

That was hardly surprising: during the first quarter hour of their gunnery duel, Hipper's ships had scored as many as a dozen hits on Beatty's battle-cruisers. Salvos were crashing out from the muzzles of the guns of both squadrons with almost clockwork regularity. With the constant roar of the guns in their ears and their attention tightly focused on the German warships, it is hardly surprising that Beatty and his staff did not take immediate notice of Q turret's devastation.

Four of Beatty's six ships took multiple hits within the first 15 minutes of the action. In addition to the devastating strike on her Q turret, *Lion* took three other hits, all apparently from *Lützow*. Likewise *Tiger* was hit multiple times by *Moltke; Princess Royal* was struck by two shells from *Lützow* and *Queen Mary* by *Seydlitz*. Only *Indefatigable* and *New Zealand* seemed immune.

Not that Hipper's ships were getting away unscathed. The British battle-cruisers quickly corrected for their embarrassing overshoots in the opening minutes of the battle, and within minutes were scoring powerful hits of their own. At 1555 a shell from *Queen Mary* exploded in *Seydlitz*' battery deck, while *Lion* scored two hits on *Lützow* at about this same time, and *Derfflinger* was hit once. A near-miss from a shell fired by *Tiger* at *Moltke* shook the entire ship, jarring fittings loose and creating electrical problems. *Seydlitz* then took yet another hit from *Queen Mary*, which crashed into the German battlecruiser's forward midships turret, putting it out of action for the remainder of the battle. Moments later, a near-miss along *Seydlitz*' starboard side buckled her armor belt for almost 40 feet, causing flooding in several compartments.

Astern of them, *von der Tann* and *Indefatigable*, each the oldest battle-cruiser in its respective squadron, were having their own private gunnery duel, each ship having fired nearly 50 shells at the other. At 1602, a salvo from the *von der Tann* came crashing down on *Indefatigable*. The British ship staggered out of the battle line—whether by accident or as an intentional course change no one would ever know—with smoke pouring from her stern, but before she could give any indication of the extent of her damage, another shell hit her near A turret, and yet another hit the turret itself. For some seconds she seemed unhurt by these last two but then she blew up violently, rent by sheets of orange flame and shrouded in billows of brown cordite smoke. The exploding shells had either ignited the cordite charges inside the turret trunk, and the flash fire passed down to the magazines, or the shells themselves penetrated the armor over the battlecruiser's magazines and exploded inside. Whichever was the case, the results were catastrophic: *Indefatigable* was torn apart in a single tremendous blast.

Signaller Charles Falmer, whose action station was in the foretop, remembered that moment with startling detail:

> There was a terrific explosion aboard the ship, the magazines went. I saw the guns go up in the air just like matchsticks—12-inch guns they were—bodies and everything. She was beginning to settle down. Within half a minute the ship turned right over and she was gone.

"There's Something Wrong with Our Bloody Ships Today!" **149**

Posted in the forward topmast, 180 feet above the water, Falmer was thrown clear of the sinking ship as she rolled over onto her starboard side and then went under in less than a minute. Only Falmer and one other crewman survived; 1,017 died with *Indefatigable.*

With the loss of *Indefatigable* and Evan-Thomas's Fifth Battleship Squadron still not yet within range, the two battlecruiser fleets were now evenly matched in numbers. *Lion* was hit by five shells from *Lützow,* one of them carrying away her transmitting aerial, leaving Beatty with no means of contacting his ships or Jellicoe directly by wireless—*Lion* could receive signals but not send them. There was neither the time nor the opportunity for Beatty to shift his flag to another ship, so he resorted to the awkward alternative of sending signals via flags or searchlight to *Princess Royal,* who then passed them along via wireless. Beatty needed time to reassert control over the situation and so ordered the squadron to alter course a point to starboard, opening the range to 18,000 yards. For the moment the guns on both sides fell silent.

It was just now that the Fifth Battle Squadron reappeared on the scene, finally overtaking both Beatty and Hipper. It was a timely intervention for Beatty: while there was something approaching parity between the lighter German guns versus the thinner British armor and the heavier British guns versus the better-protected German ships, Hipper's battlecruisers could not stand up to the 15-inch guns of the four *Queen Elizabeth* class battleships. At 19,000 yards, more than a mile beyond the maximum range of the German guns, Evan-Thomas's ships opened fire.

The Germans recognized their unmistakable silhouettes and knew what was coming. Georg von Hase, *Derfflinger's* gunnery officer, remembered how:

> Behind the [British] battlecruiser line appeared four big ships. We soon identified these as the *Queen Elizabeth* class. There had been much talk in our fleet about this class.... They fired a shell more than twice as heavy as ours. They engaged at portentous ranges.

Endless drills and target practice had produced gunnery in these four dreadnoughts that was among the best in the Grand Fleet. They quickly found the range.

The first German ship to feel the Fifth Battle Squadron's fire was *von der Tann.* At 1410 she took a hit aft, the 1,920 pound shell tearing through her armor belt, allowing 600 tons of seawater into her hull. Even the near-misses were punishing, as the explosions shook the ship from stem to stern. All four of the Fifth Battle Squadron's ships were within range, allowing *Barham* and *Valiant* to shift their fire to *Moltke,* while *Warspite* and *Malaya* engaged *von der Tann.* A shell from one of them punched through *Moltke's* side armor and detonated in a starboard coal bunker, setting off a coal dust explosion, which wrecked one of her 5.9-inch guns.

Hipper ordered his ships to begin zigzagging in order to throw off the British gunnery, even though he knew it would affect his own squadron's shooting. *Von der Tann* was close to being overwhelmed, as she was the target of not only *Warspite* and *Malaya,* but *New Zealand* as well. At 1617 the British battlecruiser put a shell into the German ship's forward 11-inch turret, jamming both guns and flooding the magazine. At the same time a 15-inch shell striking aft plunged through *von der Tann's* armored deck and knocked out her rear turret. Her remaining two turrets continued to fire, though, scoring a hit on *New Zealand* in return, although the damage was slight and there were no casualties.

At the head of the two columns, however, one of the most spectacular incidents of the entire battle was about to unfold. Because of faulty British gunnery distribution reminiscent of Dogger Bank, *Derfflinger* found herself completely unengaged by any of Beatty's ships. Both she and *Seydlitz* concentrated her fire on *Queen Mary,* and before long the accuracy of their shelling extracted an awful toll.

Queen Mary had already been hit several times by this point, with her aft secondary armament wrecked; at least one 11-inch shell had landed near X turret. Observers on *Seydlitz* saw an ammunition fire flare up in *Queen Mary's* after superstructure near the ruined 4-inch battery. Q turret then took a hit that put the right gun out of action, and five minutes after that two shells landed simultaneously on *Queen Mary.* One hit the left gun of Q turret, breaking it in two, the other seemed to strike somewhere between A and B turrets. According to Midshipman Jocelyn Storey, who was stationed in Q turret,

> A heavy shell hit our turret and put the right gun out of action, but killed nobody. Three minutes later an awful explosion took place which smashed up our turret completely. The left gun broke in half and fell into the working chamber and the right one came right back. A cordite fire got going and a lot of the fittings got loose and killed a lot of people.

Petty Officer Ernest Francis, whose battle station was in X turret heard more shells crash into *Queen Mary,* then there was a sudden, eerie silence; in his words, "Everything in the ship went as quiet as a church." Francis immediately sensed that something was wrong and, looking out a hatch at the back of X turret, saw that the after superstructure was a shambles and the ship was taking on an ominous list to port. A and B turrets' magazines had blown up.

Queen Mary's back was broken and the fore part of the ship beyond the forward funnel had already gone under. Von Hase in *Derfflinger* watched as

> a vivid red flame shot up from her forepart. Then came an explosion forward, followed by a much heavier explosion amidships. Black debris flew into the air and immediately afterward the whole ship blew up with a terrific explosion. A gigantic cloud of smoke rose, the masts collapsed inwards, the smoke cloud hid everything and rose higher and higher. Finally nothing but a thick, black cloud of smoke remained where the ship had been. At its base the cloud covered only a small area, but it widened toward the summit and looked like a monstrous pine tree.

An officer on the bridge of *Tiger,* only five hundred yards astern of *Queen Mary,* saw much the same thing as did von Hase:

> I saw one salvo straddle her. Three shells out of four hit.... The next salvo straddled her and two more shells hit her. As they hit, I saw a dull red glow amidships and then the ship seemed to open out like a puffball.... There was another dull red glow forward and whole ship seemed to collapse inwards. The funnels and masts fell into the middle, the roofs of the turrets were blown a hundred feet high....

A passing gust of wind parted the smoke cloud, and, as they passed, *Tiger* and *New Zealand* were able to see all that was left of *Queen Mary.* Only the stern of the ship was afloat, listing hard to port, her screws out of the water and still turning. *New Zealand's* gunnery officer reported seeing men crawling out of the after turret and along her decks, and just as *New Zealand* was passing by, what remained of *Queen Mary* suddenly rolled over and blew up. Out of a crew of 1,275, there were nine survivors.

The loss of *Queen Mary* left Beatty stunned. He had engaged Hipper fully confident of his numerical superiority of six battlecruisers to the German five. Now within the space of three quarters of an hour he had lost two of them. No sooner had the report of *Queen Mary's* destruction reached him than *Princess Royal* was engulfed in a torrent of shell splashes that completely hid her from view, and a signalman on *Lion's* bridge reported in dismay, "*Princess Royal* blown up, sir!" Nonplussed, Beatty turned to Captain Chatfield and blurted out, "There seems to be something wrong with our bloody ships today!" Just then *Princess Royal* steamed out of the splashes, smoke, and spray and spat a broadside at *Moltke.*

It was at this moment that an *ad hoc* flotilla of British destroyers, a dozen in all led by Commander Edward "Barry" Bingham in *Nestor,* finally caught up with the battlecruisers, and Beatty immediately ordered them to attack Hipper's squadron with torpedoes. What happened next was so confusing that no two eyewitness accounts agree on more than the most general outline of events. The British destroyers charged toward Hipper's battle line at 34 knots, only to be met by the light cruiser *Regensburg* and 15 German destroyers. A free-for-all quickly ensued as the little ships dodged and weaved back and forth, narrowly missing one another, 3- and 4-inch guns barking and banging, torpedoes hissing out of their tubes; the secondary batteries of the battlecruisers joined in whenever an enemy destroyer was careless enough to come within range. The German destroyers managed to launch 18 torpedoes at the British battlecruisers; the British destroyers launched 20. Both battlecruiser squadrons turned away from the torpedo attacks, and all 38 missed, save for one, which managed to find its way into *Seydlitz'* port side.

Seydlitz was rapidly acquiring the reputation for being at once the unluckiest and the luckiest ship in the High Seas Fleet—unlucky in that she seemed to attract enemy shells and torpedoes and lucky in that they never caused enough damage to sink her. Severely damaged at Dogger Bank, she had come within a few seconds of blowing up, but escaped, though with the loss of almost 90 crew. Here at Jutland half of her guns were already out of action, and she was badly holed above and below the waterline, though she was able to maintain her position in the German battle line. Now a British torpedo exploded close to A turret, tearing a hole 40 feet long and 13 feet wide in her hull plating. Still she was able to maintain her position, but her situation grew increasingly perilous as hundreds of tons of seawater began flooding her forward lower decks.

This sort of success came at a price, however, as the destroyers *Nomad* and *Nestor*—the latter Bingham's own ship—both took hits in their boiler rooms, leaving them powerless and sinking, wallowing helplessly between the two fleets. The British exacted measure for measure, however, as the German destroyers *V-27* and *V-29* were sunk in the melee.

Though only one British torpedo found its mark, the attack by Bingham's destroyers had bought time for Beatty. It was desperately needed, for the tactical situation had been utterly transformed, and now the British battlecruisers were suddenly faced with a far greater threat than any Beatty had ever imagined. He had been lured toward a German trap.

At 1638 Hipper's squadron unexpectedly made a 180 degree turn to port and began steaming northward again. At first Beatty had no idea why the Germans had turned about. There is no denying that for the first hour of the Battle of Jutland the Royal Navy came off second-best. Not only had the Germans sunk two of the British battlecruisers, they had inflicted serious damage on three of the survivors, and while some of them had taken significant damage—*Seydlitz* was, in fact, already in serious trouble and *von der Tann* was reduced to a single working turret—yet turning back into the North Sea would simply prolong the engagement, increasing the likelihood that one or

"There's Something Wrong with Our Bloody Ships Today!"   **153**

more of Hipper's ships would join *Indefatigable* and *Queen Mary* on the bottom. A signal received by *Lion* at the same moment Hipper turned suddenly made it all clear, laying bare the German admiral's stratagem as well as his masterful execution of it.

For Hipper had performed his reconnaissance and entrapment role to perfection: he had lured Beatty far enough to the south for Scheer's dreadnoughts to be able to bring their guns to bear. While the British battlecruisers might face their German counterparts as more or less equals, they were never designed to stand up to the German battleships. It was to be the culmination of Scheer's strategy of catching a section of the Grand Fleet unawares and destroying it in detail, simultaneously erasing the Royal Navy's numerical superiority and dealing a psychological blow from which the British fleet—and, indeed, the British people—might never recover.

The signal delivered to *Lion's* bridge at 1638 was from the light cruiser *Southampton*. It read, "URGENT. PRIORITY. Have sighted enemy battlefleet, bearing approximately southeast."

When Beatty had turned his force to the south and formed the battlecruisers into a line of battle at 1545, the 12 ships of his three light cruiser squadrons increased speed, straining to take up their proper scouting positions in front of the battlecruisers. By 1635 they had overtaken the big ships and were again acting as an advance screen, pounding southward at better than 28 knots. Standing on the bridge of HMS *Southampton,* flagship of the Second Scouting Squadron, Commodore William Goodenough looked off to the southeast and watched in amazement as the pale grey battleships of the High Seas Fleet, along with a horde of escorting cruisers and destroyers, emerged from the North Sea mist. "We saw ahead of us first smoke, then masts, then ships," he later wrote, "sixteen battleships with destroyers around them on each bow." Goodenough waited a few moments before sending out a signal alerting the rest of the British fleet to the High Seas Fleet's presence, wanting to be sure of his sighting. Then his commander (the Royal Navy's equivalent of the U.S. Navy's executive officer) cooly reminded him, "Sir, if you're going to make that signal, you'd better do it now. You may never make another."

It was not an idle comment—Goodenough's four cruisers were already within range of the German dreadnoughts' guns. The only thing that saved them from annihilation was a case of mistaken identity: seen from bows-on, the British cruisers were mistaken for German ships and were momentarily spared an onslaught of 11- and 12-inch shells. At 1638 Goodenough's first sighting report went out to the British fleet.

Still Goodenough pressed closer, wanting to gather as much information as he could, until the range was down to barely 13,000 yards—6.5 miles, almost point-blank range for a battleship's guns. Finally, at 1648, he ordered his ships to turn away, and as the four-funneled profiles of the British cruisers were exposed, Scheer's battleships opened fire on them. Desperately twisting and turning, dodging salvos by turning into the shell splashes of the previous shot, Goodenough was able to make his escape, all the while transmitting to Beatty and Jellicoe what he had learned. "URGENT. PRIORITY. Course of enemy's battlefleet is north, single line-ahead. Composition of van is *Kaiser*-class…. Destroyers on both wings and ahead. Enemy's battlecruisers are joining battlefleet from the north." The trap for Beatty had been set. The question now was whether or not he would fall into it.

Chapter 8

The Thunder of the Guns

The Chinese ideogram for "crisis" is a combination of two others—"danger" and "opportunity"—and it was precisely such a situation that now confronted David Beatty, for if his impetuous nature got the best of him, he could lead the British battlecruisers to wholesale destruction; at the same time, a canny maneuver executed at precisely the right moment could deliver the whole of the High Seas Fleet into the maw of the Grand Fleet.

It has been said that even the most incompetent military leader is capable of one stroke of inspired genius, and whatever his shortcomings as a strategist or tactician, David Beatty was no incompetent. Perhaps because many of his operational habits were more impulsive than considered, it was in a flash of tactical insight that Beatty suddenly sensed the opportunity lurking within the danger in which the Battlecruiser Fleet now found itself. It was possible that Beatty could turn the tables on Franz Hipper and lure the German fleet into a British ambush, for clearly Hipper believed that the British battlecruisers were on their own, operating as a single, independent squadron, without the support of the Grand Fleet. If the German admiral had the slightest inkling that the British battle fleet was at sea and lurking just over the horizon, he would have never tried to lure Beatty's ships into range of the guns of the High Seas Fleet: the last thing Hipper or Scheer wanted was to face the combined strength of the entire Grand Fleet.

Hipper and Reinhard Scheer expected the British battlecruisers to turn away from the advancing German battle fleet. Knowing that Beatty had already lost two of his ships and that at least one other had been hit hard, Hipper would certainly follow, hoping to pick off any stragglers or possibly inflict further damage. The challenge for Beatty was to turn back to the north and make it appear as though he were in full retreat, rather than merely withdrawing: one was an apparent admission of defeat, the other a pause to regroup and renew the fight. It was a fine distinction, but one that would make the difference between luring Hipper into a British trap and tipping his hand to the Germans and giving them a chance to escape.

It was not that difficult a deception: *Lion* had been hit 15 times, as had *Princess Royal,* while *Tiger* had taken 17 hits in that furious first 45 minutes of gunfire. With visible damage and trailing smoke from hits on their decks and superstructures, it was easy to imagine that any of these ships might be crippled. At 1440 Beatty instructed a new signal to be hoisted: "Alter course in succession 16 points to starboard." The maneuver Beatty ordered was a 180 degree turn, with each ship in the line turning at the same spot, thus preserving their order in line as well as the distance interval between them. There was a risk to such a turn: by making all four ships turn at the same place, Beatty gave Hipper's battlecruisers, as well as the lead dreadnoughts of the First Battle Squadron, the opportunity to find the range exactly and blanket that small corner of the sea with shells.

But at that moment, as with so many other times in his career, Beatty was lucky. The turn was executed just out of range of the German battleships, and there was not enough time for Hipper's battlecruisers to concentrate all their guns before Beatty's four ships had swung round and were now headed north. If Beatty's luck held, in less than an hour it was Hipper and Scheer who would be on the receiving end of a particularly nasty shock.

In the meantime, though, yet another signaling error by the incorrigibly inept Lt. Ralph Seymour brought Hugh Evan-Thomas's Fifth Battle Squadron perilously close to disaster. Neither *Lion* nor *Tiger* had relayed Beatty's course change to *Barham,* Evan-Thomas's flagship, and so the quartet of battleships continued on their southerly course. By now they were making close to 25 knots, while the High Seas Fleet was storming northward at 22, leaving the old predreadnoughts of the Second Battle Squadron to catch up as best they could. Thus, the two forces were closing at a rate of nearly 50 miles an hour, with Evan-Thomas outnumbered four to one. It was not until Evan-Thomas's battleships and Beatty's battlecruisers passed each other going in opposite directions that Beatty realized what had happened and had Lt. Seymour repeat the flag hoist for the course change.

The signal went up at 1648, but rather than lower it—which was the signal to execute the order—after the regulation two minutes had passed, Seymour apparently forgot that it was hoisted and left it up for more than six minutes. By the time he realized his mistake and lowered the signal, the Fifth Battle Squadron was within range of Admiral Paul Behncke's four *König*-class battleships—*König, Grosser Kurfürst, Kronprinz Wilhelm,* and *Markgraf*—the four most modern and powerful ships in the fleet.

Fortunately for Evan-Thomas and his quartet of ships most of their shells fell short, but the sight of the German fleet blazing away was something never to be forgotten. *Warspite's* commander later recalled,

> I saw on the starboard quarter the whole of the High Seas Fleet—masts, funnels, and an endless ripple of orange flashes all down the line…. I felt one or two very heavy shakes but it never occurred to me that we were being hit…. I distinctly saw two of our salvoes hit the leading German battleship. Sheets of yellow flame went right over her masts and she looked red fore and aft like a burning haystack. I know we hit her hard.

It was in these moments that the four magnificent *Queen Elizabeths* justified every shilling spent on their construction, for as they defied the power of the High Seas Fleet, they lashed out furiously at their tormentors. The impact on the German ships of the 15-inch shells, which weighed nearly a ton apiece, was literally staggering. No warships in history had ever been subjected to the punishment now being meted out on the German battlecruisers and battleships by these four dreadnoughts. *Barham* and *Valiant* first combined their fire against *Seydlitz,* then turned on *Lützow* and *Derfflinger; Warspite* and *Malaya* threw salvos at *König, Grosser Kurfürst, Kronprinz Wilhelm,* and *Markgraf. Barham's* hits on *Seydlitz* were devastating, demolishing one gun turret and starting a flash fire in another. In a moment that almost mirrored the horrible fate of *Queen Mary* and *Indefatigable,* the fire roared down the turret trunk toward the magazines, but the German magazine crews closed the flash doors in time to prevent the flames from reaching the powder or the shells, sparing *Seydlitz* the fate of the two British battlecruisers. Nonetheless, the fire had incinerated the gun crews and all the men inside the turret trunk.

There is really no other experience that is even roughly equivalent to that of being aboard a ship when it is struck by a heavy shell. For most of the crew there is little or no warning before the impact: apart from a handful of officers and ratings stationed in exposed positions like the bridge, the spotting top, and the signaling platforms, the rest of the crew is cut off from the outside world. When "Action Stations" is sounded, every watertight door is dogged down, every hatch is closed and latched, and every porthole is covered with a heavy metal scuttle to reduce to the absolute minimum the number of apertures through which the sea might gain access to the interior of the ship. Consequently, the crew is unaware of the approaching shells—no whistling, warbling, or express-train-like roar is heard with their approach, as is customary on land. Instead, it is only in that split second when the incoming projectile crashes into the ship that the men inside her know that she has been struck.

In that moment of impact and detonation, lasting less than half a second, a surprising range of sounds are heard, separated by barely milliseconds, but which the mind absorbs and can with astonishing clarity later separate into discrete segments. If the incoming shell strikes the thin shell plating of the superstructure or upper decks, there first comes a sharp, piercing shriek of ripping metal as the heavy projectile punches its way through, shedding its thin streamlining cap along the way. When it strikes the armor belt or an armored deck, there comes a dull, deep bell-like ringing, a basso-profundo "clang" as the mass of the shell itself drives itself into the massive steel plates meant to stop it. At this point the shell begins to expend its kinetic energy into the structure of the ship, causing deck plates and bulkheads in the immediate proximity to ripple, heave, and sometimes buckle or split open. Sharp "cracks" are heard as rivets sheer apart and plates are wrenched apart. If the armor is sufficiently thick, the forward progress of the shell is stopped at this point. If not, the shell will literally tear the armor plate apart and continue on until it no longer carries sufficient kinetic energy to defeat whatever obstacles it encounters. In either case, by this time the shell's fuse, located in its base, has been activated and begins the detonation process.

Because ships, especially warships, are among the strongest structures built by mankind, the effect of a large-caliber shell bursting inside a ship's hull is nothing short of devastating, for the structure of the ship tends to confine the blast. The explosive filling of a British 15-inch shell was just over 60 pounds of lyddite, which when detonated in a confined space filled it with an instantaneous pressure wave of several tons per square inch, pulverizing any soft matter in its path, warping, buckling, and tearing apart bulkheads and decks. At the same time, the heat of the detonation, which can reach well over 1200°F, will vaporize anything flammable within its radius, including human beings; fragments of the shell, called splinters, whiz about like giant bits of shrapnel, shredding anything softer than themselves they encounter. As the blast, heat, and flame recede, they leave behind them toxic gasses that quickly suffocate anyone unfortunate enough to be left alive in their wake.

Unknown to the British on May 31, 1916, a large number of their shells were defective in design, the flaw causing many of the projectiles to break up when striking German armor at oblique angles, others bursting prematurely when striking light sheet metal or shell plating, exploding prematurely. This meant that numerous hits scored by the Grand Fleet's dreadnoughts appeared to cause insignificant damage, as the energy of their impact and explosive blast was mostly expended outside the hulls of their German targets.

But for 12- and 13.5-inch shells, and particularly the 15-inch shells fired by the *Queen Elizabeth* class ships, even such glancing blows struck powerfully. Warships are immensely strong, but they are also exceedingly complex and, consequently, are particularly vulnerable to shock and excessive vibration. A 15-inch shell, even if it did not explode within the hull of its target, carried a tremendous amount of kinetic energy that expended itself ferociously on the ship's structure. The target shuddered down its entire length momentarily, while the structure immediately around the point of impact rang like a bell. The effects of the jarring and shuddering are subtle but significant. Secondary batteries were smashed, the guns jarred from their mountings; auxiliary machinery—pumps, motors, hoists—were knocked out of alignment; pipes ruptured at joints; valves began to leak; hatches and doors were suddenly frozen closed as their frames became distorted; speaking tubes became blocked or broken; electrical equipment, including wireless, failed as power lines were cut or mountings disturbed. Eventually the structure of the ship itself began to suffer as riveted joints began to loosen and seams opened to the sea. Even the British shells that struck home but exploded prematurely were taking a toll on the ships of the High Seas Fleet.

Still the German battlecruisers and battleships survived: when he began building the High Seas Fleet two decades earlier, Alfred von Tirpitz had set down as his primary construction directive that a warship's first priority was to stay afloat. This they did, but little by little, their effectiveness as fighting ships was being eroded. Perhaps even more critical was the crews' growing apprehension, as their ships were being struck again and again, because they had no way of knowing what damage, if any, their own shells were meting out to the enemy. It was an experience that came to haunt the High Seas Fleet.

From the bridge of *Friedrich der Grösse*, Reinhard Scheer felt that he was on the verge of a tremendous victory. From every indication he had, all that was facing the First Scouting Group and the High Seas Fleet was the British Battlecruiser Fleet—already badly depleted in numbers—and a single squadron of battleships. Believing he was pursuing a badly damaged, disorganized enemy, he abandoned the formality of the High Seas Fleet's steaming formation and ordered the signal "Give chase" raised. This meant that each ship was now free to pursue any foe of its choosing at the best speed it could make. The new *König* class dreadnoughts surged forward, pushing past 23 knots as they strove to catch up to the escaping British battleships and battlecruisers, while the predreadnoughts of the Second Battle Squadron fell even farther behind. The once compact and effective formation of the High Seas Fleet now straggled out into a ragged line nearly 25 miles long. Scheer had no way to know it, of course, but he was on the verge, not of a great victory, but of losing tactical control of the battle, and with it his entire fleet.

Hipper was pushing his battlecruisers as hard as he could, but the best speed his ships could make was 25 knots, and Beatty was steaming away at close to 28, the four battleships of the Fifth Battle Squadron making 26 knots.

A gap was opening between the German and British fleets, but this was not a serious concern for Hipper: sooner or later, he knew, Beatty would have to turn and fight, and this time, with the High Seas Fleet supporting him, Hipper was certain that none of the British ships would ever reach the Firth of Forth again. Grimly, cigar still clenched in his teeth, he watched as Beatty gradually began altering his course toward the east, apparently in an attempt to cut across Hipper's bow. This he would not allow: if the British were going to fight, they would do so broadside to broadside. After having watched the twin immolations of *Queen Mary* and *Indefatigable*, Hipper had no illusions about the outcome.

All this time Beatty, who had taken advantage of the lull in the firing as the range opened between the two fleets to allow his crews to begin damage control, was shaping a very deliberate course as he steamed northward. He was determined to continue to draw the High Seas Fleet toward the Grand Fleet, but at the same time conceal the presence of the British battle fleet until the last possible moment. Consequently, rather than steam directly toward John Jellicoe, Beatty began easing his squadron to starboard, his course describing a gentle arc from the north to the northeast. What Beatty was counting on was that Hipper would adhere to one of the fundamentals of naval tactics—never let the enemy "cross your T."

"Crossing the T" is a tactical situation where one battle fleet steams across the bow of an enemy fleet, a position where it can bring the full weight of all of its broadside guns to bear on the enemy, who can reply only with his forward armament. Also, because the shells are falling down the length of the target ships rather than across their beam, the number of hits achieved increases dramatically. For a battle fleet so caught out, such a situation is a recipe not for disaster but for annihilation.

Hipper refused to be so drawn, and so as Beatty eased his course eastward, the German battlecruisers followed. The tactical situation was deteriorating for the Germans in other ways: the light mist that had persisted throughout the afternoon was beginning to thicken in patches, and the late afternoon sun was now shining almost directly into the eyes of the German gunners, while the pale grey German warships were silhouetted in stark relief against the darkening eastern horizon. If Beatty was willing to continue the action, however, these would be minor inconveniences.

Continuing the action was precisely what Beatty had in mind. At sometime around 1730 he signaled to his four battlecruisers and Evan-Thomas's battleships "Prepare to renew the action," and 31 gun turrets swung round to starboard, drawing a bead on the German ships. Hipper's battlecruisers steamed into one of those patches of mist and was lost to sight for a few moments, while three miles behind him, Admiral Paul Behncke's four *König* class dreadnoughts strove to catch up with them. It was actually Behncke who first saw the dreadful sight, rather than Hipper. Cutting through a bank of mist, *König* emerged on its north side at 1759, and there stretching across the northern horizon, Behncke beheld the embodiment of the High Seas Fleet's worst nightmare: deploying in battle line, the massive gun turrets training on Behncke's four ships, prepared to instantly open fire, were 24 British dreadnoughts—the entire might of the Grand Fleet.

As the British battlecruisers were steadily drawing the High Seas Fleet up from the south, the Grand Fleet had been thundering down from the north. The 24 dreadnoughts, formed into six divisions of four ships each steaming in line astern, were drawn up in six columns proceeding abreast of each other. This formation kept the fleet relatively compact while at the same time offering the best protection against torpedo attack, whether from enemy destroyers or submarines. Ahead of them was a widely spread screen of heavy and light cruisers, as well as several flotillas of destroyers, all of which acted as a screen to prevent surprise and scout out the way forward; additionally the Third Battlecruiser Squadron under Rear Admiral Horace Hood was stationed some 25 miles ahead of the main body of the Grand Fleet.

It was a formation ideal for high-speed sweeps of the North Sea and for protection from submarine attack, but it was ill-suited for bringing a fleet into battle—the lines of dreadnoughts would interfere with each others' arcs of fire, masking each others' guns and making spotting impossible. For Jellicoe to be able to bring the full weight and power of the Grand Fleet's guns against the enemy, he would have to order a change of course and formation that would bring all six divisions into one long battle line. To do so properly he needed to know the bearing and course of the German fleet. Repeated requests for this information went out to Beatty from *Iron Duke*, but no reply was forthcoming. (Jellicoe could not know that *Lion's* transmitter had been smashed by an early hit from *Lützow*.)

Earlier that afternoon, by piecing together the scattered wireless signals sent between Beatty's battlecruisers, Evan-Thomas's battleships, and their escort screens, Jellicoe had been able to quickly deduce that more than just German light cruisers and destroyers were out in force. At just about the time when the Grand Fleet was to rendezvous with the Battlecruiser Fleet, the battleship *St. Vincent* was picking up strong wireless signals on a frequency used exclusively by the High Seas Fleet itself, and Jellicoe ordered an increase in speed to 18 knots. *Galatea's* wireless signal sent at 1451, "Smoke seems to be from seven vessels besides destroyers and cruisers," seems to have made up Jellicoe's mind, for at 1500 he gave the order for the Grand Fleet to clear for action.

Bugles sounded throughout the ships, followed by the thud of running feet, the clang of watertight doors closing, and bangs and thumps as hatches and scuttles were secured. Machinery and equipment variously whined, hummed, or moaned, as turrets were swung round, shell hoists were put into motion, and guns were elevated. A peculiar sense of urgency communicated itself to the officers and ratings, and suddenly every man in the Grand Fleet knew that this was no ordinary sweep and not just another drill. The Germans were out!

It was a midshipman in *Neptune* who first noticed it, but soon every man with a telescope or a set of glasses became aware of it, then it was clear even to the naked eye. From yardarms, signal halyards, funnel stays, and jackstaffs, snowy-white billows of silk began spreading, white silk quartered by the red Cross of St. George, the upper inside quarter bearing a Union Jack: the White Ensign of the Royal Navy. Evoking the pride, traditions, courage, discipline, and fighting spirit of the Nile, the Saints, Copenhagen, the Glorious First of June, and Trafalgar, the Royal Navy had broken out its battle ensigns.

At 1651, Jellicoe informed the Admiralty, "Urgent. Fleet action is imminent." Three signals from Goodenough reached the flagship, at 1700, 1740, and 1750, informing Jellicoe that the enemy battle fleet was still steaming north, but the positions the commodore gave were so clearly wrong that they did nothing to aid Jellicoe in formulating his instructions for deploying the fleet. When, at 1733, the two escort screens, Beatty's and Jellicoe's, made contact, it did little to clarify the situation: the Grand Fleet was still steaming south-southeast, while Beatty had bent his course around to almost east-north-east; thus the two fleets met on courses that were almost 90 degrees apart. It was another 20 minutes before the battlecruisers themselves were actually in sight, but when a query was flashed from *Iron Duke* to *Lion*—"Where is the enemy battlefleet?"—Beatty's reply at 1806—"Enemy battlecruisers bearing southeast"—was essentially worthless: it was hardly certain that Scheer had followed Hipper or that, if he had, was on the same course as the German battlecruisers. Another seven minutes passed before the signal came from Beatty at 1813: "Enemy battlefleet in sight bearing south. The nearest ship is seven miles." But still he provided neither bearing nor course, the two pieces of information most vital to Jellicoe in his decision to deploy the fleet. Standing alone on the bridge of Iron Duke, a small figure in a belted blue greatcoat, each passing minute bringing him and the Grand Fleet another half mile closer to what could well be the battle that would decide the fate of the British Empire, Jellicoe had to make a choice. He could deploy the fleet on either the right or the left wing, that is, have his 24 dreadnoughts fall into line behind the lead ship of the squadron that was on the far left or right of the fleet. But he would have only one chance to make the right

The Thunder of the Guns 163

choice—deploy on the wrong wing and he could find the whole of the Grand Fleet steaming away from the High Seas Fleet—or, worse, could find itself steaming directly toward it, with Scheer's dreadnoughts in perfect position to cross the British T and rain an annihilating fire down on the Grand Fleet.

And yet....

If he deployed his ships correctly, Jellicoe could well create a circumstance that was nearly unique in naval warfare—he could not only cross the German T, but he could achieve tactical surprise as well, opening fire on Scheer's battleships before the German admiral even knew that the Grand Fleet was within range, or even anywhere nearby. The choice then was left or right, port or starboard. And the decision must be made *now,* for perhaps the worst circumstance of all would be for a meeting of the Grand Fleet and the High Seas Fleet while the British ships were still deploying, a maneuver that would take 20 minutes to complete.

There on the bridge of *Iron Duke,* Jellicoe pieced together everything he knew and everything he suspected about the position of the High Seas Fleet, along with everything he knew about his own ships, as well as everything he had learned, intuited, and experienced in more than four decades service in the Royal Navy. Though Jellicoe had no way of knowing, it would be the decisive moment of the First World War. In less than two minutes he had made up his mind: the fleet would deploy on the port—left—wing. *Iron Duke's* captain, Frederic Dyer, never forgot that moment:

> [Jellicoe] stepped quickly onto the platform around the compasses and looked in silence at the magnetic compass card for about twenty seconds.... Then he looked up and broke the silence with the order in his crisp, clear-cut voice to the Fleet Signal Officer "Hoist equal speed pendant southeast." This officer said, "Would you make it a point to port, sir, so they will know it is on the port wing column." Jellicoe replied, "Very well, hoist equal speed southeast by south."...

A moment later, while the other battleships were still acknowledging the signal, Jellicoe turned to Dyer and simply said, "Commence the deployment." Two blasts immediately sounded from *Iron Duke's* siren, the seagoing signal for "I am turning to port," and the battleship's helm was put over. The leading ships in the other five columns instantly followed suit, and within minutes all 24 battleships were beginning to turn to port, one by one falling into line behind *King George V,* the lead ship of the squadron on the far left of the Grand Fleet's formation.

It was not a moment too soon, for just as the battleships were turning into line, the High Seas Fleet appeared on the horizon, just as Jellicoe had anticipated—silhouetted against the setting sun to the west. As the German dreadnoughts loomed out of the mist, rangetakers began dialing in their rangefinders, reading the distances off their dials, transmitting the numbers to the gun turrets, which swung minutely as gun barrels nudged up or down, making final adjustments for the first salvo.

While Professor Arthur Marder perhaps went too far in describing Jellicoe's deployment order as "the peak moment of the influence of seapower upon history"—that honor more rightly belongs to Trafalgar or, arguably, Midway—it was, as Sir Julian Corbett so eloquently put it, "the supreme moment of the naval war." Events unforeseen, unanticipated, and unimagined took shape over the next two years as a consequence of what transpired in the next two hours, the result of Jellicoe's brilliant deployment. The very course of the war was shaped, altered, and irretrievably changed by the outcome of this battle—and the outcome had already been decided by Jellicoe.

For the officers and men of the High Seas Fleet, awareness that they were confronting the entire Grand Fleet came in a series of short, sharp shocks. The first inkling anyone had that there might be more British ships out there than just Beatty's battlecruisers and Evan-Thomas's battleships came at 1750, when Hipper's light cruisers, three miles ahead of his flagship *Lützow,* signaled that they were under fire from British dreadnoughts—from their position it was clear that these ships were not the four *Queen Elizabeths* of the Fifth Battle Squadron. But who were they? Hipper, who at the moment was passing through a bank of mist, could see nothing ahead of him and so had no idea.

It was Admiral Behncke, coming up behind Hipper with the four *König* class battleships, who first sighted the Grand Fleet. He watched, stunned, as the great dreadnoughts swung round from their cruising formation into line of battle, and jets of flame spat from the muzzles of their guns as they trained on his battleships. A few moments later, shells began falling around *König* and her sisters, one of the first striking *König's* bridge and seriously wounding the admiral before he could report the situation to Scheer. Instinctively, the First Battle Squadron followed Hipper's battlecruisers, unconsciously leading the High Seas Fleet into the maw of the British dreadnoughts.

At first Scheer refused to believe that any British forces other than those engaged by Hipper were at sea. At the same time that Jellicoe was deploying the Grand Fleet, Scheer's battleships were exchanging salvos with Evan-Thomas's Fifth Battle Squadron, firing on a pair of armored cruisers that had suddenly charged toward the German battle line and then focusing their fire on *Warspite,* which had suddenly fallen out of the Fifth Squadron's battle line and begun inexplicably describing circles between the two fleets. Scheer's flagship, *Friedrich der Grösse,* was almost two-thirds of the way back in the long German line, stretched out as it was by its headlong pursuit of Beatty,

The Thunder of the Guns

165

so the commander in chief was in a poor position to see for himself anything of the action ahead. When the sound of the gunfire ahead grew in volume and an increasing number of shell splashes began rising around his ships, Scheer began to suspect that there might be other British warships lurking in the mist, but he still refused to consider the possibility that it might be the whole of the Grand Fleet. Then, at 1825, he was handed a message from the commander of the Fifth Torpedo Boat Flotilla—prisoners captured from the sunken British destroyer *Nomad* confirmed that the Grand Fleet was indeed at sea, and even now was lying in wait for the High Seas Fleet. The biter had been bitten: the trap Scheer had laid for the Battlecruiser Fleet and the Fifth Battle Squadron had instead been sprung on *him.*

The seemingly weird dance of HMS *Warspite* in front of the High Seas Fleet was the unintentional climax to one of the most amazing incidents of a day already overfull with drama. As the Grand Fleet began its deployment, the screening force of cruisers and destroyers had to scramble to take up new positions. Into this melee of twisting, turning ships stormed a pair of armored cruisers, HMS *Defence* and HMS *Warrior.* The two ships were the last of their kind ever built by the Royal Navy, being superseded by the battlecruiser, but they were powerful ships in their own right. However, the middle of a gunnery duel between two fleets of battleships was no place for them, yet there they were, for the commander of the First Cruiser Squadron, Rear Admiral Sir Robert Arbuthnot, had spotted the crippled German light cruiser *Wiesbaden* dead in the water between the battle fleets and was determined to finish her off. Turning his flagship *Defence* toward the hapless German ship, he ordered *Warrior* to follow—the squadron's other two cruisers, *Black Prince* and *Duke of Edinburgh,* had been separated from the squadron by the fleet's deployment.

Storming in on *Wiesbaden,* Arbuthnot cut across *Lion's* bow, passing so close that the battlecruiser had to make an emergency turn to avoid running down the smaller ship. *Defence's* guns were firing as rapidly as possible, pumping shell after shell into *Wiesbaden,* joined moments later by *Warrior.* But Arbuthnot had apparently forgotten that he was well within the range of the German battlecruisers: *Lützow* and *Defflinger* quickly reminded him of his mistake. A pair of 12-inch shells crashed into *Defence's* quarterdeck near her aft gun turret, then a moment later, at 1820, another salvo struck at the base of her forward turret. Her magazines exploded in sympathetic detonation, and, in a single great gout of smoke and flame, *Defence,* Rear Admiral Arbuthnot, and all 900 officers and men of her crew vanished.

This left *Warrior* all alone less than 8,000 yards from the German battlecruisers. The German gunners began systematically tearing her apart, shells exploding on her decks, her upperworks, and in her hull. As steam pipes

166   Distant Victory

ruptured, her speed began to fall off, while one by one her guns were silenced. It appeared as if *Warrior* would soon go the way of *Defence,* when suddenly and quite unintentionally, *Warspite* came to her rescue.

When Rear Admiral Evan-Thomas spotted the Grand Fleet, he immediately turned toward it, knowing that in this situation his proper position was in the main battle line. As *Warspite* followed *Barham* and *Valiant* into a sharp turn to starboard in order to allow the First Battle Squadron to pass, a 12-inch shell from *Kaiserin* struck her stern, causing the rudder to jam hard over. Lurching out of line toward the German fleet, she came under fire from eight different German battleships. Her captain, Edward Phillpotts, wisely kept her speed up, and she swung back into line behind *Malaya,* but, when the rudder refused to break free, *Warspite* swung back into another turn toward the High Seas Fleet.

This evolution was different, however, as it took her right around the crippled *Warrior,* diverting the German battleships' fire from the hapless cruiser and onto herself. *Warrior's* crew made good the opportunity *Warspite* unintentionally gave them and were able to get the cruiser to limp away from the battle. For her part, though she was finally able to free her rudder while making her second circle, *Warspite* suffered 13 of the 29 hits she took that day during those two turns. When her captain tried to bring her back into the battle line, he found that, at any speed over 16 knots, flooding from holes punched in *Warspite's* hull overwhelmed her pumps. The ship had become more of a liability than an asset to the Grand Fleet, so the captain chose to leave the battle and steam northwest for Rosyth in the Firth of Forth.

At almost the same time that *Defence* was being annihilated, *Warrior* was being crippled, and *Warspite* was making her unintentionally heroic circles, the Third Battle Cruiser Squadron was racing through the Grand Fleet to reinforce Beatty. The Third Squadron had been detached from the Battlecruiser Fleet to undergo gunnery training at Scapa Flow, and had just begun when the order to sail arrived on May 30. Under the command of Rear Admiral Horace Hood, the Third Squadron had sailed with Jellicoe, but as the Grand Fleet approached its action with the High Seas Fleet, Jellicoe decided that Hood's proper place was with Beatty. The three battlecruisers, *Invincible*—Hood's flagship—*Inflexible,* and *Indomitable,* were the oldest in the fleet, the first three such ships ever built, but Hood had honed their gunnery to a fine edge in the previous two months, and the crews were keen for action. Racing ahead of the Grand Fleet, Hood's squadron actually outran Beatty's battlecruisers and found itself engaging the leading light cruisers of Hipper's First Scouting Group. Four German cruisers, *Wiesbaden, Elbing, Frankfurt,* and *Pillau,* had ambushed the light cruiser *Chester* and were pummeling that newly commissioned ship when Hood's three battlecruisers

The Thunder of the Guns

loomed up and waded into the fray. *Wiesbaden* was quickly put out of action —her damage would eventually sink her—while *Frankfurt* and *Pillau* took hits as well; meanwhile *Chester* made good her escape.

German and British torpedo boats and destroyers then dashed in to make torpedo attacks. One of the British destroyers, HMS *Shark,* was hit and left dead in the water, but with her guns still firing, one of them served by her captain, Commander Loftus Jones. When the destroyer *Acasta* pulled alongside to take off *Shark's* surviving crew, Jones refused to be taken off and continued to load and fire his gun. A few minutes later, a German shell took off his right leg; as *Shark* went under, the handful of crewmen who had also remained behind got him into a life raft but Jones died before they were picked up. His courage, though, had earned him a posthumous Victoria Cross.

Hood, meanwhile, was rushing to his own moment of posthumous glory. Almost simultaneously he spotted Hipper's battlecruisers off his port bow and Beatty's battlecruisers off his starboard bow. Immediately he swung his squadron round to take position in front of the Battlecruiser Fleet, steaming parallel to the five German battlecruisers at a range of 9,000 yards. Instantly all three ships demonstrated their superior gunnery, bringing *Lützow* and *Derfflinger* under a rapid, accurate fire, hitting Hipper's flagship eight times and her sister five. Standing on *Invincible's* bridge, a clearly elated Hood called through a speaking tube up to the spotting top, telling the gunnery officer, Lt. Commander Hubert Dannreuther, "Your firing is very good! Keep it up as quickly as you can! Every shot is telling!" They were the last words Hood ever spoke.

At that moment, 1830, a salvo from *Derfflinger* landed on *Invincible's* Q turret, and within seconds her midships magazines detonated, literally disintegrating the center section of the ship. A gigantic ball of crimson flame erupted from *Invincible's* hull, the tripod masts toppled inward and a huge column of black smoke soared into the sky. Lt. Cdr. Dannreuther was thrown from the forward tripod mast into the sea, one of six survivors out of a crew of 1,031. Hood was not among them. The bow and stern of the wreck were left standing almost vertically in the relatively shallow water—it was less than 200 feet deep, and when *Lion* passed by and saw the handful of survivors clinging to the bilges, she signaled to the destroyer *Badger* to pick them up. Minutes later, *Iron Duke* passed by, and Jellicoe signaled to *Badger,* "Is wreck one of our ships?" *Badger* replied simply, "Yes. *Invincible*."

Whatever satisfaction Hipper may have felt over the destruction of *Invincible* was short-lived, for his own situation was becoming increasingly desperate. *Lützow's* wireless had been out of action for some time, leaving Hipper to resort to semaphore to signal his ships; the battlecruiser was barely afloat, having already taken 18 hits, great waves of water washing over her foredeck as she struggled to keep pace with the rest of the squadron. *Derfflinger's* condition was hardly better, having taken 20 hits herself; *Seydlitz* was a shambles, listing five degrees to starboard, half of her guns inoperable, a great hole in her starboard side allowing seawater to pour into her hull. All of von der Tann's guns were out of action, although her hull was largely intact, but was also suffering from wireless problems. Only *Moltke* was relatively undamaged, and it was to this ship that Hipper had proposed to shift his flag and regain control over the First Scouting Group.

It was not an easy decision to make; in fact, Hipper at first seemed incapable of making it. When advised that it was imperative that he leave *Lützow* for another ship, his chief of staff, Captain Erich Raeder recalled that "a kind of paralysis seemed to descend on Hipper.... It was the first time he had nothing to say." Hipper, who had become genuinely fond of *Lützow* in the month she had been his flagship, refused to leave the bridge. Only when Raeder, in language forceful enough to border on insubordination, reminded Hipper that he could not function as an admiral as long as he was aboard a ship that could not function as a flagship did Hipper give way. At 1900 *Lützow* stopped and lowered a boat, which was immediately picked up by the torpedo boat *G-39*. *Lützow* then turned to starboard to begin the long journey back to Wilhelmshaven alone, her day of battle over.

Unfortunately for Hipper, he was unable to quickly take his place on the bridge of another battlecruiser. *G-39* steamed directly for *Moltke,* but just as she drew alongside, the battlecruiser suddenly picked up steam, leaving the little torpedo boat and the commander of the First Scouting Group bobbing in her wake as she sped off to answer some silent summons. Unknown to Hipper, Scheer had ordered the German battlecruisers to charge headlong at the dreadnoughts of the Grand Fleet, for Scheer had brought the High Seas Fleet not once but twice to the brink of disaster.

Long after the war, Scheer's flag lieutenant, Ernst von Weizäcker, maintained that throughout that afternoon the High Seas Fleet's commander in chief "had but the foggiest idea of what was happening," and, while the words are harsh, they are not without a certain degree of justification. Even Scheer later gave the impression that he still did not believe that what had happened had actually taken place. Despite the intelligence from *Nomad's* survivors and the evidence of his own eyes, he seemed to be unable to grasp that he was confronting the whole of the Grand Fleet. As he described it,

> It was now obvious that we were confronted *by a large portion of the English fleet* [author's emphasis]. The entire arc stretching from north to east was a sea of fire. The flash from the muzzles of the guns was seen distinctly through

the mist and smoke on the horizon although the ships themselves were not distinguishable.

It is not overstating the case to say that Scheer was literally shocked. Deprived by bad weather of the zeppelin reconnaissance on which he so heavily depended, taking the silence of the U-boats posted off the Grand Fleet's anchorages to mean that the British ships had not sailed, Scheer found himself in a tactical and strategic position for which he had never formulated a response. The Grand Fleet was now steaming south-southeast with the High Seas Fleet to the west, silhouetted against the setting sun, the dark grey British ships all but invisible in the dusk; the Grand Fleet's course carried it directly across Scheer's most direct route to Wilhelmshaven, cutting off his retreat. The British dreadnoughts had quickly found the range, and a storm of shells was crashing down on Hipper's battlecruisers and Scheer's leading battleships. The straggling German fleet stretched out across more than nine miles of sea, while the whole of the Grand Fleet, drawn up into a compact line little more than five miles long, was passing across its bow. For 15 agonizing minutes the ships of the High Seas Fleet were hammered by a blizzard of 12-, 13.5-, and 15-inch shells. All thoughts of victory were abandoned—what the High Seas Fleet must do now was *escape.*

Fortunately for Scheer, a maneuver that lent itself splendidly to the High Seas Fleet's dilemma had long been practiced by the Imperial German Navy. This was the *Gefechtskehrtwendung*—the "simultaneous battle turn." Instead of the "turn in succession" used earlier by Beatty, where each ship in the battle line turned only upon reaching the point where the first ship in line made its turn, thus preserving the order of the line, this maneuver called for all of the ships in the fleet to make a 180 degree turn in the same direction *at the same time.* It was daring, it was untried except in peacetime, and it was the only hope the High Seas Fleet had, for to turn in succession would have invited destruction in detail by the British guns as they ranged in on the turning point.

At 1833 the signal was hoisted to Friedrich der Grösse's masthead: *Gefechtskehrtwendung nach steuerbord*—"simultaneous battle turn to starboard." The signal was relayed forward to the ships of the First Scouting Group, and the German torpedo boats surged forward to lay down a covering smoke screen. At 1836, Scheer gave the signal to execute the turn, and in what seemed like the blink of an eye, the German fleet vanished from British rangefinders.

No one in the Grand Fleet realized what had happened for some moments. At first it seemed that the increasingly fickle North Sea mist had intervened and blocked the Grand Fleet's view of the High Seas Fleet, but as the minutes

170   Distant Victory

passed and the German dreadnoughts did not reappear, it became clear that some sort of turnaway maneuver had been executed. It is hardly surprising that the British did not expect it: the Royal Navy had no equivalent maneuver, and there is little evidence to indicate that it had any knowledge that the Germans had introduced and perfected it. Nine minutes passed before Jellicoe reacted, and then he only altered course, slightly at first, then directly to the south. He had no desire to attempt to directly pursue Scheer until he knew where the German fleet had gone; as it was, the new course would still keep the Grand Fleet between the High Seas Fleet and Wilhelmshaven. This was a singular consideration of Jellicoe's, for he was determined to if at all possible force Scheer to fight, and, by cutting off the German retreat, he made such confrontation all but inevitable.

But now a new trouble appeared—German torpedoes. As the German torpedo boats had surged forward to lay down the covering smoke screen for Scheer's turn, they launched torpedoes that were now closing in on the rear of the Grand Fleet's line. Ships began to turn to avoid them, for the most part successfully, but the new battleship *Revenge* was hit by one that failed to explode, while *Marlborough* was less fortunate. Striking on her starboard side, the torpedo opened up 30 feet of her hull, flooded a boiler room as well as an auxiliary engine room, and killed two men. A list of 8 degrees set in, and her speed was reduced to just over 17 knots, but she grimly maintained her place in the battle line.

Jellicoe, exercising the caution of a man with the fate of an empire in his hands, took the torpedo attack as a warning and refused to turn westward in pursuit of Scheer. Long before the war had even begun, he had steadfastly maintained that "if an enemy battlefleet were to suddenly turn away from me, I would believe its intent would be to lead me across mines or submarines, or both, and would refuse to be so drawn." If Scheer was planning some sort of ambush, Jellicoe was not about to oblige him by steaming into it. The Grand Fleet's course to the south remained unchanged.

Having escaped the guns of the Grand Fleet, albeit not without serious damage, the High Seas Fleet steamed southwest for 20 minutes. At this point, the battle could be considered a significant German victory, and Scheer could well have congratulated himself on his success. But now he made the most baffling decision of his entire naval career, one that at the time and in the years to come he could never explain satisfactorily to his superiors, his subordinates, or himself.

At 1855, the same signal rose to the top of *Friedrich der Grösse's* yardarm, *Gefechtskehrtwendung nach steuerbord*. Scheer was calling for another simultaneous turn, this one taking the High Seas Fleet back toward the deadly embrace of the Grand Fleet that it had only just escaped. Scheer later

The Thunder of the Guns 171

explained that he had hoped to pass behind the Grand Fleet, possibly inflicting some nuisance damage on the rearmost British ships, and try to rescue the crew of the sinking *Wiesbaden* at the same time. But it does not wash: without sure knowledge of exactly where the British ships were, this was an enormous gamble that could well result in even more destruction being rained down on the German battleships.

The simple truth is that Scheer really had no idea what he was doing: he felt the need to do *something*, rather than just steam aimlessly into the North Sea, but there was little he could accomplish given his strategic and tactical circumstances. Nevertheless, the order was given and carried out. The results were inevitable: the ever-reliable Commodore Goodenough in *Southampton* was the first to spot the returning German fleet and quickly sent a signal to Jellicoe. The officers and ratings of the British dreadnoughts quickly scrambled back to their action stations, and once again the great guns were brought to bear on the approaching enemy. Scheer was about to give Jellicoe a second chance to annihilate the High Seas Fleet, and Jellicoe was determined to seize it.

Chapter 9

Steel Maelstrom

The senior officers of the Grand Fleet were baffled by the sudden disappearance of the High Seas Fleet: one moment it had been there, and the next it was gone. The exchange of fire, such as it was, lasted for less than 20 minutes—the flagship, *Iron Duke,* had only enough time to fire nine salvos at the German ships before they vanished, others only three or four. Observers on the light cruisers *Canterbury* and *Falmouth* had actually seen the Germans turn away, but apparently did not realize *what* they were seeing and so made no report to John Jellicoe.

All in all, it had been a rather one-sided exchange, as damage reports quickly made it clear that the guns of the High Seas Fleet had not scored a single hit on any of Jellicoe's dreadnoughts, while all the battleships of Reinhard Scheer's leading squadron had taken a pounding. Reassured of the readiness of his command to continue the battle, Jellicoe grimly pursued his southward course after losing sight of the Germans, determined to retain his position between Scheer and Wilhelmshaven.

Consequently, when the High Seas Fleet reappeared, Jellicoe may have been amazed at Scheer's audacity—or folly—but he was neither tactically nor strategically surprised. As the battlecruisers and dreadnoughts of the High Seas Fleet emerged from the swirling smoke, mist, and sunset haze to the west, straight toward the center of the British battle line, Jellicoe realized that they had been granted a second chance to annihilate his enemy. At 1910 the battleships in the center of the Grand Fleet opened fire again, and by 1914 the entire British line was hurling salvos at the German ships. At 1915 David Beatty's battlecruisers, now in the proper place at the vanguard, that is, the leading formation, of the British fleet, joined in.

174 Distant Victory

There had never been a bombardment like it, and there never would be such a one again: the next 15 minutes were the climax of the age of the great gun, which had dominated naval warfare for five centuries. It was also the apogee of the Royal Navy, for never again was the British fleet able to speak with such unchallengeable might and authority. The thunder of the guns was endless, the muzzle flashes from their barrels a solid wall of flame as 30 battleships and battlecruisers, between them mounting forty 15-inch, ten 14-inch, one hundred thirty-four 13.5-inch, and one hundred twenty-eight 12-inch guns, concentrated their fire on Scheer's battle fleet. This was the moment for which the British dreadnoughts had been built, and they would not be denied: even *Marlborough*, with a gaping torpedo wound in her side, kept her place in line, hurling out 14 salvos, hitting with four of them.

Under this terrible barrage, the German fleet began to fall apart. The battlecruiser squadron, hampered by the crippled *Lützow* and *Seydlitz,* was slowing down, while the battle fleet was rapidly overtaking it. Desperately putting their helms over to port or starboard to avoid running down the battlecruisers, the battleships began falling out of formation. Some actually stopped or began running astern, adding to the confusion. The German gunners and spotting officers had little opportunity to retaliate: they could see nothing of the British except that endless chain of gun flashes ahead of them—the enemy ships were invisible in the murk and accurate ranging was impossible.

From the moment the first British guns opened fire Scheer realized he had made a disastrous mistake. The High Seas Fleet was in the same position it had been less than an hour earlier, with the Grand Fleet crossing its "T" and raining a withering fire down upon it, but it was in much worse shape this time: two of Franz Hipper's battlecruisers were near sinking, all but one had their guns put out of action, the First Battle Squadron was being repeatedly hammered, and his own Third Battle Squadron had come within range of the British guns and was beginning to take hits as well. Ten minutes passed, though, before Scheer decided that persisting on this course was simply a short route to destruction, and finally chose to execute another simultaneous battle turn.

At 1912 the signal went up *Friedrich der Grösse's* halyards, *Gefechtskehrtwendung nach steuerbord*. A minute later another signal was made, this one an amazing signal to von Hipper's battlecruisers: "*Schlachtkreuzer ran an den Feind, voll einsetzen!*" perhaps best translated as, "Battlecruisers, full speed at the enemy! Give it everything." Eight minutes after that, a third signal was made, calling for a massed destroyer attack on the Grand Fleet to cover the High Seas Fleet's turnaway.

It was that second signal that had caused *Moltke* to suddenly pull away from the torpedo boat *G-39* just as von Hipper was attempting to make his transfer. Gathering themselves for one last burst of speed, the four remaining German battlecruisers drove straight for the center of the British battle line. The next five minutes have often been described as a "death ride": the attack of the four German battlecruisers was the last offensive action ever taken by the High Seas Fleet. The quartet of ships quickly became the focus for the attention of the entire Grand Fleet. *Derfflinger,* the lead ship, was hit 14 times; *Seydlitz,* already perilously close to sinking, took five more hits; *von der Tann* was struck at least three times, while *Lützow,* trying vainly to limp away, was battered by *Monarch* and *Orion,* five more 13.5-inch shells striking home. Only *Moltke* escaped serious damage.

Mercifully, just as he gave the command to execute the "simultaneous battle turn," Scheer sent a signal to the battlecruisers—"Operate against the enemy's van"—which allowed them to sheer away from the British guns. They had done their job: they masked the latest turnaway by the High Seas Fleet and distracted the British from the 14 torpedo boats dashing toward the British battle line at 30 knots.

This turn by the High Seas Fleet lacked the crispness and precision of the first two such maneuvers. By now all of the German captains were anxious to escape the British guns: nothing would be achieved by throwing away their lives, their crews, and their ships in loitering about while the British shelled them into oblivion. Some ships turned to starboard as instructed, others to port; helm and engine orders rang out as headings and speeds were constantly adjusted to avoid collisions. Some ships got off one last, defiant salvo in the direction of the British fleet, but none of their shells hit. That there were no collisions was a testament to the quality of German seamanship. For many of the German ships, the return to Wilhelmshaven tested that quality to the utmost.

Jellicoe, who had spent the entire engagement on *Iron Duke's* bridge, watched as Scheer had once more turned away, then recognized the distinctive, lean profiles of the German torpedo boats as they made their attack runs toward the Grand Fleet. Some of them, commanded with a courage and dash that even the British sailors had to admire, closed to within 8,000 yards of the British battle line before launching their torpedoes and turning away, laying down a thick smokescreen as they departed.

The phrase "a hail of fire" is one that is often used inappropriately, but in this instance it was entirely applicable. Every 4- and 6-inch secondary battery aboard the British dreadnoughts that could be brought to bear on the German torpedo boats began spitting out shells as rapidly as their crews could load and train them. The Germans came on in three successive waves, launching a total of 31 torpedoes. Nearly every one of the attacking boats was hit by the British barrage, one of them—*S-35*—sinking in a matter of minutes; four others were later lost to the damage they sustained in this attack. But they were able to make their attack, and by doing so compelled Jellicoe to turn the Grand Fleet away from Scheer, buying even more time for the High Seas Fleet to escape.

It had long been Jellicoe's belief that German torpedoes posed a greater danger to his dreadnoughts than did German guns, and so he had worked out a carefully planned response should the Grand Fleet ever be subjected to a massive torpedo attack, such as the one that had just been launched. His considered response was to have the entire fleet turn 22 degrees *away* from the torpedoes, presenting them with the ships' sterns rather than their broadsides. Not only did this make the target dramatically smaller, it also had the added benefit of putting additional distance between the torpedoes and the target ships, while at the same time reducing the speed at which the two closed by more than half. The closure rate between a 20-knot battleship attempting to outrun a 30-knot torpedo was a mere 10 knots. This not only increased the time it took for the torpedo to reach its target—and increased the likelihood that the torpedo would run out of fuel first—the slow rate of closure also made evading the torpedo that much easier.

Now, at 1922, Jellicoe instructed that the Grand Fleet Battle Order response to a torpedo attack be implemented; the entire fleet immediately turned 22 degrees to port. Three minutes later, just to be sure, Jellicoe ordered another 22 degree turn. Just how successful were Jellicoe's tactics can be determined from the knowledge that of the 31 torpedoes fired by the German boats, 21 made it close enough to the British battleships for their white wakes to be spotted—and not one of them hit a British ship.

Still, Jellicoe was later subjected to considerable criticism, particularly by armchair admirals, for his decision to turn away from the torpedo attack rather than toward it. To many of his more vocal—and ignorant—critics, such a tactic amounted to turning away from the enemy, a cardinal sin in the orthodoxy of the Royal Navy. But Jellicoe knew what he was doing: prewar studies by the Admiralty had estimated that in theory 35 percent of torpedoes randomly fired at a battle line would find a target. In practice, Jellicoe's carefully thought-out tactics reduced that figure to absolutely zero.

After the torpedo attack had spent itself, the Grand Fleet continued on its new course for just over one-half hour, then turned back to its original heading, expecting to find the High Seas Fleet waiting to continue the battle. But Scheer had had enough: as soon as the battle turnaway was complete, he had ordered a new course to the southwest, away from the Grand Fleet. At some point, Scheer knew, the High Seas Fleet would have to change course yet again, first to the south and eventually back to the east, in order to return to the safety of Heligoland Bight and Wilhelmshaven. At 1945 he gave the order to alter course to the south, counting on the growing darkness to conceal his ships from the searching eyes of the British. Until the sun set and the twilight faded, he desperately wanted to avoid another encounter with Jellicoe's battleships.

Beatty, though, believed he was in a position to intercept Scheer. The Battlecruiser Fleet—or what was left of it—had been steaming ahead of the Grand Fleet, and as the German torpedo attack had come nowhere near, it never changed course. Now Beatty believed he knew where the High Seas Fleet could be found and wanted to lead Jellicoe's battleships to it. Steaming almost due south, Beatty signaled to *Iron Duke,* "Submit van of battleships follow battlecruisers. We can then cut off whole of enemy's battlefleet." To Jellicoe, Beatty's suggestion stopped just short of insubordination, not for its content, but for its tone. Beatty's signal could not be ignored, however, for it implied that he knew the German position and course. Accordingly, Jellicoe signaled to Vice Admiral Sir Martyn Jerram's Second Battle Squadron, led by *King George V,* "Follow our battlecruisers." Jerram did his best, but he could see neither Beatty nor the German fleet, and so steamed due south in the hope of making contact with one or the other.

Meanwhile, Beatty, who, in fact, had no idea where the High Seas Fleet was, held to his current south-by-southwest course, and as he did so, luck favored him one last time. The fading rays of the setting sun managed to break through the evening mist one last time, silhouetting the German battlecruisers, which were just over a mile east of the German battleships. The range was on 10,000 yards, and at 2012, the six surviving British battlecruisers opened fire. All four of the German ships were hit almost immediately. Once again *Seydlitz,* in particular, took a pounding, receiving five hits in as many minutes. The first was the worst, as it struck squarely on her bridge, killing or wounding everyone there, ruining her compasses and destroying her charts and navigation equipment.

Konteradmiral Mauve, commanding the Second Battle Squadron, quickly proved that there was no lack of courage aboard his six obsolete predreadnoughts. Turning toward the British battlecruisers, the old German battleships opened fire, with *Posen* scoring a hit on *Princess Royal*—and in turn *Pommern, Schlesien,* and *Schleswig-Holstein* were all hit at least once. Mauve's intervention was short but timely, providing enough of a distraction for the four German battlecruisers to slip off into the growing murk and escape. At 2019 the sun set, and Beatty broke off the engagement; for the moment at least, the High Seas Fleet had escaped.

Sunrise would come early—in just over five hours—and the British were prepared to remain at sea and once again try conclusions with the Germans in the morning. Jellicoe had reason to be satisfied with the current tactical

178 Distant Victory

situation and to feel confident that the morning would deliver the High Seas Fleet into his hands.

At this moment, though Jellicoe did not know it, the two fleets were actually on converging courses, but when Beatty lost sight of the Germans after the exchange with the Second Battle Squadron, at 2028 Jellicoe altered course once again, this time slightly to the east, forming a single line. He was determined to simultaneously stay across the German line of retreat by continuing to head southward, and at the same time draw away from the High Seas Fleet and avoid a night action. He was justifiably concerned about the Grand Fleet's limited night-fighting skills and especially worried about the danger of torpedo attacks in the darkness. As events showed, it was a wise decision.

The time had come for Scheer to make a crucial decision: he had to choose between two routes back to Wilhelmshaven. One was southeast to Horns Reef, past Heligoland Bight, and from there to the Jade Roads and Wilhelmshaven. This had the advantage of being the shortest, most direct course, little more than 100 miles distant. It was, however, heavily patrolled by British submarines, and the Royal Navy had also laid huge minefields in the waters to the north of Heligoland. The other route lay to the east, down the coast of Schleswig-Holstein, past the mouth of the Ems and down to Wilhelmshaven, a distance of about 180 miles, virtually the reverse of the course the High Seas Fleet had taken when it sortied out. Given the battered condition of many of his ships, in particular the battlecruisers and the Third Battle Squadron, Scheer really had no choice: he had to make for Horns Reef. With several of his most valuable ships heavily damaged and some near sinking, he was going to take the shortest route, straight for Horns Reef. The High Seas Fleet would press on with all possible speed, and any stragglers would simply have to take their chances. Scheer knew that the Imperial German Navy was far better trained in the tactics and coordinated action required for night fighting, and trusted this advantage would see the fleet through any British opposition he encountered. At 2110 he sent the signal to the fleet: "Battle fleet's course southeast by a quarter east. This course is to be maintained. Speed sixteen knots."

Naval combat at night was a far different prospect than in the daytime. It was not a long-range slugfest between the main batteries of the battleships, but more like a knife fight at close quarters between the ships' secondary batteries and the destroyers that would range in attempting to launch torpedoes. The big guns were essentially ineffective beyond point-blank range: range-finding equipment was useless at nighttime, and the secondary batteries could react to the swiftly moving destroyers more readily than the main guns. What was necessary was coordinated action between a ship's searchlights and its secondary battery. The Germans had perfected this: searchlight crews would open a small aperture in the shutter of their light, which would shine a thin, almost pencil-like beam on a suspected target. Once it was identified, the target would be fully illuminated as the searchlight's shutter snapped completely open, and the secondary battery would instantly open fire. Drills endlessly repeated in the Baltic had honed these skills for the German crews to a keen edge.

Jellicoe, on the other hand, was not at all sanguine about the Grand Fleet's proficiency at night fighting. In his memoirs his language was blunt:

> It was known to me that neither our searchlights nor their control arrangements were at this time of the best type...the fitting of Director Firing Gear for the guns of the secondary armament of our battleships had only just begun.... [O]ur own destroyers would be no effective antidote at night since...they would certainly be taken for enemy destroyers and fired on by our own ships.

Any attempt at a night action with the battleships would have "inevitably led to our battle fleet being the object of attack by a very large German destroyer force throughout the night." Jellicoe, then, was determined to avoid a night action if at all possible, simply maintaining the Grand Fleet's position between the High Seas Fleet and Wilhelmshaven and waiting patiently for the morning.

The question that Jellicoe then had to answer was, "Which route would Scheer take to get back to port?" Knowing that several of the German ships had taken considerable damage, he gave no credence to the idea that Scheer might try to sail up through the Skaggerak, around Denmark to Kiel. Nor did it seem likely that he would choose to sail down the coast of Schleswig-Holstein. Scheer would try to make the direct passage to Horns Reef and Heligoland Bight, passing *behind* the Grand Fleet: it was utterly implausible that, having twice run directly into the center of the British battle line that afternoon, Scheer would risk another head-on engagement, even at night. Jellicoe gave instructions that the fleet should "steer south where I should be in a position...to intercept the enemy should he make for...Heligoland...." At 2101 Jellicoe ordered the fleet to take up its nighttime cruising formation—three divisions of line abreast, designed to avoid the possibility of friendly ships mistaking each other for an enemy in the gloom, while leaving the fleet ready to reform the battle line within minutes. The destroyers were positioned astern of the battleships, the better to intercept any German attacks and to keep them well clear of the British dreadnoughts.

The result of Scheer's and Jellicoe's orders were to direct their respective fleets onto converging courses, like the arms of a giant "V." A flurry of small-scale actions broke out in the darkness as light cruisers and destroyers encountered one another, and one side or the other failed to properly respond to challenges flashed out in the night. It was Commodore William Goodenough who first became aware that the British fleet had company. Sometime around 10:30 PM he and his officers aboard *Southampton* noticed a handful of unidentified ships barely 800 yards off the starboard quarter. HMS *Dublin* opened fire on the strangers, and instantly a half-dozen searchlights switched on, catching the British light cruisers in their glare. Four German light cruisers concentrated their fire on *Southampton,* leaving 35 crewmen killed and 41 wounded, but the British cruiser gave better than she got, one of her torpedoes striking SMS *Frauenlob* and sending her to the bottom with her entire crew of 320.

Hard on the heels of the German light cruisers came the German battleships, and for the next 90 minutes an unequal battle raged astern of the Grand Fleet as the High Seas Fleet drove through the British destroyer flotillas. When the German ships were challenged by the destroyer *Tipperary* at the suicidal range of 700 yards, three battleships, *Rheinland, Nassau,* and *Westfallen,* opened fire on her, reducing the little ship to flaming slag in minutes. Trying to launch torpedoes, HMS *Spitfire* rammed *Nassau,* leaving behind 60 feet of hull plating. (*Spitfire* somehow made port the next day.) HMS *Broke,* under fire from two battleships and a light cruiser, spun out of control, wildly careening back toward the rest of the British destroyers, where she rammed *Sparrowhawk,* which was later abandoned and sunk. The confusion was not all one-sided, however, as the light cruiser *Elbing* was rammed and nearly cut in two by the battleship *Posen.* The little British ships peppered the superstructures of the German battleships with their 4-inch guns, causing numerous casualties and inflicting considerable damage to light equipment. HMS *Achates* was able to put a torpedo into *Rostock,* which sank shortly after sunrise, but she and the destroyer *Fortune* were soon sunk in turn by the German battleships.

So desperate was the action that not one of the British destroyers was able to send a contact report to Jellicoe. When he heard the sound of gunfire to the north, he believed it was from the attack by the German destroyer screen he had earlier anticipated. What he did not know was that the "V" of the two fleets' converging courses had now become an "X" as the High Seas Fleet was passing astern of the Grand Fleet. Room 40 had intercepted and deciphered Scheer's signal sent at 2110—"Battle fleet's course southeast by a quarter east. This course is to be maintained. Speed sixteen knots"—and passed it on to Jellicoe, but, because of the earlier bungling by Rear Admiral Jackson, who had advised him that the High Seas Fleet was still in harbor when, in fact, it was already at sea, Jellicoe had come to mistrust the reliability of these intercepts. Coupled with the lack of any reports from the British destroyers that they were engaging the German battleships, this mistrust led Jellicoe to believe that the action astern was only light forces.

Unfortunately for the British and fortunately for the Germans, it was not only the destroyer captains who failed to report the presence of German battleships. *Marlborough,* no longer able to keep her place in line, was slowly slipping astern of the Grand Fleet, accompanied by the battleships *Revenge, Hercules,* and *Agincourt,* as well as Rear Admiral Hugh Evan-Thomas's Fifth Battle Squadron. These seven ships, now at the rear of the Grand Fleet, were less than three miles from the destroyer melee, and spotters on *Malaya* made a positive identification of the German battleship *Westfallen.* Evan-Thomas himself saw the flashes of gunfire and watched as *Southampton* was set ablaze. Yet for reasons never properly explained, although it seems to be a case where everyone assumed someone else would do it, no one reported what they saw to *Iron Duke.* Jellicoe's last chance to catch the High Seas Fleet was irretrievably lost.

The fighting between the German battleships and the British light forces continued until near daybreak. Just after midnight the armored cruiser *Black Prince,* which had become detached from the British fleet in the confusion earlier that afternoon, steamed in between two columns of what she apparently believed were friendly ships. It was a terrible mistake, as she actually blundered into the middle of Scheer's First Battle Squadron. The main guns of *Friedrich der Grösse, Thüringen,* and *Ostfriesland* swung around and at point-blank range began shelling her. What happened next was awesome even when compared to the immolation of the three British battlecruisers. The thin armor of *Black Prince's* hull was no protection against the 12-inch shells of the German battleships, and inevitably at least one struck her forward magazine. Horrified, the Germans watched as the blast traveled the length of the ship, as one by one her magazines exploded in succession, blowing turrets and guns into the air, the cruiser's funnels toppling down into her gutted hull, the blasts tearing the ship to pieces. All 900 of her crew perished.

But it was the High Seas Fleet that suffered the last act of destruction in the battle. At 0145 on the morning of June 1, the Twelfth Destroyer Flotilla, under the command of Captain Anselan Stirling in HMS *Faulknor,* spotted a long line of ships 28 miles north of Horns Reef. It was Scheer's battleships. Somehow he had succeeded, his iron determination and repeated exhortations of *"Durchalten!"*—"Maintain course!"—had brought the High Seas Fleet through the rear of the Grand Fleet essentially intact. Stirling knew his duty and signaled to *Iron Duke,* "PRIORITY. URGENT. Enemy battlefleet steering southeast…. My position ten miles astern of 1st Battle Squadron." Stirling

182   Distant Victory

repeated the signal at 0156, 0208, and 0213, but German jamming kept it from reaching Jellicoe.

That did not stop Stirling from attacking, however, and his six destroyers charged in, launching 17 torpedoes. Only one of them found its mark, and it was not in one of the modern German battleships; instead, it exploded deep inside the old predreadnought *Pommern*. An officer aboard one of the attacking destroyers, *Obedient*, watched as it happened:

> Amidships on the waterline of the *Pommern* appeared a dull, red ball of fire. Quicker than one can imagine, it spread fore and aft, until, reaching the foremast and mainmast, it flared up the masts in big, red tongues of flame, uniting between the mastheads in a big black cloud of smoke and sparks. Then we saw the ends of the ship come up as if her back was broken.

The two halves of the ship remained afloat, upside down, for about ten minutes before they vanished. All of *Pommern's* crew of 844 were lost.

While the High Seas Fleet was battling its way through the British destroyer screen, two German ships were doing their best to remain inconspicuous. *Seydlitz* and *Lützow* had both become separated from the German battlefleet, *Seydlitz* when her bridge was smashed and her navigating gear destroyed, and *Lützow* when she was abandoned by von Hipper moments before the first confrontation with the Grand Fleet. Each ship was sailing alone; they were both very near to sinking. *Seydlitz* had taken 21 heavy shell hits, and *Lützow* at least 24—some sources later said as many as 40—and both were moving at barely 5 knots, their foredecks awash, *Seydlitz* with an 8 degree list to port. Their crews struggled to keep the ships afloat, but for *Lützow* it ultimately proved to be a losing battle. By 0030 she had taken on more than 8,000 tons of water, her dynamo rooms were flooded, depriving her of electrical power, and as she took on an increasing bows-down trim, her screws and rudder gradually rose out of the sea, leaving her motionless. At daybreak Captain Harder ordered his surviving crewmen into the ship's boats, then called the torpedo boat *G-38* alongside to put two torpedoes into the battlecruiser's hull. As the crew gave three cheers for the Kaiser, Scheer, and von Hipper, then sang "Deutschland über Alles," *Lützow* rolled over onto her starboard side and slowly disappeared. Her crew were picked up by the torpedo boats that had been *Lützow's* escort.

Seydlitz was a floating charnel house, carrying within her hull 98 men killed and 55 injured. Her rudder machinery failed, and she was being steered by hand. During the night she passed within a mile of *Marlborough* and the six battleships escorting her. Neither side wanted to give its position away, however, so no one opened fire. At 0140, when she reached Horns Reef, she ran aground, not once but twice, managing to free herself both times. By

Steel Maelstrom

183

0440, though, she was 11 feet down by the head, and she grounded again. Pulling herself off with the aid of a favoring wind and tide, she scraped the Amrum Bank as she passed, straining her interior bulkheads while her crew was literally bailing her out with buckets. Her speed reduced to a crawl, *Seydlitz* finally made a hard grounding just outside of Wilhelmshaven late in the afternoon of June 1. Her wounded were taken off at that point, but she spent four days sitting on the bottom while the forward gun turret was dismantled in order to reduce her weight sufficiently to allow her to be refloated.

Moltke had an adventure of her own. Finally able to pick up von Hipper around 9:00 PM, she, too, became separated from the rest of the High Seas Fleet during the night. She was the only German battlecruiser that was relatively undamaged. With his ship still able to make her top speed of nearly 25 knots, *Moltke's* captain, Johannes von Karpf boldly chose to pass in front of the Grand Fleet and reach Heligoland from the west. At one point she came within 2,000 yards of HMS *Thunderer,* but with a quick turn to port she was soon lost to sight. By midnight she was past the Grand Fleet and was steaming home, reaching Wilhelmshaven by midmorning. In the meantime, the light cruisers *Elbing* and *Rostock,* both severely damaged, were sunk by German torpedo boats after their crews had been safely taken off.

Dawn found the High Seas Fleet still 16 miles from Horns Reef: every officer and rating expected the Grand Fleet to suddenly appear at any moment. When after a time it became clear that the British were not going to show, the crews gradually relaxed. By 0330 the old predreadnoughts of the Second Battle Squadron were passing through the protective minefields of Heligoland. At 0520 *Ostfriesland* was struck by a drifting mine, but was still able to make her way into port. By 1445 that afternoon, the last ship of the High Seas Fleet had safely reached Jade Roads at the entrance to Wilhelmshaven Harbor. Scheer began collecting reports of the damage to his ships as well as after-action details of what damage had been inflicted on the Royal Navy. By the time he had written his official report and transmitted it to Berlin, a perilous affair that nearly resulted in the destruction of most, if not all, of the High Seas Fleet had been transformed into a glowing account of a magnificent German naval victory.

Dawn brought disappointment to John Jellicoe. Having rested fitfully during the night on a cot in *Iron Duke's* chart room, he was prepared to renew the battle at daybreak. But the fleet was badly dispersed—*Marlborough* and her escorts had fallen far astern, and Jellicoe soon sent her on her way to the Tyne for repairs, the other ships rejoining the battle fleet. The destroyers were scattered far and wide, a consequence of the confused night action, and it took some time to get them reorganized and repositioned. Meanwhile Beatty,

184   Distant Victory

who was 15 miles to the southwest, persisted in believing that the High Seas Fleet was still to the southwest of him and at 0404 asked for permission to sweep in that direction. Jellicoe knew better: five minutes earlier an Admiralty signal had arrived advising him that Scheer had wirelessed his position at 0230 as being 16 miles from Horns Reef. Though still skeptical of Admiralty deciphers, this one arrived with sufficient authority that Jellicoe believed it. If it were true, then there would be no battle this morning: somehow Scheer had managed to pass behind the Grand Fleet and was now safely in heavily defended and protected waters.

At 0413 Jellicoe ordered the Grand Fleet back into its cruising formation and laid out a course to the north-northwest, back to Scapa Flow. It took almost five hours for all of the light cruisers and destroyers to finally resume their stations, all the while the fleet was steaming across the waters that had witnessed the previous day's battle. Immense patches of oil stained and colored the water, while masses of wood—ship's fittings, decking, paneling, furniture, mess tables, partitions—bobbed about. Scattered across the surface of the sea were hundreds of bodies, British and German mingled together in death, while here and there a survivor waved and shouted in the hope of being rescued.

The fleet made its grand progress to the north, as majestic as it had been the day before when it was thundering southward, though somewhat diminished in numbers, but still the most powerful battle fleet on the planet. Jellicoe already knew that *Invincible* had been lost—he did not yet know about *Indefatigable* or *Queen Mary*. Nor did he know of the extent of the damage done to the other battlecruisers. Still, apart from *Warspite* and *Marlborough*, the strength of the Grand Fleet's battleships was undiminished. The armored cruisers *Defence* and *Black Prince* had been lost, and *Warrior* sank later that day; eight destroyers had been sunk. It would take some time to make an assessment of the enemy's losses, for Jellicoe was not prepared to make false claims. Until he was as sure as he could be of all the facts, his report to the Admiralty could wait. At 1100 Jellicoe ordered a new course, this one for Scapa Flow.

The Battle of Jutland was over.

Chapter 10

The Reckoning

Standing on the bridge of *Friedrich der Grösse,* safely docked in Wilhelmshaven, *Vizeadmiral* Reinhard Scheer received the reports of his senior officers late in the afternoon of June 1. Earlier he had toasted them with champagne, a gesture that was perhaps as much a silent acknowledgment of their survival as it was a tribute to their apparent success. He then sent the Admiralty in Berlin a rather hastily composed telegram sketching the outlines of the battle; by nightfall the telegram had been reworked into a hyperbolic official communiqué, carefully worded and highly sensationalized, that was distributed to all the major German newspapers as well as the foreign press bureaus resident in Berlin.

The resulting news stories across Germany generated a wave of near-hysterical celebration among the German public. Suddenly, and for the first time, the Imperial Navy rather than the Imperial Army was the toast of the German Empire. Patriotic bunting and national flags were hung everywhere as June 2 was declared a national holiday and a day of mourning for those lost in the battle. The German people were told that the High Seas Fleet had lost only the old battleship *Pommern* and the light cruiser *Wiesbaden;* no mention was made of *Lützow,* while *Frauenlob, Rostock,* and "several destroyers…had not yet returned to base." The Kaiser showed up at Wilhelmshaven the following Monday, delirious with joy and handing out Iron Crosses left and right. Scheer and Franz Hipper were presented with Germany's highest decoration, the Ordre pour le Mérite, and each was promoted a grade, Scheer to full *Admiral* and Hipper to *Vizeadmiral.* Both men were also offered elevation to the German nobility, Scheer by the Kaiser and Hipper by the King of Bavaria, as he was Bavarian-born. Scheer declined his "von"; Hipper accepted his.

186 Distant Victory

While German losses were concealed from the German people, British losses were exaggerated. Some allowance can be made for the latter due to wartime passions and the need for morale-boosting propaganda on the home front. According to the German Admiralty, the High Seas Fleet had sunk not only the battlecruisers *Indefatigable* and *Queen Mary,* but, in a case of mistaken identity, the battleship *Warspite* as well; whether the latter was a deliberate falsehood or a genuine misidentification of *Invincible* as the larger ship remains unknown. The British also lost, read the communiqué, two armored cruisers, two light cruisers, and 13 destroyers.

To some extent the exaggerations of the German press were understandable, even forgivable. When Scheer made his report to Berlin, he couched it in terms of having openly challenged the Grand Fleet, destroying a trio of their largest ships, and successfully escaping a British trap, losing only one modern vessel in the process. Not mentioned were the two frantic retreats made by the High Seas Fleet as it turned away from the Grand Fleet, or the desperate nature of the nighttime thrust through the British destroyer screen. Careful examination, however, reveals that Scheer was casting the best possible light on what even the most favorable interpretation could only be considered an inconclusive engagement. Underlying the language of his report was a tone of near-hysteria reminiscent of an innocent man who had been given a last minute reprieve from an execution, which in a way he was. Scheer never had any intention of engaging the whole of the Grand Fleet: the High Seas Fleet's sortie had not been some pointless "death-or-glory" charge into the guns of the Royal Navy. His reaction in putting the best possible face on the battle was symptomatic of a man who had been profoundly shaken by what he had just experienced.

The plain truth was that what happened to the German fleet at Jutland haunted Scheer: he had lived his worst nightmare—having the combined strength of the entire Grand Fleet materialize before him without warning as he stood on the bridge of *Friedrich der Grösse,* the British guns blazing and their ships crossing the "T" of the High Seas Fleet. He understood all too well that only a combination of extraordinary luck and superb seamanship had saved the German battle fleet from annihilation. He knew he could always count upon the quality of German seamanship; what he could never again count upon was such a stroke of luck. It is a grave injustice to suggest that Scheer had lost his nerve; what he did lose was that aggressively keen edge that had set him apart from his predecessors as commander in chief of the High Seas Fleet.

The surveyors' reports of the damage done to his ships made for dismal reading. *Lützow* was, of course, sitting at the bottom of the North Sea. *Seydlitz, von der Tann,* and *Derfflinger* were all a shambles. *Von der Tann's* entire main armament had to be replaced or repaired—every one of her main turrets had been hit and either crippled or destroyed outright. Three out of four of *Derfflinger's* gun turrets had been hit, two of them reduced to burnt out shells, while internal explosions had devastated her interior spaces. *Seydlitz* took the longest: all of her guns needed to be replaced, while her hull had suffered almost fatal damage, and her engines and boilers needed work as well. Both ships remained in dry dock for nearly six months. Of the German battlecruisers only *Moltke* was in reasonably good shape, yet even she required several weeks' worth of attention in the Germaniawerft docks before she was fully restored to fighting trim.

The condition of some of Scheer's battleships was hardly more encouraging: *Grösser Kürfurst* had been hit by five 15-inch and three 13.5-inch shells; *König* had taken one 15-inch and nine 13.5-inch hits; *Markgraf* had been struck by three 15-inch projectiles and a pair of 13.5-inch and 12-inch shells. *Ostfriesland* had a hole in her hull the size of a barn door, caused by the mine struck in Heligoland Bight. Numerous others had damage done to searchlights, signaling equipment, secondary guns, and superstructures. When Scheer had reviewed all the dockyard reports, it was clear that it would be at least two months before the High Seas Fleet would be ready to put to sea again.

John Jellicoe and the Grand Fleet were still at sea when the Amsterdam Bureau of Reuters picked up the German Admiralty's official communiqué on June 1 and sent it along to its London office. Because all British news services were under strict wartime censorship, the information was not directly released to the public; at the same time, the Admiralty knew that it was impossible to prevent news of the battle from eventually leaking to the public. For this reason Whitehall began pressing Jellicoe for details, specifically those of ships lost and casualties suffered.

Jellicoe did not immediately respond, for the simple reason that not all of his squadron commanders had made their complete reports; Beatty for one had yet to confirm the loss of *Queen Mary* and *Indefatigable*. Moreover, he had more weighty matters at hand than putting together a half-baked report based on incomplete information, which the Admiralty would probably get all wrong anyway before it was made public. The Battlecruiser Fleet reached Rosyth in the Firth of Forth during the very early morning hours of June 2, but it was past midmorning before the Grand Fleet reached its anchorage at Scapa Flow. *Warspite* and *Marlborough* were still out in the North Sea, both heavily escorted and limping home at just over 10 knots. Several cruisers and destroyers were still unaccounted for, while a large number of destroyers were running dangerously low on fuel.

188 Distant Victory

Yet when all the returns were in, the results were surprising. True, *Queen Mary, Indefatigable,* and *Invincible* had blown up, while *Defense, Black Prince,* and *Warrior* were lost as well, along with eight destroyers. But only one of the Grand Fleet's battleships, *Marlborough,* had to go into dry dock—and only one other, *Colossus,* had even been hit by the High Seas Fleet. The Battlecruiser Fleet and the Fifth Battle Squadron, which had seen the heaviest action, were still viable fighting units. While *Warspite* was undergoing repairs, her place was taken by *Queen Elizabeth; Malaya's* stay in the dockyard amounted to a matter of days. And while *Lion, Tiger,* and *Princess Royal* were out of action for some weeks, their places were taken by the return of *Inflexible* and *Indomitable,* as well as *Australia* coming fresh out of the shipyard from a refit: while von Hipper's First Scouting Group had essentially ceased to exist for the time being, the Royal Navy could still field a potent force of battlecruisers.

Had all the numbers been known on both sides of the North Sea, the outlook for the High Seas Fleet would have seemed even more bleak: by the time most of the German warships had completed their repairs, their British counterparts would be coming out of their dockyards as well, essentially restoring the prebattle numerical status quo; however, at the same time, two new battlecruisers and a pair of new battleships—all four armed with 15-inch guns—would be joining the Grand Fleet. Scheer could count on receiving only one new battleship and one new battlecruiser in that same span. Despite the losses inflicted by the High Seas Fleet, its inferiority in numbers would only continue to grow.

Yet before the Admiralty became aware of all this, it took note of the rising swell of rumor and speculation that was stirring among the British public— fueled in part by the Admiralty orders to dockyards all along England's east coast to be prepared to receive heavily damaged warships. Lacking solid information from Jellicoe, the Admiralty chose to make the German communiqué public, but did so without any explanation or qualification. It was one of the worst public-relations blunders in the history of the Royal Navy. No attempt was made to explain that the news release was official German propaganda, nor was there any accompanying announcement about German losses; likewise there was no explanation that the orders alerting the dockyards had been purely precautionary. Consequently, the public took all of it at face value, and soon newspapers in Great Britain and around the world were declaring that the Royal Navy had suffered a terrible defeat—one so devastating that it was said the Admiralty refused to even acknowledge it, but instead was attempting to conceal the news from the public.

The Reckoning

That same day, the First Lord of the Admiralty, Arthur Balfour, compounded the blunder when he produced a statement that was released at 7:00 PM. It read in part:

> On the afternoon of Wednesday, May 31, a naval engagement took place off the coast of Jutland. The British ships on which the brunt of the fighting fell were the Battle Cruiser Fleet and some cruisers and light cruisers supported by four fast battleships. Among these the losses were heavy…. The battle cruisers *Queen Mary, Indefatigable,* and *Invincible* and the cruisers *Defence* and *Black Prince* were sunk. The *Warrior* was disabled…and had to be abandoned…. No British battleships were sunk…. The enemy's losses are serious. At least one battle cruiser was destroyed, one battleship was reported sunk by our destroyers during a night action; two light cruisers were disabled and probably sunk.

Though he later claimed that he was motivated by a desire to "let the people know the best and the worst that I knew"—and there is no reason to doubt Balfour's honesty or sincerity in the matter—the First Lord had unwittingly begun a bitter controversy over what was to be called the Battle of Jutland by the British and the Battle of the Skaggerak by the Germans, which raged in varying degrees of intensity for the next nine decades.

Balfour's mistake was to focus almost solely on the numbers and types of ships lost: by failing to mention that the High Seas Fleet had twice turned and run from the Grand Fleet, Balfour gave the impression that the battle had been a stand-up, toe-to-toe confrontation between the two, rather than an encounter where, despite its losses, the dominance of the Grand Fleet had been so overwhelming that the Germans refused to stand and fight. Thus to the British public, and to much of the world, the Royal Navy had lost more ships and men than had the Imperial Navy; therefore Jutland was at best a draw or at worst an outright defeat.

Yet the results, effects, and consequences of the battle went far beyond mere arithmetic. In strategic terms, Jutland served only to institutionalize the High Seas Fleet's numerical weakness and strategic impotence compared to that of the Grand Fleet. Despite all of Scheer's bravado in his dispatch to Berlin and all of the bombast in the official German communiqués, one overarching fact remained: nothing had changed. The High Seas Fleet was still trapped and impotent behind Heligoland Bight, while the Grand Fleet commanded all of the entrances to the North Sea. For all of its sound and fury, Jutland had done nothing to alter this strategic balance. The London *Globe* pointedly asked "if the German people, for all their flag-waving," would get "any more of the copper, rubber, and cotton their government so sorely needs? Not by a pound. Will meat and butter be cheaper in Berlin? Not by a *pfennig.*" Or, as the *New York Herald* succinctly put it on June 3, "The German fleet has assaulted its jailer, but it is still in jail."

And yet, the Battle of Jutland had a profound effect on the strategic thinking of the German Naval High Command and ultimately the German government. Though Jellicoe could not know it at the time, he had directed the Grand Fleet in what was one of the decisive battles of the First World War.

A "decisive" battle is one that significantly and materially alters the course of a war, through immediate outcome, its long-term strategic effects, or a combination of both. Some battles are immediately seen as decisive—Marathon, Tours, Waterloo, and Midway are particular examples—while others require months, sometimes years, for their full measure to be taken and felt. Trafalgar was one such, and in its long-term consequences, so was Jutland. What made Jutland decisive was how it altered German strategic thinking, leading the German political as well as military leadership to make decisions that ultimately brought disaster down upon Germany.

The person first and most acutely affected was Reinhard Scheer. In many ways Scheer personified the spirit of the Imperial German Navy: he wholeheartedly embraced the traditional tools of naval warfare—the battleship armed with large-caliber, long-range guns—while at the same time recognizing the value and potential of new weapons, specifically aircraft and submarines. Scheer's original strategic concept for the prosecution of the naval war against Great Britain had been built around the idea of using Germany's surface fleet and her U-boat flotillas in concert to strike at both the Royal Navy and British merchant shipping. Only by working together, as Scheer saw it, could they hope to achieve victory—neither possessed the power alone to do both.

But after the experience of Jutland Scheer's confidence in the power of the High Seas Fleet began to erode. A sortie on August 18, another planned coastal bombardment intended to once more draw out the British battlecruisers, ended when a patrolling U-boat unexpectedly reported the Grand Fleet approaching from the north, just 65 miles away. Once again Room 40 had alerted Jellicoe that the High Seas Fleet was preparing to put to sea, and once again the British ships sailed even before the Germans had left port. Scheer, wanting no part of another confrontation with Jellicoe's battleships and wondering how the British always seemed to appear whenever the High Seas Fleet sailed, turned about to the southeast and steamed straight for Heligoland. The Royal Navy had become Reinhard Scheer's personal bogeyman: he began suspecting British traps and ambushes everywhere. Another sortie on October 18 ended just outside Heligoland Bight, when a British submarine torpedoed the light cruiser *München* and Scheer, fearing the Royal Navy was lying

The Reckoning **191**

in wait, cancelled the entire operation. Two more years passed before the High Seas Fleet ever attempted to put to sea again.

By the autumn of 1916, the strategic situation had been significantly altered from what it had been in March, when the Imperial Navy had attempted to resume unrestricted U-boat warfare. While to much of the world it seemed to have shifted significantly in Germany's favor, in reality it had dramatically altered for the worse. Russia's army was once more reeling back across the steppes, but the Brusilov Offensive of June 1916 had brought the Austro-Hungarian army close to collapse, requiring the deployment of more German troops on the Eastern Front at a time when Germany's own manpower reserves were dwindling. True, the French army had been bled white at Verdun, but—and this was never part of Erich von Falkenhayn's original plan—the German Army had suffered almost as badly as the French: by the battle's end in December 1916, both armies had lost a third of a million men in the struggle for Verdun. True, the British Army had suffered horrible casualties of its own at the Somme, losing 60,000 men in the first day alone, but as the battle continued, German casualty figures soon began approaching those of the British. Germany's manpower reserve was not inexhaustible, and the German Army was being stretched to its limits. The Imperial German government finally came to believe that in order to avoid *losing* the war—let alone winning it—the absolute necessity was to break Great Britain's ability to continue the fight. This meant unleashing the U-boats once again.

The debate began on August 31, when Chancellor Theobald von Bethmann-Hollweg, Foreign Minister Gottfried von Jagow, and Admiral Henning von Holtzendorff met with Field Marshall Paul von Hindenburg, the new chief of the General Staff, and his assistant, Col. General Erich von Ludendorff, in Berlin. For the first time since March the question of another submarine campaign was raised, and pressed with some vigor by von Holtzendorff, with, surprisingly, the support of von Hindenburg and von Ludendorff. The Admiral had dusted off the study done by Admirals Alfred von Tirpitz, Hugo von Pohl, and Reinhard Scheer the previous January, revised it with up-to-date information, and made a strong case for the U-boats.

The three admirals had done their work well, for much of their eight-month-old report was still essentially valid. Their conclusions were simple: if the U-boats were permitted to wage war on *all* shipping found in British waters, they would be able to destroy enough tonnage, British and neutral alike, that British shipyards could not begin to replace the losses. The target number was 600,000 tons per month—if the U-boats could send that much shipping to the bottom of the sea for five straight months, Britain would not have enough ships left to even import the food necessary to feed her people, let alone maintain her armies in the field.

The possibility of America declaring war on Germany as a consequence was considered, but the admirals disregarded it: if the U-boats were successful, and there was every reason to believe they would succeed, the war would be over before the United States could ever effectively intervene. Von Holtzendorff made it clear that this plan had the support of all of the senior admirals of the Imperial Navy, including Scheer and himself. This was significant, for never before had Scheer propounded the idea that the U-boats alone could be decisive in the naval war; von Holtzendorff himself had opposed beginning a new unrestricted U-boat campaign in the spring of 1916. Now both men believed that only Germany's submarines could break the British blockade and strangle Britain's sea-lanes: the High Seas Fleet had, at Jutland, shot its bolt. The arguments as well as those making them were persuasive.

In truth, the Germans had no idea just how good a case it was: Great Britain was in a worse condition than they imagined. Her dependence on American industry had grown, and now was costing more than £2,000,000 ($10,000,000) a day; her negotiable securities were almost exhausted, leaving only government credit to secure the loans necessary to continue to buy the munitions and supplies the British armies needed. The American Federal Reserve warned its member banks against making further unsecured loans to any belligerent or renewing short-term loans that were soon due. Britain's back was brushing the wall: the harvest in the fall of 1916 had not been particularly good, forcing Britain to buy more of her food abroad; her finest troops already lay in Flanders' fields, and she was running out of money. A year before Britain was content to use the United States as a source of supply, but had no desire to see her become a belligerent. Now only America's entry into the war offered any hope for Britain, but President Wilson was reelected in November 1916 after campaigning under the slogan "He kept us out of war!" Once the Germans had restrained the U-boats in the spring of 1916 and no more American lives were lost, American anger toward Germany had abated somewhat. Certainly there was still a smoldering resentment, but it was not enough to go to war over. The *Lusitania*, now 15 months on the bottom, was regarded as old news.

Still, von Bethmann-Hollweg refused to allow a resumption of unrestricted submarine warfare. He remained fearful that the neutral powers would turn on Germany: America was his greatest worry, but he was concerned, too, that Holland and Denmark might well resent their ships becoming targets for the U-boats and declare war as well, creating still more strategic nightmares for the German Army by widening the Western Front.

The Reckoning   193

Acknowledging this reality, von Hindenburg agreed that the time had not yet come for such precipitate action, but also warned the Chancellor that such risks might become unavoidable.

Von Hindenburg and von Ludendorff were called to the conference because Field Marshall von Falkenhayn had fallen from Imperial favor, dismissed as chief of staff by the Kaiser. Von Bethmann-Hollweg, after the trio of disasters of Verdun, the Somme, and the Brusilov Offensive very pointedly asked Wilhelm, "Where does incompetence end and crime begin?" and recommended von Hindenburg as von Falkenhayn's replacement. The Kaiser, equally appalled at the bloodbaths initiated by von Falkenhayn, agreed, and so von Hindenburg was summoned from the Eastern Front, along with his obnoxious and neurotic but seemingly gifted subordinate, von Ludendorff. The two worked well in tandem and had done so since their triumph at the Battle of Tannenburg in August 1914, where they led an outnumbered German army that had turned back a Russian invasion of East Prussia and Silesia. Though von Ludendorff was later perceived as the true strategic genius of the duo, the truth was that his real talent lay in his ability to turn von Hindenburg's strategic ideas into workable operations. What von Hindenburg possessed despite his age—he was 66—was an understanding of the realities imposed on modern war by new technologies. He grasped almost as quickly as had Scheer and von Holtzendorff that the strategic situation demanded resorting to a renewed U-boat campaign to defeat Great Britain, before Germany's resources were completely exhausted.

The combined authority of the opinions of von Hindenburg, von Holtzendorff, and Scheer became increasingly difficult for von Bethmann-Hollweg to ignore or oppose: those of the two admirals bore a particular weight. This was the first time von Holtzendorff and Scheer endorsed the idea that the U-boat campaign alone could defeat Great Britain. In the six months between March and April, only one singular event had transpired that could have worked such a profound change of heart in both men: the Battle of Jutland.

Jutland had shown up all the flaws in the strategies and stratagems of the High Seas Fleet. The massive damage done to so many of his ships at Jutland convinced Scheer that a straightforward fight with the Grand Fleet was a hopeless proposition: however good German ships might be, they were not as good as the German Naval High Command had believed. The first premise of the High Seas Fleet's strategy had proven to be flawed. So did the others.

Scheer, of course, had no way of knowing that the second premise had simply been invalidated: the idea that the High Seas Fleet would be able to catch one of the British battle squadrons isolated from the Grand Fleet would not come about as long as Room 40 was reading the German naval ciphers.

Foreknowledge of German plans allowed Jellicoe to keep his fleet concentrated, ready to sweep down on the High Seas Fleet whenever it sortied from Wilhelmshaven. What Jutland had done for Scheer was drive home the folly of attempting to pursue such a strategy by showing him what the consequences of that strategy would be. His command decisions on August 18 and October 18 were simply further proof that while he might persist in paying lip service to such a strategy, at the same time he knew it was doomed to failure.

The blunt truth, as Scheer and von Holtzendorff finally came to see it, was that the High Seas Fleet would never possess the numerical and material strength to be able to defeat the Grand Fleet, and in so doing break the British blockade of the North Sea, opening the North Atlantic shipping lanes to attack by the Imperial Navy. Jutland had shown the dream held by the officers of the High Seas Fleet for more than a decade to be nothing more than a pipe dream.

Still, von Bethmann-Hollweg was determined to avoid taking that last, drastic step to unrestricted U-boat warfare as long as possible. Quite rightly the Chancellor understood that the majority of Americans were quite content to let the Europeans beat each other bloody and saw no good reason for the United States to get involved. Why not, von Bethmann-Hollweg argued, let the Americans remain that way? Why give them a pretext for joining the Allies where none now existed? By late autumn 1916, the worst of the diplomatic crises created by the destruction of so many passenger ships by German U-boats had begun to pass. Woodrow Wilson was campaigning for reelection to the Presidency on a decidedly pacifistic platform, so it seemed to von Bethmann-Hollweg that a diplomatic solution, not just to the problems of the British blockade and the German U-boat campaign, but to the war as a whole, might be possible. Despite such statements by Wilson that a German victory in the Great War would "change the course of civilization and make America a military nation," von Bethmann-Hollweg believed that the President was in truth more interested in peace in Europe than in seeing either side achieving a victory. The Chancellor pinned his hopes on that belief.

Wilson was no admirer of Germany or the Germans, and he did in truth believe that the world would suffer should Germany win the war. However, he was equally convinced that the way to avoid such an outcome was not to lead America into the war on the side of the Allies but to stop it altogether. He continued to profess that impartiality on America's part was the only way to get both sides to begin some form of peace negotiations. Only a negotiated peace could last, he said, but a settlement "forced on the vanquished by the victor would be accepted in humiliation, under duress, at an intolerable sacrifice, and would be a sting, a resentment, a bitter memory upon which the terms of peace would rest, not permanently, but only as upon quicksand."

"A peace between equals" or a "peace without victory" was what he hoped to offer—and it was that hope von Bethmann-Hollweg was hoping to exploit. After Wilson's reelection in November 1916, the Chancellor waited anxiously for what he believed would be some communication coming out of the White House that would formally propose the idea of a negotiated peace. The Chancellor knew his man, for that is exactly what Wilson had in mind; however, Wilson was working according to his own timetable, not von Bethmann-Hollweg's, and when a month had passed since the November election and no proposal was forthcoming from Wilson, the German Chancellor began preparing one himself.

He was, he knew, running out of time. He was fighting not just against the ruthless beliefs of the German military leadership, but also against powerful forces outside the military and far beyond their control. The grip held by the British blockade on the German economy was rapidly becoming a death grip. The winter of 1916–1917 became known as the "Turnip Winter" as that bland, starchy tuber replaced most other vegetables on German dinner tables; milk was available only for infants and small children; salt, sugar, and butter were all but impossible to obtain. Stockyards throughout the country were all but shut down as supplies of beef, pork, and poultry dwindled to the nearly nonexistent. That autumn's potato harvest had failed, creating a twofold impact on the German diet: not only had potatoes themselves become scarce, but they could no longer be used as a substitute for wheat flour in the bread made by German bakers. Once again the ubiquitous turnip was called in to stop the gap.

Fuel of all kinds—oil, petrol, gas, and coal—were in increasingly short supply as well. That winter most houses in Germany went unheated, and many schools closed down because the children were kept at home in bed all day to stay warm. In factories workers willingly put in overtime, not for the sake of increased production or a fatter pay envelope, but merely to stay warm. Bitterness and resentment against the government for the shortages and hardships was growing daily, although the outright rage was directed at the British and to some extent the Americans, who were increasingly regarded as British puppets.

None of these conditions were apparent to the world outside of Germany, however, so on December 9 the Chancellor drafted a diplomatic note that was circulated to all the neutral capitals in Europe, announcing that Germany invited all of the warring nations to open negotiations for a settled peace. It was the Chancellor's last chance: von Holtzendorff,

Scheer, von Hindenburg, and von Ludendorff had all made it clear to von Bethmann-Hollweg that if the negotiations did not come to pass they expected him to give his approval to the resumption of unrestricted submarine warfare.

Two days before von Bethmann-Hollweg's note was circulated, however, the government of H. H. Asquith collapsed and Asquith resigned as prime minister of Great Britain, his place being taken by the man who had engineered his downfall, David Lloyd George. Lloyd George was a fiery Welsh liberal who at heart was an opportunist who craved power and relished exercising it; having spent most of his political career lusting after the office of prime minister, and the previous three years conniving to replace Asquith, he was not about to embrace a course of action that might diminish his authority. Therefore almost his first official act was to reject the German invitation very nearly as soon as it arrived, a course the French government followed in a matter of hours. Imperial Russia simply ignored the German Chancellor's note.

Still, while Lloyd George's rejection of the German peace proposal may have cemented his grip on power, it was more than mere politics that compelled the new Prime Minister to such a decision and the French and Russians to endorse it. The terms under which Germany was willing to entertain such a conference amounted to an admission of defeat by the Allies. Germany would retain nearly all of the territory her armies had conquered in exchange for an immediate cessation of hostilities. In effect, there was to be very little if any actual negotiation, but rather a formal acquiescence by the Allies of Germany's new dominant position in the middle of the European continent: Berlin was offering to present a German victory under the guise of a negotiated peace. For this reason, however sincere von Bethmann-Hollweg's motives may have been, his proposal was doomed to failure from the moment it left his office.

Another proposed peace conference was likewise doomed when it was circulated a week after von Bethmann-Hollweg's. President Wilson, not realizing the absurdity of his timing in putting forward his own peace initiative at this moment, issued his own note on December 18. Seeking to take a different approach than the Germans had put forward, Wilson began by asking each of the belligerent powers to publicly state their war aims, hoping to find some middle ground as a basis for negotiation. Such a request revealed just how out of touch Wilson was with the realities of the war, for the aims of the Allies and the Central Powers were so far apart that there simply was not any common ground.

Germany was the first to reply, on December 26, very carefully avoiding making any specific mention of war aims while politely pointing out that the German government preferred to deal directly with her adversaries, without the participation of the United States in any possible peace settlement. The Allies, who issued a joint reply two weeks later, were somewhat less courteous in their rejection. Knowing the strength of their position, they felt that Wilson's attempt at mediation would simply allow the Central Powers to avoid their inevitable defeat. Until Germany and her allies were defeated and left in a position from which they could never again threaten their neighbors with aggressive war, there would be no peace talks.

This was the moment for which von Hindenburg, von Ludendorff, von Holtzendorff, and Scheer had been waiting, and which von Bethmann-Hollweg had been dreading. Now it could be argued that no reasonable objection could be raised to the resumption of unrestricted U-boat warfare. Military solutions had been tried, diplomatic compromises sought, naval action pursued, but all without result: the British blockade remained in place, the Royal Navy was undefeated, and Great Britain was still at war with Germany. With the Kaiser's senior military and naval advisors unanimous in assuring him that unrestricted submarine warfare would sever Britain's lifelines with her empire and the United States, and with von Bethmann-Hollweg no longer opposing them, Wilhelm allowed himself to be persuaded that once the U-boats were let loose in Britain's sea-lanes, the British war effort would collapse for want of food, material, and manpower in a matter of weeks. Once that had been accomplished, with Britain unable to fight and Russia wracked by revolution, France would have no choice but to sue for peace—a peace Germany could dictate. America, he was told, could be discounted entirely: even if the United States chose to declare war on Germany, the fighting in Europe would be over long before any significant American intervention could make itself felt. On January 31, 1917, Wilhelm finally approved the unrestricted submarine campaign, to begin February 1. The orders now to the U-boats were simple—sink any ship, of any type and any nationality, on sight.

No one was more stunned by the German announcement than Woodrow Wilson. He was furious: had the Germans forgotten that the cause of every dispute that had arisen between Germany and the United States during the war had always been related to the U-boats? Had they forgotten that Wilson had threatened to break off diplomatic relations a year earlier when the Germans announced their first unrestricted U-boat campaign? The German announcement was tantamount to telling Wilson that they took neither him nor the United States seriously. Within 48 hours Wilson ordered his passports returned to the German ambassador, Count Johannes von Bernstorff, and all diplomatic ties with Germany were severed. It was not war, but it was close to it.

Yet even then it was difficult for Wilson to believe the Germans had gone that far. Going to Congress on February 3 to explain his decisions and his actions, Wilson remarked, "...only overt acts on [the Germans'] part can make me believe it even now." Incredibly, the Germans were not long in providing the most overt act imaginable.

Chapter 11

The Fatal Blunder

The Germans are nothing if not thorough, even in situations where such thoroughness provides the means for their own undoing, and Germany's provocation of the United States in early 1917 was a convincing demonstration of this propensity. Once word of President Wilson's reaction to the resumption of unrestricted U-boat warfare reached Berlin, the Kaiser and his ministers, though convinced that Wilson's diplomatic break was merely bluster, began to take precautions to guard against the event that it was not. What followed was one of the greatest diplomatic blunders of all time.

Above all else, it was imperative that Germany prevent any effective American intervention in Europe. The United States Army in the spring of 1917 was almost laughably small—just 140,000 officers and men—and in organization and equipment it was in many ways still better suited to the role of a frontier constabulary than a full-fledged fighting force. But America's manpower potential was awesome: fully 23 million men between the ages of 21 and 30 were registered by the newly formed selective service for a possible draft, and ultimately 4 million of them were called up to service. It was a pool of manpower that was utterly beyond Germany's capacity to match. Something had to be done to divert such immense numbers away from the Western Front.

The solution was provided by Germany's new foreign minister, Arthur Zimmermann, who had replaced the aging and ailing Gottfried von Jagow in December 1916. Big, beefy, red-haired, and red-faced, Zimmermann was the very antithesis of the prewar professional diplomat. He was blunt, aggressive, rude, and lacked polish and poise. He was, above all, ambitious, and it was his ambition that had brought him to his present overly elevated post. Unquestionably a hard worker, which facilitated his rise, he was more shrewd

Distant Victory

than intelligent and seemed to believe that to be properly conducted diplomacy need consist only of threat and bluster.

At the same time that Berlin informed Ambassador Johann von Bernstorff in Washington of the resumption of unrestricted U-boat warfare, instructions were being sent to Ambassador Hugo von Eckhardt, the Imperial German Minister in Mexico City, Mexico. Playing on years of mutual suspicion and sporadic hostilities between Mexico and the United States, and in particular the still smoldering animosity created by the intervention of the United States Marines in Vera Cruz during the Mexican Revolution of 1914, as well as the punitive expedition against Pancho Villa, led by General John J. Pershing, in northern Mexico in 1916, Germany sought a military alliance with the government of President Venustiano Carranza. Von Eckhardt's brief was contained in a telegram sent to him on January 17 that read:

> On the first of February we intend to begin unrestricted submarine warfare. In spite of this, it is our intention to endeavor to keep neutral the United States of America.
>
> If this attempt is not successful, we propose an alliance on the following basis with Mexico: That we shall make war together and make peace together. We shall give generous financial support, and it is understood that Mexico is to reconquer the lost territory in New Mexico, Texas, and Arizona. The details are left to you for settlement…
>
> You are instructed to inform the President of Mexico of the above in the greatest confidence as soon as it is certain that there will be an outbreak of war with the United States and suggest that the President of Mexico, on his own initiative, should communicate with Japan suggesting adherence at once to this plan; at the same time, offer to mediate between Germany and Japan.
>
> Please call to the attention of the President of Mexico that the employment of ruthless submarine warfare now promises to compel England to make peace in a few months. Acknowledge receipt.
>
> *Zimmermann*
> *(Foreign Minister)*

The Germans had just played an ace that they believed could not be trumped. By allying with Mexico, she would divert American troops that otherwise would have gone to France to fight Germans to America's southern border to defend the American southwest, at the same time making no new manpower demands on her own resources. The U-boats would starve Britain into submission, and France, left without allies but with a shattered army, would clamor for peace. It was elegant, it was brilliant, and it would be the greatest diplomatic masterstroke in German history.

The Fatal Blunder

But if the Germans had played an ace, the British held the joker in the deck—the code and cipher wizards in Room 40 at the Admiralty. The signal from Zimmermann, which will be forever known as "the Zimmermann telegram," was intercepted as it was sent by wireless, and because its addresses and priority coding indicated that its contents were extremely sensitive and urgent, it was given absolute priority by the experts in Room 40. Within a matter of days it was decoded, but rather than hand it over immediately to Walter Hines Page, the American ambassador in London, it was placed in a safe in the Admiralty's communications department. There it sat, while Captain William Reginald Hall decided how it could be presented to the Americans without compromising how the Admiralty came by it in the first place. After two and one-half years of war, the Germans were still unaware that the British were reading almost all of their encrypted communications, and Hall was determined that Berlin continued to be kept in the dark. Eventually a carefully crafted cover story was presented, involving a German diplomat's stolen briefcase and a (possibly) fictitious file clerk at an unnamed embassy through which the cable had passed, and a copy of the telegram was presented to Ambassador Page, who in turn delivered it to Wilson on February 24.

Now Wilson was confronted with an "overt act" of unprecedented enormity. For more than three weeks after the German announcement of the resumption of unrestricted submarine warfare, Wilson had sat mute and immobile as a string of American ships and American lives were lost to German torpedoes in the North Atlantic. The sinkings had demonstrated how lightly Imperial Germany regarded the United States now that the U-boats were unleashed.

The situation Wilson now faced, with the revelation of the Zimmermann telegram, was no longer a semiabstract debate over international law and the rights of neutrals. Nor was it even just a matter of ships sunk without warning and the American lives being lost aboard them, an admittedly distant consideration for people living in the American midwest, southwest, and west. The Zimmermann telegram was something very different: an open, direct threat to the people and the territorial integrity of the United States. When the *New York Times* broke the story of the Zimmermann telegram on March 1, 1917, it caused a nationwide sensation: the complacency, even indifference, that most Americans felt about the Great War ended in an instant. For the first time since the war began, one of the warring powers had threatened the United States openly and directly. The Great War was no longer simply Europe's problem, or as the Omaha *World-Herald* put it: "The issue shifts from Germany against Great Britain to Germany against the United States."

202 Distant Victory

The change in the attitude of the American public toward Germany was as profound as it was sudden. The threat was too real and too personal to be ignored. Even the leading newspapers in the large German-American communities of the Midwest quickly came down on the side of unquestioned loyalty to the United States. The ground-swell clamor for the United States to join with the Allies in making war on Germany grew steadily, until by March 20 Wilson felt compelled to call a cabinet meeting and sound out his advisors. Though some cabinet members like Secretary of the Navy Josephus Daniels were in tears over their decision, they were unanimous in their conviction that America had no choice but to declare war. The next day Wilson called for Congress to meet in special session on April 2.

At 8:30 that next evening, he rode to the Capitol in a light rain to face a joint session of Congress. He spoke for 26 minutes in the careful tones of a university professor lecturing a hall of attentive students. "With a profound sense of the solemn and even tragical character of the step I am taking," he asked Congress to "declare that recent course of the Imperial German Government to be in fact nothing less than war" against the United States and "formally accept the status of belligerent." Neutrality was impossible when faced with an "autocratic government backed by organized force which is controlled wholly by their will and not the will of the people." Wilson spoke of submarine warfare as outside the pale of international law and cited repeated acts of German sabotage in the United States, then finally offered the Zimmermann telegram as incontrovertible proof of Germany's hostile intent toward America. "There is one choice we cannot make," he declared. "We cannot choose the path of submission."

Finally, the hushed listeners—senators and representatives, the Supreme Court and Cabinet, the Diplomatic Corps, and the invited guests in the gallery—heard that string of memorable phrases delivered as if Wilson's resolve were hardening, his determination mounting, with every word. The German government, he said, was "the natural foe of liberty"; that, he made clear to everyone who heard or read his words, was why America was adopting this course, because "the world must be made safe for democracy." It must be understood what America's aims were:

We have no selfish ends to serve. We desire no conquest, no dominion. We seek no indemnities for ourselves, no material compensation for the sacrifices we shall freely make. We are but one of the champions of the rights of mankind. We shall be satisfied when those rights have been made as secure as the faith and freedom of nations can make them.

It is a fearful thing to lead this great peaceful people into war, into the most terrible and disastrous of all wars, civilization itself seeming to be in the

The Fatal Blunder 203

balance. But the right is more precious than peace, and we shall fight for the things which we have always carried nearest our hearts.

Those were simply summed up: "America is privileged to spend her blood and her might for the principles that gave her birth...." He assured his audience with a benediction: "God helping her, she can do no other."

It was over; it was done. Five days later Congress officially declared war on Imperial Germany and her allies. To the hard-pressed French and British, America's decision to take up the sword was greeted more by sighs of relief than by cheers. Russia had already known the first of two revolutions that wracked her in 1917, and despite Premier Alexander Kerensky's pledge to continue to fight, there was no disguising that Russia's armies were collapsing. The French Army was caught up in the first waves of a near mutiny, which followed the bloody and futile Neville Offensive. Britain was gearing up for what was to be her biggest—and though no one could know it, most disastrous—offensive, trying to finally crack the Hindenburg Line: it became known to history as Passchendaele. Now, the unimaginable resources and reserves of material and manpower at America's disposal could be mobilized and hurled at the Western Front. Germany was doomed.

The German High Command did not see it that way, of course. And with good reason: the U-boats were succeeding beyond all expectations, for the first three months of the new campaign can only be described as a massacre. Henning von Holtzendorff's target figure of 600,000 tons sunk per month was still valid, and now the German Navy had even more U-boats available —over 130—with which to mount the offensive. That first month, February, the German submarines sank 520,000 tons, very close to their target figure; the next month they did even better at 564,000 tons. But in April the figure soared to 860,000 tons, a figure that crippled the British shipping industry in a matter of months and in so doing strangled the British economy even more thoroughly than the British blockade had throttled Germany's.

One key to the U-boats' success, to which the British had no counter, was the sheer ruthlessness of the German attack. Victims in the first three months of the new U-boat offensive included ships flying the flags not only of all of the Allied powers, but also the ensigns of the United States, Sweden, Denmark, the Netherlands, Brazil, Spain, and Norway. The magnitude of the threat was so great and the likelihood of being attacked so real that many skippers refused to take their ships to British ports—and those already in British ports refused to sail, 600 neutral-flagged ships doing so in February alone.

Abetting the German U-boat commanders' determination to press home their attacks was the Royal Navy's inability to adequately defend the merchant ships sailing into and out of British ports and harbors. This was not due to any lack of willingness on the navy's part, but rather from something far more basic—a lack of ships. The submarine's natural enemy was the destroyer, which had the speed, firepower, and agility to handily dispatch an attacking submarine, the mongoose to the U-boat's cobra. But the Royal Navy's destroyer forces were simply stretched too thin. There were three missions with which the destroyers were tasked: securing the Channel crossings to France, screening the Grand Fleet when it sailed from Scapa, and protecting merchant shipping sailing to and from the British Isles. In the spring of 1917 the Royal Navy possessed 260 destroyers of all types, many of them of prewar construction and showing their age. One hundred of them were at any given time assigned to screening duties with the Grand Fleet, the balance being parceled out to the remaining commands to the best of the Admiralty's ability.

The problem was that just as geography had crippled the High Seas Fleet by bottling it up in the North Sea, so geography aided the U-boats in their hunt for merchant shipping. There were only two passages to the British Isles, together called the Western Approaches. One lies above Ireland and leads past Belfast into the northern mouth of the Irish Channel, giving access to Glasgow, the Tyne, and Liverpool. The other lies to the south, in the waters of the Irish Sea and the Bay of Biscay, opening into the southern end of the Irish Channel, as well as the English Channel and ultimately the mouth of the Thames. Liverpool, Bristol, Southampton, and London were all accessible from this southern route. But these restricted waters had a funnel-like effect on merchant ships, essentially forcing them into areas where the U-boats knew they would find them. It was not difficult; in fact, the U-boats would have had to work at not stumbling across their targets: each month more than 5,000 merchant ships entered or departed British ports and harbors.

For the British destroyers, the problem was exactly the opposite: their numbers were too few, and they were attempting to hunt down opponents who were relatively few in number as well. Unless a destroyer happened to be in the immediate vicinity when a U-boat struck, there was little the British ships could do but resort to endless patrolling in the hope of forcing any U-boats in the area to depart for safer waters, and look to luck in spotting a U-boat careless enough to be cruising on the surface. The submarines, on the other hand, had the luxury of being able to pick their location, and simply wait for their targets to appear, which, given the number of ships passing in and out of British waters, was inevitable.

In December 1916, John Jellicoe passed command of the Grand Fleet to David Beatty when he was called to London to assume the duties of First Sea Lord, and with them came the responsibility for defending against the U-boats. On December 18, 1916, he created a new department, the Anti-

The Fatal Blunder   **205**

Submarine Division, and gave it to Rear Admiral Alexander Duff. Duff was energetic and imaginative, and immediately set about increasing the number of armed merchantmen, laying additional defensive minefields, laying out new protected routes for merchantmen to follow in British waters—and changing them frequently to confuse the U-boats—and assigning destroyer and trawler patrols to those routes. Yet despite his best efforts the rate of sinkings increased. On February 21, 1917, Jellicoe informed the First Lord and the Cabinet that, in his words, "The position is exceedingly grave." Before long the government would have to face the question of "how long can we continue to carry on the war if the losses of merchant shipping continue at the present rate."

The answer was not long in coming—by early April not long after the United States declared war on Germany, Jellicoe confided to Admiral William S. Sims, the newly appointed American naval liaison officer in London, that there was less than a six-weeks' supply of grain in Great Britain, and that unless something were done to stop the hemorrhaging, the U-boats were about to bleed the country dry. According to Jellicoe's figures, even with the most stringent rationing and conservation measures, if the destruction of Britain's merchant fleet continued at its present pace, it would be impossible for Great Britain to hold out beyond November 1.

Sims was, in his words, "fairly astounded." He confessed to Jellicoe that neither he nor anyone in the United States realized that the situation had become so grave. Seeking the British Admiral's advice, he then sent a long, detailed cable to the Navy Department in Washington, DC, describing in uncompromising terms the conditions in Britain. He asked for every available destroyer and light cruiser to be sent to assist the Royal Navy, characterizing the urgency as being "one of life or death."

There was, to Sims, one obvious solution to the problem: convoy. It was not a new idea to the Royal Navy: it had been forming and escorting convoys since the middle of the eighteenth century. It had experienced considerable success with convoys during the Great War, particularly in the opening days when the whole of the British Expeditionary Force was carried across the Channel to France without losing a single soldier—a practice that continued throughout the war. Troopships regularly traveled in convoy throughout the Mediterranean, and convoys had carried all the troops to and from Gallipoli without a loss. And yet, as late as January 1917, the Admiralty was still advocating that merchant ships make their sailings alone—with near-catastrophic results.

This was not, though popular belief came to hold it so, because the Admiralty lacked imagination or was too conservative, too blind, or too backward in its thinking to see the wisdom of adopting a convoy system for merchant shipping. The primary reason that convoys were not begun was a lack of escorts.

There were two specific advantages convoy bestowed on the defending forces. First, it reduced the number of opportunities any given submarine had to encounter a target—a convoy of 20 ships presented only a single chance for a U-boat to make its attack, while the same 20 ships sailing independently offered 20 separate opportunities for attack. Second, because the ships were concentrated in a relatively small area, it was possible to concentrate the escorts with them, rather than have them spread out across vast expanses of ocean, dramatically increasing their effectiveness by placing them at the spot where a U-boat attack was likely, exposing the submarines to greatly increased risk of counterattack and destruction.

The Admiralty knew all of this. What held Whitehall back from beginning convoys as soon as the Germans resumed unrestricted submarine warfare was their belief that convoys were beyond the abilities of civilian merchant ships and crews to maintain. The trooping convoys across the Channel and in the Mediterranean were made up of ships, usually commandeered passenger liners, that were commanded by officers of the Royal Navy or the Royal Naval Reserve and manned by reservist crews with a leavening of regulars. These were men with the training and experience in the precise navigation and shiphandling required for convoy work. Civilian merchantmen, on the other hand, were accustomed to following whatever courses and speeds they chose, and their navigation was often haphazard and sloppy, while the concept of steaming in formation, vital to the success of a convoy, was an utterly alien concept to most merchant skippers. In the opinion of the Royal Navy, given these circumstances convoys would be impossible to form or maintain.

This was not, as it might appear, simply a case of Royal Navy prejudice against the merchant marine. These conclusions were based on conferences in late February 1917 with merchant captains who offered these conclusions as their professional opinions based on decades of experience. Nor was it a case of reverse prejudice on the part of the merchant marine: if anything, the merchant officers and crews wanted to find some protection from the marauding U-boats as much if not more than did the Royal Navy. But the facts were blunt: in the first three months of Germany's new U-boat campaign almost 2 million tons of shipping were destroyed—at a cost to the Imperial German Navy of seven U-boats sunk. It seemed that introducing convoys for all merchant ships sailing to or from the British Isles was the only alternative.

Rear Admiral Duff took it upon himself to determine once and for all whether convoys actually provided more protection for the merchantmen. Combining all of the facts accumulated from three years of experience with convoys along with the three separate U-boat campaigns of 1915, 1916, and 1917, Duff drew up a highly detailed, carefully thought-out memorandum recommending the introduction of a convoy system. The objections of the merchant marine were noted and ruthlessly overridden: the civilian officers and crew simply had to learn the new skills convoy required. The scarcity of escorts would be overcome by the arrival of American destroyers, some of which were already on their way across the Atlantic. Duff immediately went to Jellicoe on April 23 to make his case. Jellicoe in turn instantly saw the validity of Duff's work and conclusions, circulated the memo to the Admiralty on April 25, and two days later gave his approval to the formation of the first convoys.

The results were almost instantaneous. On May 10 a convoy of 16 merchant ships accompanied by five escorts left Gibraltar for Plymouth. They arrived intact on May 20, necessity and peril being excellent teachers, the merchant crews having learned that the skills needed to keep station and follow zigzagging courses were not beyond them. The first transatlantic convoy soon followed: 12 merchantmen left Hampton Roads, Virginia, for Bristol on May 24. Two stragglers fell out, one of which was later torpedoed and sunk, while the remaining ten reached Bristol under the watchful eyes of eight destroyers. No German submarine had dared to attack them.

By the end of July the rate of sinkings dropped from 25 percent of all ships sailing to the British Isles to one-tenth of that figure, and this despite a dramatic rise in the number of ships sailing from American to Great Britain; of 354 ships crossing the Atlantic, just two were lost to U-boats.

Churchill later summed up the how and why of the convoys' sudden success:

> The size of the sea is so vast that the difference between the size of a convoy and the size of a single ship shrinks in comparison almost to insignificance. There was in fact very nearly as good a chance of a convoy of forty ships in close order slipping unperceived between the patrolling U-boats as there was for a single ship; and each time this happened, forty ships escaped instead of one.

Even better, from the Royal Navy's perspective, was that by keeping the escorts close to the U-boats' intended targets, they created more opportunities for attacking the enemy submarines. The U-boat would be irresistibly drawn to the convoy, where the destroyers and trawlers waited to pounce on it; this was a new form of offensive warfare, one that set previous thinking on its ear. For three years the Royal Navy had been trying to take the war to the U-boats, now the convoys brought the U-boats to them. The British did not have to go looking for the Germans, they came as if by invitation. Even if the submarine were not sunk, if it were prevented from making its attacks, that counted as a success.

The U-boats continued to take their toll on Allied and neutral shipping: even in the last full month of the war they accounted for 297,000 tons lost. But it was not a case of "too little, too late" with the submarine offensive: the concept of the campaign was flawed from the beginning, a direct result of the arrogance of the German Naval High Command, an arrogance it had displayed since the creation of the High Seas Fleet. In the end the Germans were undone by their own hubris: just as a fatally flawed belief in the superiority of German shipbuilding led the German admirals to believe that their ships were ton for ton better than their British counterparts, so, too, did their flawed thinking lead them to believe that the British would not be able to find an effective counter to the unrestricted U-boat campaign before Great Britain was starved into submission. The mistaken belief in the superiority of German ships led the Imperial Navy to believe in "Der Tag"—"the Day"—when German and British fleets tried conclusions and the German fleet would emerge victorious. It led to a reckless naval policy that needlessly provoked Great Britain and made the Triple Entente a reality. It led to pointless adventures that needlessly exposed German ships and their crews to destruction at the hands of the Royal Navy. And it eventually led to the adoption of the one form of naval warfare that held out a chance for a German victory while offering the certainty of American hostility.

In short, because the Germans refused to allow for the possibility that they might not succeed, they guaranteed failure. When the High Seas Fleet failed to find a way to defeat the Grand Fleet, despite the Imperial Navy's assumptions of qualitative superiority, because there was no alternative plan Germany had to turn to the U-boats. This led to America entering the war as a full belligerent, and when the U-boats failed, despite all the assurances that they would not, Germany was left bereft of choices.

The great miscalculation was made first by the German Naval High Command in the persons of Admiral Reinhard Scheer and Admiral von Holtzendorff when they created the plan for the submarine campaign was that it would inevitably succeed. It was a foolish mistake, one that they could easily have avoided if only they had understood Admiral Alfred Thayer Mahan as well as they thought they did. For Mahan taught that the purpose of sea power was to be able to protect and maintain shipping lanes and the vessels that plied them. Mahan had repeatedly drawn on the lessons of convoy to demonstrate how navies could more effectively accomplish that mission, yet the German Admiralty appears to have never considered the possibility of the British reverting to convoys for their merchant shipping, even though

The Fatal Blunder

209

they well knew that Great Britain's military convoys had proven to be nearly invulnerable to submarine attack.

Nor was this arrogance limited to the German Admiralty: the Army General Staff in the person of Col. General Erich von Ludendorff displayed the same foolish propensity. By the winter of 1917–1918, it was clear that Germany lacked the strength to continue to hold the Western Front indefinitely. The collapse of the Russian Empire had freed more than 2 million soldiers for service in the West, yet the hundred-odd divisions they formed were neither rested nor really fresh. The privations created by the British blockade had begun to be felt within the German Army itself, where rations began to decline in both quantity and quality, and new uniforms and equipment were increasingly difficult to obtain. Moreover, Germany had reached the limits of her manpower reserves: while the Allies could count on literally millions of fresh American troops arriving in the spring and summer of 1918, Germany had no replacements left to put into the field. Von Ludendorff, concluding that Germany was too weak to remain on the defensive, decided that her only hope was to take the offensive and shatter the Allies with a series of ponderous hammerblows before the American divisions could begin to arrive.

The result was the "Peace Offensive"—the German press deemed it the *Kaiserschlact,* "the Kaiser's Battle"—which began with a massive assault on the British trenches just above the point where the French and British armies met. Beginning on March 21, 1918, the attack gained ground with amazing speed in its first four days, in some places pushing the British back some 37 miles from their original lines. But the British Army refused to break, and as the attack stalled, rather than reinforce it, von Ludendorff switched his focus to a new offensive, this one launched out of the Chemin des Dames by the French on May 27. Advancing 40 miles, the German armies came almost within sight of Paris, but the French resistance stiffened and the German onslaught halted.

Von Ludendorff then shifted his focus back to the north, where he again attacked the British Army, but this time made little gain; another attack on the French produced no appreciable results. By the end of July von Ludendorff had exhausted what few reserves he had been able to scrape together: in the four offensives the German Army had lost almost a million men killed, wounded, or missing, who were literally irreplaceable. The Allies had suffered enormous casualties as well, but as the last of von Ludendorff's attacks was petering out at the end of July, there were already more than 1 million American soldiers in France on their way to the front—the same American soldiers that Scheer and von Holtzendorff 18 months earlier had assured the Chancellor and the Kaiser would never reach Europe. What had started as a trickle of Americans in olive drab uniforms in November 1917 had become a torrent, then a flood, by the summer of 1918. By autumn the Allies were on the offensive for the length of the Western Front, and the Germans, while retreating carefully and methodically, had no way of actually stopping the Allied advance. The end, when it came, came quickly.

Theobald von Bethmann-Hollweg had resigned as Chancellor in July 1917 after the disgrace of America's declaration of war. He was succeeded by a procession of nonentities until October 1, 1918, when Prince Max, the Kaiser's cousin, assumed the office—but did so on the condition that he would actively seek an armistice with the Allies. President Woodrow Wilson had issued an outline for peace in January, called the Fourteen Points, which Prince Max immediately accepted as the basis for negotiating a cease-fire, but by now events were creating their own momentum that was taking over. Max's determination to seek peace was fiercely opposed by Admiral Scheer, who was now the chief of staff of the Imperial German Navy, having taken over from Admiral von Holtzendorff, who had resigned in August when his health gave out. Scheer refused to accept the truth that the war was all but over, and continued to dream up offensive schemes for the submarine flotillas and the High Seas Fleet. It was this last, mad flurry of planning that created the catalyst that finally brought down the German Empire.

Col. General von Ludendorff was dismissed by the Kaiser on October 26, after presenting Wilhelm with a virtual ultimatum, asking the monarch to choose between von Ludendorff and Prince Max, essentially a choice between continuing a war already lost and finding a way to end the fighting. Wilhelm, seeing the future with startling clarity, understood that von Ludendorff—who by this time may have been slightly mad—was quite willing to plunge Germany into a gargantuan *Götterdämmerung* in order to preserve the German Army. As much as he loved the army, this was something Wilhelm was not prepared to do. With von Ludendorff gone—von Hindenburg remained as the chief of the Imperial General Staff in order to provide the army with a sense of stability as it began its withdrawal into Germany—Prince Max informed the Allies that Germany was prepared to accept an armistice under all the terms outlined in President Wilson's declaration. One by one her allies fell away, as Austria-Hungary concluded a separate peace on October 29, and Turkey followed suit two days after that.

It was now that Scheer and Franz von Hipper indulged in the greatest naval folly of the war. Von Hipper, now commander in chief of the High Seas Fleet, succeeding Scheer upon his promotion to chief of staff, minuted to Scheer that "an honorable battle by the fleet—even if it should be a fight to the death—will sow the seeds for a new German fleet in the future." Somehow both men convinced themselves that even if the whole of the High Seas Fleet were destroyed, if it did sufficient damage to the Grand Fleet in the process,

The Fatal Blunder

that would create a certain amount of favorable influence for Germany in any peace negotiations. Secretly Scheer began to plan for one last all-out attack on the Royal Navy. Sending a messenger with oral instructions to von Hipper on October 22—"The High Seas Fleet is directed to attack the English fleet as soon as possible"—Scheer was committing a colossal act of insubordination, for he had neither the Kaiser's nor the Chancellor's approval for such an operation.

The plan was ambitious and under other circumstances might well have worked. The High Seas Fleet was now more powerful than ever, with 5 battle-cruisers, 18 dreadnoughts, 12 light cruisers, and 72 destroyers. The basic concept was to lure the Grand Fleet into the waters roughly 100 miles north of Heligoland Bight, into freshly laid minefields and across six separate lines of lurking U-boats, which were expected to decimate the British battleships as they passed; the surviving British ships would then be engaged by the undamaged battleships and battlecruisers of the High Seas Fleet. The lure for the Grand Fleet was to be a series of hit-and-run raids by destroyers and light cruisers along the English coastline and into the Thames estuary. The tactical details were worked out by von Hipper, and Scheer gave his approval on October 27, the date for the operation being set for 30 October.

But rumors had begun to leak out, and in this case the story being spread among the crews of the High Seas Fleet was that the impending operation was a suicide mission—death and glory for the officers and a watery grave for the ordinary sailor. Two years earlier such a prospect might have been welcomed in the seamen's mess as in the wardroom, but by October 1918 the High Seas Fleet was no longer the finely trained and fiery battle fleet it had once been. Two years of idleness had sapped its strength and vigor and drained its morale, as the best and brightest of the sailors and young officers were transferred over to the submarine service, leaving the crews aboard the battleships and battlecruisers as little more than the dregs of the Imperial Navy, often the leavings of the Imperial Army, which meant that they were very poor-quality specimens indeed. The ships themselves were becoming dirty and shabby, falling into disrepair and desuetude, as the crews began neglecting the routines of maintenance that keep a ship alive.

The mutiny of the High Seas Fleet began quietly enough, when on October 27 forty-five stokers from the light cruiser *Cuxhaven* refused to return to their ship. That night a total of 300 men from the crews of the battlecruisers jumped ship and swam ashore, disappearing into the docks and warehouses of Wilhelmshaven's waterfront. When the battleships took up station in the Jade Roads the next day, the trouble began to spread more openly. Aboard *Markgraf* one seamen leaped atop a gun turret and called for three cheers for President Wilson, which the crew returned to the echo. The rot spread quickly after that, as *Helgoland, Thüringen, König, Kaiserin,* and *Kronprinz Wilhelm* were all wracked by insubordination. Von Hipper, realizing that he was losing control of the fleet, cancelled the operation and dispersed the battle squadrons, a move that only spread the mutiny further. Within a week red flags were flying in Wilhelmshaven and Kiel, as sailors paraded in the streets and loudly chanted for an end to the war and the overthrow of the monarchy. On November 9 a red flag was hoisted to the masthead of SMS *Baden,* von Hipper's own flagship, and the admiral knew that the end had come. Groups of sailors left Kiel and Wilhelmshaven for Germany's other great ports, and soon the red flags of revolution were flying all along the Baltic and North Sea coasts and spreading inland, as revolution gripped Germany and the Kaiser's throne, already teetering, began to collapse.

The same day that the red flag was raised aboard *Baden,* Admiral Scheer informed Wilhelm that the navy could no longer be counted upon to obey his orders or those of anyone else. Within hours von Hindenburg informed Wilhelm that the same situation applied to the army. That evening the Kaiser abdicated and fled to the Netherlands, never to see Germany again for the remaining 22 years of his life. The German Empire had fallen, its collapse precipitated by the mutiny of what had once been one of its greatest instruments of power, the High Seas Fleet.

The mutineers—now revolutionaries—had no way of knowing that late on the night of November 8, at the provincial French town of Compiègne, a delegation of German politicians had met with a handful of senior Allied officers, led by the French Field Marshall Ferdinand Foch, generalissimo of the Allied armies, to discuss the terms of an armistice. Although the two sides spent the better part of the next two days talking, there was little in the way of actual negotiation: the Allied representatives simply presented their terms to the German delegates with the understanding that they could take them or leave them. If they chose the latter, Foch assured the delegates, or if the German Army and Navy failed to comply with the terms within 48 hours once the armistice was signed, he could force the outright surrender of Germany within six weeks. With heavy hearts but bowing to the inevitable, the Germans agreed and signed the armistice. The cease-fire took effect at 1100 on the morning of November 11. After four years and three months of fighting, at a cost of more than 10 million lives, with more than twice that number wounded and maimed, the Great War had finally come to an end.

Chapter 12

Distant Victory

The sun had been up for barely an hour when, just over 100 miles to the southeast of Scapa Flow, the British light cruiser HMS *Cardiff* spotted the German battlecruiser SMS *Seydlitz* looming over the horizon. Behind *Seydlitz* were four more battlecruisers and nine battleships, along with seven light cruisers and 49 destroyers, the most powerful German squadron to sail this far into the North Sea since the Battle of Jutland. But there was no frantic beat to quarters aboard *Cardiff*, no desperate sighting signals sent by wireless, and no cries for assistance from the Grand Fleet. Instead, the diminutive British ship simply signaled to the leading German behemoth "Follow me," and, turning toward the Firth of Forth, led the German fleet toward a waiting assembly of 370 Allied warships off May Island. The High Seas Fleet had finally sailed from Wilhelmshaven, but not to engage the Royal Navy in one last, great fight. Instead the German fleet had sailed in order to comply with the terms of the armistice signed November 11, steaming not toward death and glory but for internment and captivity.

When the German delegation met with the Allied representatives at Compiègne, among the officers present was the First Sea Lord, Admiral Rosslyn Wemyss, who had replaced John Jellicoe at Christmastime in December 1917. Wemyss was insistent that two carefully worded clauses directly addressing the disposition of the German Navy be included in the armistice agreement. The first, Article XXI, ordered the surrender within two weeks of all German U-Boats already in service or completed, as well as the destruction of any unfinished submarines. The second, Article XXIII, named 74 warships, of all types, to be handed over to the Allies and interned in Allied or neutral ports; the peace negotiations determined their ultimate fate. That same article anticipated the possibility that the Germans might try to scuttle

214   Distant Victory

these ships, declaring, "No destruction of ships or of materials is to be permitted before evacuation, delivery, or restoration." The Allies were determined that no matter what the outcome of the peace conference the German Navy would be in no position to resume the war.

This was too much for Admiral Franz von Hipper. Though nominally still the commander in chief of the High Seas Fleet, he left the details of sailing the designated ships into internment to *Konteradmiral* Ludwig von Reuter, who hoisted his flag aboard *Friedrich der Grösse,* Scheer's old flagship. In addition to the unpleasant task of surrendering his fleet, von Reuter had serious disciplinary problems with his crews, many of whom were in varying stages of mutiny, some of them openly displaying communist and Bolshevik sympathies. It was von Reuter who took 71 German ships to sea on November 19, bound first for the Firth of Forth where the British checked that they had been disarmed according to the provisions of the armistice before moving them to other ports to be interned. The battleship *König* and the light cruiser *Dresden* both had engine problems, a consequence of having sat in harbor for so long, and had to be left behind; the battlecruiser *Mackensen* was not yet sufficiently finished to be seaworthy. During the crossing to Scotland the torpedo boat *V-30* strayed off course and struck a mine, which broke her back and sank her. (Four additional ships eventually took the places of those that were missing.) Still it was a powerful force at von Reuter's disposal, and had he been so inclined he might have believed he could cause a great deal of damage before his command was overwhelmed.

The sight of the waiting Allied fleet would have soon dispelled that notion: 32 battleships—four of them American—nine battlecruisers, and a virtual cloud of armored cruisers, light cruisers, and destroyers. Every British ship was flying two, three, sometimes four White Ensigns, just as they had at Jutland. The German fleet was outnumbered by a margin of more than five to one. Still, the Royal Navy was taking no chances. As the German ships approached May Island, the Allied fleet formed into two long lines, steaming parallel to each other, six miles apart, with the single line of German warships in between them. While all the ships' guns remained trained fore-and-aft, shells and powder charges were at the ready, and the rangefinders and spotters kept a wary eye on the Germans, continually updating range, course, and speed data and working out new firing solutions.

They need not have bothered: when the German ships arrived at the Firth of Forth and teams of British inspectors had an opportunity to examine them, it was found that all powder and ammunition had already been removed, and on some ships the breechblock mechanisms were missing as well, rendering the guns useless. An inkling of the actual condition of the German warships had been given when one of the German squadrons, instructed to increase its speed to 17 knots, replied, "Unable to comply. We cannot do better than 12 knots due to lack of lubricating oil."

At noon the German fleet anchored at the mouth of the Firth of Forth, and the great Allied fleet steamed majestically past, its numbers alone seeming to emphasize the totality of the German defeat. The last ship to enter the Firth was David Beatty's flagship, now the battleship *Queen Elizabeth,* and as she dropped anchor a signal was sent to the German vessels: "The German flag will be hauled down at sunset today and will not be hoisted again without permission." It was the first of a series of slights and insults that were directed toward the ships and crews of the High Seas Fleet over the next seven months and that set the stage for the fleet's spectacular demise.

Over the next five days the interned ships were sent to Scapa Flow, where they were moored in a lonely corner of Pentland Firth, east of Hoy. Eventually there were 74 ships at anchor there, drawn up in sullen rows: 11 battleships, 5 battlecruisers, 8 light cruisers, and 50 destroyers. Technically they remained the property of the German government, and no British naval personnel were allowed aboard except when on official business. All wireless equipment and most signal lamps were removed, and the crews were quickly reduced to care-taker levels. Battleships were allotted 165 officers and men, battlecruisers 200, light cruisers 80, and destroyers 20, barely enough to do the most basic of essential maintenance. These numbers were actually higher than the British thought necessary, but the Germans insisted and the British gave way. Still, of the more than 20,000 crewmen who had crossed the North Sea with these ships, 15,000 were sent home to Germany by the middle of December.

Conditions were worse than spartan for the remaining German crewmen, while relations between the Germans and British in general were formal and rather strained. The unspoken but still very real truth that the armistice was only a cease-fire, not a permanent peace, was an undercurrent running through everything that happened in Scapa Flow. There was no fraternizing between the two fleets, the only German officer who could initiate any com-munication with the British was Admiral von Reuter, who was only allowed to contact the commander of the ships guarding the German fleet in writing.

The Germans were openly unhappy with being interned at Scapa Flow, as they felt that internment should have been in a neutral port and that the Brit-ish had violated the spirit, if not the actual wording, of the armistice. They could do nothing about it, however. The British had, in fact, approached both Spain and Norway as possible locations for the interned ships, but with the rot of revolution aboard, no nation was willing to take them. Scapa Flow had become, almost by default, the only place the German ships could go.

Before long disciplinary problems became commonplace among the remaining crewmen, many of whom openly proclaimed themselves revolutionaries. Von Reuter was forced to shift his flag to the cruiser *Emden* after rebellious crewmen made life aboard *Friedrich der Grösse* impossible. A large measure of the breakdown in discipline was due to boredom—there simply was not enough work to keep the men busy, and idleness bred insolence. There was enough food—the British required that all rations come from Germany, and supply ships arrived twice monthly, also bringing the sailors' mail—as well as generous allowances of tobacco and alcohol. But neither officers nor seamen were allowed ashore, nor were they permitted to leave their ships; ships could communicate with one another by signal flag only, while mail, incoming as well as outgoing, was censored. There were no German-language newspapers available, only British dailies, and these usually ran four days late when they arrived at Scapa. They were the German fleet's only source of news apart from the crews' mail.

This last inconvenience became a source of rising friction between von Reuter and his British "hosts." In almost every way the German admiral was a model of cooperation and goodwill, but he was understandably galled by the lack of news that did not have an unmistakably pro-British bias. Von Reuter, along with his officers and remaining crewmen, was anxious to follow the progress of the peace conference being held at Versailles. Among the many details being determined was not just the fate of Germany but, of more immediate interest to the internees at Scapa Flow, the fate of the High Seas Fleet as well. The peace talks dragged on through the winter and spring, with the Armistice being extended several times, and the peace treaty, which became known as the Treaty of Versailles, was not ready to be approved and signed until mid-June 1919.

Meanwhile the fate of the ships had divided the Allies: giving them back to Germany was out of the question, of course, but what was to actually be done with them became an almost acrimonious issue. France and Italy both wanted a significant share of the German fleet, hoping to dramatically increase the size of their own navies without having to make a corresponding expenditure of time and money. Great Britain and the United States, who now possessed, respectively, the largest and second-largest navies in the world, were less than keen on that idea, and preferred that all the German warships be scrapped. On one subject, at least, all the Allies agreed: the entire German U-boat fleet was summarily ordered destroyed, save for a handful of boats that were given to France.

Rumors began spreading, though, even before the final draft of the peace treaty was given to the German delegates at Versailles. The word quickly spread that the ships of the High Seas Fleet were to be formally surrendered and given to the Allies. Among the German officers and ratings, it was believed that once the Armistice expired, when the Treaty of Versailles was signed, the Royal Navy would move quickly to seize the interned ships. It was a prospect that none of them relished: though Wilhelm had fled the throne and Imperial Germany as such had ceased to exist, there was not an officer aboard any of the 74 German warships at Scapa Flow who had forgotten his oath to the Kaiser that he would never let any vessel of the High Seas Fleet fall into enemy hands. Seizure of the fleet by the Royal Navy was still only a rumor, but if it came to that, many of them silently vowed, they would scuttle the fleet before it could happen.

And yet, whether or not the High Seas Fleet chose a path of self-destruction ultimately mattered very little, for its presence alone in Scapa Flow was sufficient testimony to its defeat, as abject and complete as a formal capitulation. Many of the senior German officers argued—fruitlessly—that interning the High Seas Fleet in a British anchorage was, if not a violation of international law, at the very least an act of dishonor to a fleet that had never been beaten in battle. It was a specious argument, for the only time the High Seas Fleet had faced an opponent in battle—at Jutland—it had fled, not once but twice, in order to prevent its wholesale destruction. It could even be argued in return that there had never been a need for the Grand Fleet to confront and defeat the High Seas Fleet in an open sea fight, since as long as the German warships remained confined to the waters of the North Sea and the Baltic, they had no more effect on Britain's command of the seas than if they were sitting on the bottom. The truth was that the High Seas Fleet had never sought a straightforward confrontation with the dreadnoughts of the Royal Navy, preferring instead to pursue a strategy designed to erode the British numerical superiority until the two fleets achieved approximate parity in numbers. And even then there is little evidence to show what or how the Germans planned for exploiting such a success, or how they intended to bring about the decisive battle with the Grand Fleet. There was nothing wrong with adopting and following such a cautious strategy: never had it been expected in warfare that an army or navy would deliberately present its enemies with an opportunity to crush it. But for the officers of the Imperial German Navy to argue that it had somehow been "dishonored" by never being defeated in a battle it was never willing to fight was little more than an exercise in the most hypocritical form of self-justification.

In the end, what had happened was that the High Seas Fleet had been unequal to the task for which it had been constructed—contending with the Royal Navy for supremacy on the world's oceans. When the German warships anchored at the Firth of Forth on the morning of November 21, 1918, their arrival was a tacit confession of the failure of all of Kaiser Wilhelm II's ambitions, as well as those of the finest naval minds in Germany who had been unequal to the task given them, that of turning Wilhelm's dreams into

Distant Victory

a reality. The whole history of the High Seas Fleet must be regarded as a bitter failure: aside from a few minor skirmishes and the Battle of Coronel, the Imperial German Navy could boast of no victories. Its proudest moment was when it turned away from a greatly superior enemy and returned to port to celebrate not its victory but its survival.

In the evening of the day the High Seas Fleet steamed into internment, Admiral Beatty sat down to a celebratory dinner in *Queen Elizabeth's* wardroom, after having received the cheers of the Allied fleet earlier that afternoon. Ironically, although the Grand Fleet was under his command as it escorted the German ships into internment, Beatty was not the man who had made the Allied victory possible. That man, Admiral Sir John Jellicoe, was now retired, and that same evening was sitting down to a dinner of his own, a much smaller, more intimate affair—in London with his wife and their four surviving daughters. Across the North Sea, both Admiral Reinhard Scheer and Admiral Franz von Hipper were preparing to retire from the naval service. By the end of 1918, only one of the four flag officers who led the fleets at Jutland was still on active service—David Beatty.

The aftermath of Jutland seemed to bring out the worst in Beatty and gave full rein to a grasping side of this ambitious character. The guns had barely grown cold when Beatty began subtly undermining Jellicoe, privately encouraging those who believed that the commander in chief had, through incompetence and timidity, lost a chance to destroy the High Seas Fleet, all the while publicly appearing as the senior admiral's staunch supporter. Uninformed criticism of Jellicoe as being unnecessarily cautious in refusing to engage the Germans unless he had overwhelming superiority, criticism that Beatty could have easily discredited, gradually coalesced into the belief that Jellicoe was no longer fit to command the dreadnought fleet. But Beatty had his eye on the command of the Grand Fleet, and as the chorus of criticism grew, so not surprisingly did the sentiment that a younger, more aggressive commander was required, one who was willing to engage the Germans wherever and whenever they were to be found.

This whispering campaign against Jellicoe rose to a crescendo in the latter months of 1916, and Jellicoe was finally brought to the Admiralty as First Sea Lord, opening the way for Beatty, by now regarded as his natural replacement, to assume the post of commander in chief of the Grand Fleet. Just as his original advancement to rear admiral had done, his promotion to the top seagoing command in the Royal Navy, over the heads of eight more senior admirals, created considerable resentment within the fleet. Ironically, Beatty turned out to be a disappointment for many of his supporters, as he discovered the responsibilities of this supreme command demanded carefully thought-out planning rather than the impulse and dash that

Distant Victory

had characterized his command of the Battlecruiser Fleet. In the end, Beatty proved to be every bit as cautious as Jellicoe, if not more so, as he came to recognize that his first priority was the preservation of the Grand Fleet—he never sought a major confrontation with the Imperial German Navy.

However, unlike Jellicoe, Beatty knew how to play political games, and he was careful to back the right horse in the Cabinet crisis of December 1916, which resulted in H.H. Asquith's resignation as Prime Minister, with David Lloyd George taking the office. Lloyd George had lusted after the Prime Minister's seals of office for nearly a decade, and once he was secure in his new position, he ruthlessly exercised its power with an almost visible glee. While perhaps the cleverest politician to ever become Great Britain's Prime Minister, Lloyd George was suspicious of anyone who was more intelligent, better educated, or more professionally competent than himself. In his dealings with the Royal Navy the Prime Minister's favorite phrase, uttered with abandon whenever the Admiralty refused—or was unable—to do things the way Lloyd George wanted them done, was "Sack the lot!"—threatening to summarily dismiss anyone who disagreed with him. Yet somehow Lloyd George took a liking to Beatty (who publicly charmed the Prime Minister while privately referring to him as a "dirty dog" and "a demagogue") and the admiral exploited the sentiment to the fullest advantage: the Prime Minister specifically promoted Jellicoe to the office of First Sea Lord in part to create the vacancy that Beatty filled.

When Lloyd George decided that the best way to make sure the Admiralty did things his way was to have his own man in charge, he brought in a political crony, Sir Eric Geddes, formerly a civilian railway official who knew nothing of ships and the sea, to replace Sir Edward Carson as First Lord in July 1917. Geddes and Jellicoe, who was still First Sea Lord at this time, often disagreed, Jellicoe politely, Geddes less so, and the admiral was frequently compelled to point out to Geddes where the man's own incompetence was creating more problems than his presence was solving. This gave Lloyd George, who had never liked Jellicoe, the opening he sought, and on Christmas Eve, 1917, Geddes, at Lloyd George's prompting, sent a special messenger to the Admiralty offices to hand deliver a letter requiring Jellicoe's resignation.

The other Sea Lords threatened to resign *en masse* in protest, while angry rumbles were heard in wardrooms and messdecks throughout the fleet: it was not just that it was Jellicoe who had been relieved, it was how it was done that deeply offended the officers and ratings of the Royal Navy. Carson, already too familiar with Lloyd George's methods, even took the issue to Parliament. The deed, however, was done, and Jellicoe, reminding his colleagues that their

220 Distant Victory

overriding allegiances were to the Crown and the Royal Navy, not to him, kept a politic silence until the war had ended.

Beatty meanwhile found that, while he could occupy Jellicoe's post as commander in chief of the Grand Fleet, he was hardly able to fill his predecessor's shoes. Never popular with his officers and crews, Beatty was all pomp and bluster, and it is stretching the truth to deem him anything more than a competent fleet commander. The Grand Fleet was, in point of fact, the product of Jellicoe's creation: he had organized, trained, drilled, and led it for two and one-half years: his stamp had been indelibly placed on it, and as such it was a near-perfect instrument for the exercise of Great Britain's sea power in the decisive theater of the naval war. While he may have been the senior officer on the bridge of the flagship when the High Seas Fleet steamed into the Firth of Forth on November 21, 1918, there was no doubt among the officers and ratings in the Grand Fleet that what they were really witnessing was the vindication of Admiral Sir John Jellicoe and his strategy.

In 1919, Beatty was appointed an admiral of the Fleet—a rank he held until his retirement eight years later; in October of that same year he was also appointed First Sea Lord. He was granted a peerage and became Earl Beatty, Baron Beatty of the North Sea and Brooksby; Parliament voted him £100,000 in recognition of his service to Great Britain. He remained the darling of the British public, in part because of his fierce battles with politicians bent on cutting back the size of the Royal Navy in the name of economy. When he retired from the Navy he also retired from public life, but remained an active and vigorous man for the rest of his days; he remained in his bizarre marriage to Ethel Field until his death in March 1936. His body rests in St. Paul's Cathedral in London.

Franz von Hipper and Reinhard Scheer had very similar careers after the end of the First World War, which is to say that they had no careers whatsoever. Both men were brokenhearted by the defeat of Imperial Germany and the disbanding of the High Seas Fleet they both loved so much. There was no place for them in the rump of a navy allowed Germany by the Treaty of Versailles: in personality, in skill, and in reputation, their stature was simply too great to be able to fit into a "navy" that was barely the size of a single battle squadron in the Imperial Navy. So both men retired to a quiet life of semi-seclusion, living with their memories and their dreams. There is no evidence that either Scheer or von Hipper ever sought the other out after the war— they had been colleagues and comrades, but they were never truly friends.

Von Hipper kept almost entirely to himself in the years that followed the war, writing no memoirs and leaving few close friends behind. He flirted briefly with some of the more conservative political movements in the Weimar Republic during the 1920s, but never made the sort of mistake that

Distant Victory

Erich von Ludendorff made when he aligned himself with the fledgling Nazi Party and lost all remaining credibility as a consequence. Von Hipper lived long enough to watch the Nazis begin their rise to power, but was never invited to take any part in laying the foundations of the new High Seas Fleet. His name and reputation were carried on, however, in the new 10,000-ton heavy cruiser launched in 1938, named *Admiral Hipper;* however, by then the real Admiral von Hipper was long gone, having died in May 1932. His body was buried in Hamburg.

Reinhard Scheer's last decade was marred by personal as well as professional losses. The folly that drove him to formulate the High Seas Fleet's abortive final mission soon burned out, and with the dissolution of the Imperial government, the Imperial Navy as such ceased to exist. In the 18 months following the Armistice Scheer composed his memoirs, an eminently readable perspective on the naval war, though one with a rather questionable perspective. Still embracing the same arrogance that had led to the Naval High Command's reassurances that the U-boat campaign would succeed in defeating Great Britain whether or not the United States entered the war, Scheer concluded that Germany had not been defeated by the Allies, but rather that she had defeated herself. According to Scheer, Germany's unquestionable superiority in all aspects of military endeavor led the army and navy to overreach themselves, allowing the Allies to wait until Germany's economy and her population were exhausted.

As an exercise in self-justification, Scheer's memoirs are a masterpiece, but the thread of sour grapes that runs through them is unmistakable. All the same, it is understandable: the fall of the German Empire left Scheer without a career, and he found civilian life tedious in the extreme. It became worse in October 1920: his wife Emillie was killed in their home by an intruder; their daughter Else was seriously wounded in the same incident. One evening at dinner time, Scheer asked the housemaid to fetch a bottle of wine from the cellar; after some time had passed and she did not return, Emillie went looking for her, followed by their daughter Else. Scheer himself found all three in the cellar: they had been shot, his wife and the maid killed and Else seriously wounded. The intruder, a painter with a history of mental illness, had committed suicide in an adjoining cellar. Scheer spent his remaining years in near solitude; in 1928, he accepted an invitation from his old adversary at the Battle of Jutland, Admiral Jellicoe, to visit England, but just prior to his trip he died in Marktredwitz. He is buried in Weimar.

After the war was over, the Battle of Jutland was refought with an even greater ferocity than it had been originally, as both pro-Beatty and pro-Jellicoe partisans brought out books and monographs that sought to burnish the reputation of one at the expense of the other. The battle lines were clearly drawn, with Beatty the hero of the popular press, while Jellicoe had the weight of professional opinion—including that of several German officers—on his side; the only British officers who openly sided with Beatty were those who were professionally indebted to him in some way. Jellicoe, who had remained silent while storms of criticism raged around him during the war, now felt free to speak out in his own defense, and did so eloquently and convincingly. Beatty had his share of equally eloquent defenders, and so the "Jutland Controversy" raged for the next eight decades, as historians and naval experts, professional and amateur alike, weighed in with their opinions as to who "won" the Battle of Jutland. Yet for all their sound and fury they quibbled over "might have beens" instead of taking a longer view to see and understand what had really happened as a consequence of those furious hours on the afternoon of May 31, 1916.

Eventually Jellicoe grew tired of the debate and rose above it. Of all the four admirals of Jutland, it can be safely said that Jellicoe had the happiest life once the war ended. Very much in love with his wife Gwendolyn, he doted on his four surviving daughters. Husband and wife were astonished and delighted in 1918, when, Jellicoe then 59 years old, Gwendolyn at last gave birth to a baby boy, George Patrick.

In January 1918 he was raised to the peerage as Viscount Jellicoe of Scapa, although Parliament, under the thumb of the still-vindictive Lloyd George, voted him only half the sum granted to Beatty—£50,000; he was promoted admiral of the Fleet in 1919. In 1919 and 1920, Jellicoe was an expert naval advisor to the colonies and dominions, assisting them in organizing their fleets according to their specific defensive needs. In this role he visited Canada, New Zealand, Australia, and India, and one of his recommendations resulted in the construction of a major naval base at Singapore. He was appointed Governor General of New Zealand in 1920, a post he held for almost five years and by all accounts enjoyed immensely. In 1924 he was raised from viscount to earl; he retired from government service shortly thereafter.

His was not a sedentary retirement, though, as he served a term as president of the British Legion, got actively involved in the Boy Scouts and Boys' Brigade, and took a strong interest in Britain's National Rifle Association. His twilight years were not cloudless, however: as he grew older Jellicoe began to lose his hearing as well as his senses of smell and taste, and his eyesight began to fail. He attributed this decline of his senses to the many years' exposure to the concussion of battleships' heavy guns. Age eventually overtook him, and he died at his home in Kensington on November 20, 1935; he was 75 years old. Like Beatty, he was laid to rest in St. Paul's Cathedral, where he is in very good company—beside him are Admirals Horatio Nelson and Cuthbert Collingwood, the victors of Trafalgar.

Distant Victory

Jutland had been no Trafalgar, but then it never could have been. The "wooden walls" of Nelson's three-deckers were nearly indestructible: the Royal Navy won its victories in the "Age of Fighting Sail" by slaughtering enemy crews and then capturing their ships, not demolishing them. In the Age of Fighting Steel, that was no longer true: the ships themselves were now far more vulnerable than their crews, and were almost irreplaceable. The fate of the three British battlecruisers at Jutland proved only too well the validity of Churchill's analogy of dreadnoughts being "eggshells armed with hammers."

Nor could Jellicoe place his faith in the measure of his crews' competence over their adversaries: time and again in the course of the Great War the officers and ratings of the German Navy proved themselves every bit as proficient and courageous as their Royal Navy counterparts. The yawning chasm that separated the fighting skills of the British seamen of 1805 from their French and Spanish opponents did not exist in 1914.

And so Jellicoe fought a very different battle, one meant to maintain the Grand Fleet's quantitative supremacy over the High Seas Fleet and ensure that the German warships remained locked in the North Sea, utterly impotent, far from the Atlantic shipping lanes that were Great Britain's lifelines. As Churchill so correctly observed, Jellicoe was "the only man on either side who could lose the war in an afternoon." Thus to Jellicoe nothing but the preservation of the battle fleet mattered: all of his strategies, all of his tactics, were drawn up with this overarching requisite in mind.

Like Trafalgar, Jutland's consequences were not immediately felt, but they possessed a long reach and proved decisive. The myth that Jutland was somehow a German victory, or even just a draw, is simply that—a myth. For all of the bluster and posturing in his official report, Reinhard Scheer could not alter the fundamental fact that when dawn broke on June 1, 1916 the High Seas Fleet was limping back into its home port, while the Grand Fleet was cruising the open waters of the North Sea, ready to renew the battle. No amount of rhetoric or circumlocution could disguise the fact that the High Seas Fleet turned away from the enemy not once but twice within the span of an hour. If any more convincing demonstration of the Grand Fleet's ascendency was needed, it can be found in the signals each commander sent to his admiralty upon arriving in port: Scheer told Berlin that the High Seas Fleet would require at least two months to repair and refit before it would be able to put to sea; the Grand Fleet, Jellicoe informed London, needed only to refuel before it would be ready to sail again.

In the end, though, when taken in the longest view, Jutland can finally be seen for what it was—one of the decisive battles of the First World War. There is more to winning and losing a battle than simply numbers: victory or defeat cannot be determined by simply counting the killed, wounded, and missing —or in the case of a naval battle, by the number of ships sunk; it would be an exercise in superfluity to recount the major, decisive battles where the victors' losses exceeded those of the defeated forces. Jutland was decisive not because one fleet failed to destroy the other, but because something else was destroyed: Reinhard Scheer's faith in the High Seas Fleet's ability to defeat the Royal Navy. After Jutland, Scheer never again advocated a major fleet action as a strategic option for the Imperial Navy. Having seen first hand the power of the Grand Fleet, he instinctively understood that the High Seas Fleet simply lacked the strength to cripple the Grand Fleet, and that nothing less would be required if German warships were to ever reach the North Atlantic. Instead, he threw his wholehearted support behind what became the panacea of German naval strategy: unrestricted submarine warfare; so great was his newfound enthusiasm that it carried his commanding officer, Admiral Henning von Holtzendorff, with it.

Scheer never fully articulated how his change of heart came about, yet the inescapable conclusion is that it was produced by his experience at Jutland. Certainly Scheer was no coward, but something broke within him that May afternoon, for he was never again the fiercely aggressive sailor he had been before the battle. Jutland disabused Scheer and his fellow admirals of any illusions they may have held about a triumphant High Seas Fleet. The decisive effect of the Battle of Jutland was that it drove them to choose the path of risk; in the end by accepting, even embracing, that risk, Germany paid the price in defeat.

After the Battle of Jutland, almost a year passed before the United States joined the Allies in making war on Germany, nearly two and one-half years went by before that cool, brisk November morning when the warships of the High Seas Fleet steamed into internment off the Firth of Forth. And yet, when they did, they were silently confirming that for the Royal Navy, for Great Britain, and for the Allies, the Battle of Jutland had, indeed, been a victory. It had just been a distant victory.

Epilogue

Scapa Flow

It was Saturday, June 21, 1919, when some 400 local school children were patiently waiting at Stromness, a small port in the northwest corner of Scapa Flow, to board an Admiralty tender, *Flying Kestrel,* which would take them on a tour of the Flow, including a cruise past the now infamous fleet of interned German warships off Hoy. It was a special occasion, for the Royal Navy rarely permitted sightseers near the German ships. The morning was sunny and breezy, and as the tender cast off at about 9:30 AM, some of the children were almost hopping with excitement. As a sort of added treat, they got to watch as the Grand Fleet, now renamed the Home Fleet and under the command of Admiral Sir Sydney Fremantle, weighed anchor and steamed majestically out of Scapa Flow for gunnery practice in the North Sea. It promised to be an exciting outing: they had no idea just how exciting it would be.

With the fleet gone, only a handful of trawlers and destroyers were left to guard the German ships. This was the moment for which Rear Admiral Ludwig von Reuter had been hoping and preparing during the previous months. Sometime around 10:00 AM he strode out onto the quarterdeck of his makeshift flagship, SMS *Emden,* wearing his full dress uniform. At 1030 a string of flags ran up the signal halyards, bearing a curious, plain-text message. It read: "Paragraph 11. Confirm." It was the prearranged signal for ships of the High Seas Fleet to commence the systematic scuttling of the entire fleet.

Aboard every German warship the forbidden ensign of the Imperial German Navy rose to the masthead, while officers and seamen set to work, opening sea cocks, knocking the heads off condenser valves, jamming open torpedo tube doors, and prying up bilge plates. Portholes, hatches, and watertight doors were jammed open, some were taken off their hinges, while others had been removed altogether days in advance. On some ships bulkheads had

226 Distant Victory

been deliberately weakened so that they would collapse as the pressure from the incoming water rose, accelerating the sinkings. The crews were making certain that, once the flooding began, there would be no way to stop it.

The possibility that the German fleet would be scuttled had been widely feared by the Royal Navy, but the British knew that in reality there was little they could do to prevent it. Rear Admiral von Reuter had decided that if the peace talks at Versailles failed to produce a treaty before the Armistice expired—at which time the war would technically be resumed—he would order the entire Fleet sunk rather than let the British have the ships. Unfortunately for von Reuter, his decision to send the ships to the bottom came about because he had to rely on four-day-old copies of *The Times* for information on the peace conference.

The newspaper reported that talks at Versailles were in chaos, a final peace agreement was nowhere in sight, and the expiration of the Armistice appeared to be inevitable. The British government, in the person of the Prime Minister, David Lloyd George, was growing exasperated with what it regarded as Germany's intransigence in accepting the terms and conditions that the Allies presented to her and finally gave the German representatives an ultimatum: accept the peace terms already laid down by noon on June 21 or face a resumption of the war. Von Reuter read this in mid-June and decided that the time had come for what was left of the Imperial Navy to act. What he did not know is that on the same day Great Britain issued her ultimatum, Germany capitulated, accepted the terms, and the Armistice was extended until June 23 to finish the details of the final draft of the treaty.

Having given the possibility—in truth almost a certainty, for in his heart von Reuter must have known that there was no realistic chance of the German ships ever being sent home—that scuttling the fleet would be necessary, the admiral had carefully thought out a plan for making it happen, designed to prevent any possibility of the British being able to intervene to immediately save the ships or raise them later and return them to service. Orders and instructions were passed from *Emden* throughout the fleet via signal flags and semaphores, and soon every remaining officer and crewman aboard the interned warships knew what was expected of him. When von Reuter's cryptic signal was hoisted at 1030 that morning, the fate of the High Seas Fleet was sealed.

So widely scattered were the German ships that it took nearly an hour before they all acknowledged the signal. But it took far less time than that before the effects of the crewmen's action became apparent: within a quarter hour some of the German ships were listing noticeably, others were rocking as their stability gradually deteriorated. The first German ship to sink was *Friedrich der Grösse*—Scheer's flagship at Jutland. She rolled over onto her starboard side and went under at 1216. *Bayern* soon followed, also rolling over before disappearing into the waters of the Flow. *Hindenburg,* moored in shallow water, began slowly settling on an even keel. All over Scapa Flow, steam, oil, and odd bits of debris were blasting out of hatch covers and port-holes as the 74 German ships anchored there began sinking.

As soon as their work was done, the German crews quickly fled the sinking ships, some taking to their ships' boats, many of which displayed white flags as a measure of protection lest the scuttling provoked an armed response from the British guardships. On some of the German ships the crews simply jumped into the water, depending on the goodwill of the British patrol craft to pick them up. There were a few violent incidents: in one case a German sailor was shot as he attempted to cut his boat free of a sinking ship; in another the captain of one of the German warships was shot in the head while waving a white flag. All told, nine German sailors were killed as the crews of the guardships responded spasmodically to the confusion surrounding them; no one lost his life through drowning.

The only British warships present, as opposed to trawlers and smaller craft, were the destroyers *Vespa* and *Vega,* which were frantically signaling the First Battle Squadron of the suddenly chaotic developments in Scapa; soon the British Fleet was thundering back to its anchorage, arriving at 1400. Desperate attempts were made to save some of the German ships: the battleship *Baden* and the cruisers *Nürnberg, Emden,* and *Frankfurt* were all beached before they sank, along with a handful of destroyers. But the rest of the High Seas Fleet was inexorably sinking into the dark waters of the Flow; at 1700 the last ship still afloat, *Hindenburg,* finally settled on the bottom.

It was a spectacle that the schoolchildren aboard *Flying Kestrel* never forgot. Decades later James Taylor, who was among them, recalled how:

> Suddenly without any warning and almost simultaneously these huge vessels began to list over to port or starboard; some heeled over and plunged head-long, their sterns lifted high out of the water. Out of the vents rushed steam and oil and air with a dreadful roaring hiss. And as we watched, awestruck and silent, the sea became littered for miles round with boats and hammocks, life belts and chests....

One of his companions later recalled:

> During that time we watched the marvelous display as the German ships sank all around us. I counted them, 12 capital ships going down. Some went up by the bows, some by the stern and some stood up in the water....

By the time the British fleet returned to Scapa, the Flow was in chaos. Some battleships were falling over onto their sides, others had already turned

228   Distant Victory

turtle and sunk. Admiral Fremantle, furious over what he considered a serious breach of good faith and naval etiquette, immediately sent word that Rear Admiral von Reuter be brought aboard the flagship. When von Reuter appeared, Fremantle angrily demanded to know why the German fleet had been scuttled. Von Reuter replied, "The stain of dishonor has been washed from the escutcheon of the German Navy." Within a matter of days, the British, disgusted with von Reuter and his men, shipped them back to Germany.

Publicly the British Government and the Royal Navy were outraged, but privately there was a realization that the Germans had, in a way, done the British a favor. With the German ships at the bottom of Scapa Flow, the question of dividing them between the victorious powers was now moot. At the same time British Intelligence tried to establish that the scuttling had been authorized by Berlin, but proof, if any ever existed, was never found. In all, five battlecruisers, *Seydlitz, Moltke, Von der Tann, Derfflinger,* and *Hindenburg;* ten battleships, *Kaiser, Prinzregent Luitpold, Kaiserin, König Albert, Friedrich der Grösse, König, Grösser Kurfürst, Kronprinz Wilhelm, Markgraf,* and *Bayern;* five cruisers; and 31 destroyers were sunk. The rest were beached and saved, only to later be seized by the Royal Navy, sold, and cut up for scrap.

Inevitably the question of salvaging the remains of the High Seas Fleet arose. Originally the British Admiralty was content to simply let the wrecks rust where they lay, but many of them were hazards to navigation. It was not until 1922 that the first efforts at raising any of the wrecks were made: a handful of destroyers lying in shallow water were brought up rather easily. The deeper wrecks—and these included almost all of the capital ships—were a different story: throughout the 1920s and 1930s most of these boats were raised by a London scrap metal dealer named Ernest Cox. In 1923 he bought the salvage rights to most of the battleships and battlecruisers, as well as more than 20 of the scuttled destroyers; by the end of 1925, 18 of the latter had been salvaged. For the larger ships, entirely new methods of underwater salvage had to be devised, and Cox set out on what became the most complex salvage operation ever conducted up to that time. Work began on *Hindenburg* in 1926, but the first effort failed as a gale struck Scapa Flow just as the wreck was being brought up. After two more unsuccessful attempts on *Hindenburg,* Cox turned to *Moltke,* which was lying nearly upside down in fairly shallow water; bringing her up took nine months. Next was *Seydlitz,* which lay on her side in 60 feet of water: after two years of work she was raised in November 1928. The wreck of *Kaiser,* sitting even deeper at 140 feet, was next; she came up in March 1929 and, like the wrecks already raised, went to the breakers' yard in Rosyth to be broken up and scrapped. After bringing up the cruiser *Bremse,* it was the turn of *Hindenburg* again, and she was finally salvaged in July 1930.

The recovery of *von der Tann* and *Prinzregent Luitpold* followed, and proved to be the most dangerous jobs yet, as explosive gasses trapped inside the wrecks were accidentally ignited from time to time, one of the resulting blasts killing one diver. These ships were the last brought up by Cox, who gave up the salvage as a bad business: in eight years the salvage had lost £10,000 but had made his name as an innovative salvager. In 1933 he sold the salvage rights to the remaining ships to the Alloa Shipbreaking Company.

The last five ships to be raised—*Bayern, Grösser Kurfürst, Kaiserin, Friedrich der Grösse,* and *Derfflinger*—were brought up by Alloa during the 1930s. As the Second World War loomed in 1939, all salvage efforts were suspended. Minor recovery efforts on the remaining wrecks were made after the war, but they lie so deep that today there is no real economic incentive to bring them up. Apart from the occasional piece of radiation-free steel, essential to certain types of scientific instruments unavailable in steel produced since the explosion of the first atomic device, recovered from time to time, the wrecks are left undisturbed.

In the little village of Stromness it is hard to avoid the history of the German scuttle. Mugs, whisky glasses, shirts, tea towels, and other souvenirs commemorating June 21, 1919, are sold in local shops. In the summer dive boats venture out to the site of the wrecks daily, carrying scuba divers intent on exploring the remains of the ships; the water is cold and the currents are swift, so only the most experienced divers are permitted to go down to the wrecks. Stromness Museum has a remarkable collection of artifacts from the scuttled Fleet—crockery, uniforms, navigational instruments, and ships' bells. Another museum, this one in Lyness on the island of Hoy, within sight of where most of the German ships were anchored and sank, tells the story of Scapa Flow in the two wars; outside, boats filled with sightseers tour the hauntingly beautiful waters. Until they take such a tour, few aboard those boats would ever know that they were passing over the remains of the Kaiser's navy. Once the Royal Navy's mightiest anchorage, now all but forgotten, Scapa Flow remains the grave of the High Seas Fleet, a ghost fleet forever entombed in the stronghold of its most powerful enemy.

Appendix I

Royal Navy Order of Battle—The Grand Fleet at Jutland

Order of Battle, 1400 hours, May 31, 1916

The Battle Fleet

First Battle Squadron

HMS *Marlborough* (Flagship of Vice Admiral Sir Cecil Burney; Capt. G.P. Ross) *Iron Duke*-class battleship

HMS *Hercules* (Capt. L. Clinton-Baker) *Colossus*-class battleship

HMS *Agincourt* (Capt. H.M. Doughty) ex-*Rio de Janiero,* ex-*Rashidieh,* 1914, 14–12-inch guns; 27,500 tons

HMS *Colossus* (Flagship of Rear Admiral E.F.A. Gaunt; Capt. A.D.P.R. Pound) *Colossus*-class battleship

HMS *St Vincent* (Capt. W.W. Fisher) 1910, 10–12-inch guns; 19,250 tons

HMS *Collingwood* (Capt. J.C. Ley) *St. Vincent*-class battleship

HMS *Neptune* (Capt. V.H.G. Bernard) 1911, 10–12-inch guns; capacity 19,900 tons

Second Battle Squadron

HMS *King George V* (Flagship of Vice Admiral Sir Martyn Jerram; Capt. F.L. Field) 1913, 10–13.5-inch guns; 23,000 tons

HMS *Ajax* (Capt. G.H. Baird) *King George V*-class battleship

HMS *Centurion* (Capt. M. Culme-Seymour) *King George V*-class battleship

HMS *Erin* (Capt. The Hon. V.A. Stanley) 1914, 10–13.5-inch guns; 23,000 tons

HMS *Orion* (Flagship of Rear Admiral A.C. Leveson; Capt. O. Backhouse) 1912, 10–13.5-inch guns; 22,500 tons

Appendix I

HMS *Monarch* (Capt. G.H. Borrett) *Orion*-class battleship

HMS *Conqueror* (Capt. H.H.D. Tothill) *Orion*-class battleship

HMS *Thunderer* (Capt. J.A. Fergusson) *Orion*-class battleship

Fourth Battle Squadron

HMS *Iron Duke* (Fleet Flagship of Admiral Sir John Jellicoe; Capt. F.C. Dreyer) 1913, 10–13.5-inch guns; 25,000 tons

HMS *Superb* (Flagship of Rear Admiral A.L. Duff; Capt. E. Hyde-Parker) *Bellerophon*-class battleship

HMS *Canada* (Capt. W.C.M. Nicholson) 1914, 10–13.5-inch guns; 25,000 tons

HMS *Benbow* (Flagship of Vice Admiral Sir Doveton Sturdee; Capt. H.W. Parker) *Iron Duke*-class battleship

HMS *Bellerophon* (Capt. E.F. Bruen) *Bellerophon*-class battleship

HMS *Temeraire* (Capt. E.V. Underhill) *Bellerophon*-class battleship

HMS *Vanguard* (Capt. J.D. Dick) *Bellerophon*-class battleship

Third Battlecruiser Squadron

(temporarily attached to Grand Fleet)

HMS *Invincible* (Flagship of Rear Admiral The Hon. H.L.A. Hood; Capt. A.L. Cay) 1908, 8–12-inch guns; 17,250 tons

HMS *Inflexible* (Capt. E.H.F. Heaton-Ellis) *Invincible*-class battlecruiser

HMS *Indomitable* (Capt. F.W. Kennedy) *Invincible*-class battlecruiser

First Cruiser Squadron

(armored cruisers)

HMS *Defence* (Flagship of Rear Admiral Sir Robert Arbuthnot; Capt. S.V. Ellis)

HMS *Warrior* (Capt. V.B. Molteno)

HMS *Duke of Edinburgh* (Capt. H. Blackett)

HMS *Black Prince* (Capt. T.P. Bonham)

Second Cruiser Squadron

(armored cruisers)

HMS *Minotaur* (Flagship of Rear Admiral H.L. Heath; Capt. A.C.S.H. D'Aeth)

HMS *Shannon* (Capt. J.S. Dumaresq)

HMS *Hampshire* (Capt. H.J. Savill)

HMS *Cochrane* (Capt. E. La T. Leatham)

Fourth Light Cruiser Squadron

HMS *Calliope* (Commodore C.E. Le Mesurier)
HMS *Constance* (Capt. C.S. Townsend)
HMS *Caroline* (Capt. H.R. Crooke)
HMS *Royalist* (Capt. The Hon. H. Meade)
HMS *Comus* (Capt. A.G. Hotham)

Attached Light Cruisers

HMS *Active* (Capt. P. Withers)
HMS *Bellona* (Capt. A.B.S. Dutton)
HMS *Blanche* (Capt. J.M. Casement)
HMS *Boadicea* (Capt. L.C.S. Woollcombe)
HMS *Canterbury* (Capt. P.M.R. Royds)
HMS *Chester* (Capt. R.N. Lawson)

Fourth Destroyer Flotilla

HMS *Tipperary* (Capt. C.J. Wintour)
HMS *Acasta*
HMS *Achates*
HMS *Ambuscade*
HMS *Ardent*
HMS *Broke*
HMS *Christopher*
HMS *Contest*
HMS *Fortune*
HMS *Garland*
HMS *Hardy*
HMS *Midge*
HMS *Ophelia*
HMS *Owl*
HMS *Porpoise*
HMS *Shark*
HMS *Sparrowhawk*
HMS *Spitfire*
HMS *Unity*

Eleventh Destroyer Flotilla

HMS *Castor* (light cruiser) (Commodore J.R.P. Hawksley)
HMS *Kempenfelt*
HMS *Magic*
HMS *Mandate*
HMS *Manners*
HMS *Marne*
HMS *Martial*
HMS *Michael*
HMS *Milbrook*
HMS *Minion*
HMS *Mons*
HMS *Moon*
HMS *Morning Star*
HMS *Mornsey*
HMS *Mystic*
HMS *Ossory*

Twelfth Destroyer Flotilla

HMS *Faulknor* (Capt. A.J.B. Stirling)
HMS *Maenad*
HMS *Marksman*
HMS *Marvel*
HMS *Mary Rose*
HMS *Menace*
HMS *Mindful*
HMS *Mischief*
HMS *Munster*
HMS *Narwhal*
HMS *Nessus*
HMS *Noble*
HMS *Nonsuch*
HMS *Obedient*
HMS *Onslaught*
HMS *Opal*

Miscellaneous Ships

HMS *Abdiel* (Minelayer)

HMS *Oak* (Destroyer tender to the fleet flagship)

The Battlecruiser Fleet

Flagship

HMS *Lion* (Flagship of Vice Admiral Sir David Beatty; Capt. A.E.M. Chatfield) 1912, 8–13.5-inch guns; 26,270 tons

First Battlecruiser Squadron

HMS *Princess Royal* (Flagship of Rear Admiral O. de B. Brock; Capt. W.H. Cowan) *Lion*-class battlecruiser

HMS *Queen Mary* (Capt. C.I. Prowse) modified *Lion*-class battlecruiser

HMS *Tiger* (Capt. H.B. Pelly) *Lion*-class battlecruiser

Second Battlecruiser Squadron

HMS *New Zealand* (Flagship of Rear Admiral W.C. Pakenham; Capt. J.F.E. Green) *Indefatigable*-class battlecruiser

HMS *Indefatigable* (Capt. C.F. Sowerby) 1911, 8–12-inch guns; 18,800 tons

Fifth Battle Squadron

(temporarily attached to the battlecruiser fleet)

HMS *Barham* (Flagship of Rear Admiral H. Evan-Thomas; Capt. A.W. Craig) *Queen Elizabeth*-class battleship (1915, 8–15-inch guns; 27,500 tons)

HMS *Valiant* (Capt. M. Woollcombe) *Queen Elizabeth*-class battleship

HMS *Warspite* (Capt. E.M. Philpotts) *Queen Elizabeth*-class battleship

HMS *Malaya* (Capt. The Hon. A.D.E.H. Boyle) *Queen Elizabeth*-class battleship

First Light Cruiser Squadron

HMS *Galatea* (Commodore E.S. Alexander-Sinclair)

HMS *Phaeton* (Capt. J.E. Cameron)

HMS *Inconstant* (Capt. B.S. Thesiger)

HMS *Cordelia* (Capt. T.P.H. Beamish)

Second Light Cruiser Squadron

HMS *Southampton* (Commodore W.E. Goodenough)

HMS *Birmingham* (Capt. A.A.M. Duff)

236   Appendix I

HMS *Nottingham* (Capt. C.B. Miller)

HMS *Dublin* (Capt. A.C. Scott)

Third Light Cruiser Squadron

HMS *Falmouth* (Flagship of Rear Admiral T.D.W. Napier; Capt. J.D. Edwards)

HMS *Yarmouth* (Capt. T.D. Pratt)

HMS *Birkenhead* (Capt. E. Reeves)

HMS *Gloucester* (Capt. W.F. Blount)

First Destroyer Flotilla

HMS *Fearless* (light cruiser) (Capt. C.D. Roper)

HMS *Acheron*

HMS *Ariel*

HMS *Attack*

HMS *Badger*

HMS *Defender*

HMS *Goshawk*

HMS *Hydra*

HMS *Lapwing*

HMS *Lizard*

Ninth and Tenth Destroyer Flotillas (combined)

HMS *Lydiard* (Commander M.L. Goldsmith)

HMS *Landrail*

HMS *Laurel*

HMS *Liberty*

HMS *Moorsom*

HMS *Morris*

HMS *Termagent*

HMS *Turbulent*

Thirteenth Destroyer Flotilla

HMS *Champion* (light cruiser) (Capt. J.U. Farie)

HMS *Moresby*

HMS *Narborough*

HMS *Nerissa*

HMS *Nestor*

Appendix I   **237**

HMS *Nicator*

HMS *Nomad*

HMS *Obdurate*

HMS *Onslow*

HMS *Pelican*

HMS *Petard*

Seaplane Carrier

HMS *Engadine*

Appendix II

Imperial Navy Order of Battle— The High Seas Fleet at Jutland

The High Seas Fleet

Order of Battle, 1400 hours, May 31, 1916

The Battle Fleet

First Battle Squadron

Friedrich der Grösse (Fleet Flagship of Vice Admiral Reinhard Scheer; Capt. T. Fuchs) *Kaiser*-class battleship

Ostfriesland (Flagship of Vice Admiral E. Schmidt; Capt. von Natzmer) 1911, 12 guns 305 mm, 22,400 tons

Thüringen (Capt. H Küsel) *Ostfriesland*-class battleship

Helgoland (Capt. von Kameke) *Ostfriesland*-class battleship

Oldenburg (Capt. Höpfner) *Ostfriesland*-class battleship

Posen (Flagship of Rear Admiral Engelhardt; Capt. Lange) *Nassau*-class battleship

Rheinland (Capt. Rohardt) *Nassau*-class battleship

Nassau (Capt. H. Klappenbach) 1910, 12 guns 280 mm, 18,570 tons

Westfalen (Capt. Redlich) *Nassau*-class battleship

Second Battle Squadron

Deutschland (Flagship of Rear Admiral Mauve; Capt. H. Meurer) 1906, 4 guns 280 mm, 14,200 tons

Pommern (Capt. Bölken) *Deutschland*-class predreadnought

Hannover (Flagship of Rear Admiral F. von Dalwigk zu Lichtenfels; Capt. W. Heine) *Deutschland*-class predreadnought

Schlesien (Capt. F. Behncke) Deutschland-class predreadnought

Schleswig-Holstein (Capt. Barrentrapp) Deutschland-class predreadnought

Hessen (Capt. R. Bartels) Braunschweig-class predreadnought 1904, 4 guns 280 mm, 13,200 tons

Third Battle Squadron

König (Flagship of Rear Admiral Paul Behncke; Capt. Brüninghaus) 1914, 10 guns 305 mm, 25,390 tons

Grosser Kurfürst (Capt. E. Goette) König-class battleship

Kronprinz Wilhelm (Capt. C. Feldt) König-class battleship

Markgraf (Capt. Seiferling) König-class battleship

Kaiser (Flagship of Rear Admiral Nordmann; Capt. F. von Kayserlink) 1912, 10 guns 305 mm, 24,330 tons

Kaiserin (Capt. Sievers Heuser) Kaiser-class battleship

Prinz Regent Luitpold (Capt. K. Heuser) Kaiser-class battleship

Fourth Scouting Group (Light Cruisers)

Stettin (Broad pendant of Commodore von Reuter; Capt. F. Regensburg)

München (Capt. O. Böcker)

Hamburg (Commander von Gaudecker)

Frauenlob (Capt. G. Hoffmann)

Stuttgart (Capt. Hagedorn)

Torpedo Boats

Rostock (Light cruiser) (Broad pendant of Commodore Michelson; Capt. O. Feldmann)

First Flotilla (half)—4 boats under Commander C. Albrecht in G39

Third Flotilla—7 boats under Captain Hollmann in S53

Fifth Flotilla—11 boats under Captain Heinecke in G11

Seventh Flotilla—9 boats under Captain von Koch in S24

First Scouting Group (Battlecruisers)

Lützow (Flagship of Vice Admiral Franz von Hipper; Capt. Harder) Derfflinger-class battlecruiser

Derfflinger (Capt. Hartog) 1914, 8 guns 305 mm, 26,200 tons

Seydlitz (Capt. M. von Egidy) 1913, 10 guns 280 mm, 25,000 tons

Moltke (Capt. von Karpf) 1912, 10 guns 280 mm, 22,600 tons

Von der Tann (Capt. Hans Zenker) 1911, 8 guns 280 mm, 19,100 tons

Second Scouting Group (Light Cruisers)

Frankfurt (Flagship of Rear Admiral Bödicker; Capt. T. von Trotha)

Wiesbaden (Capt. Reiss)

Pillau (Capt. Mommsen)

Elbing (Capt. Madlung)

Torpedo Boats

Regensburg (Light cruiser) (Broad pendant of Commodore Heinrich; Capt. Heuberer)

Second Flotilla—10 boats under Captain Schuur in *B98*

Sixth Flotilla—9 boats under Captain Schultz in *G41*

Ninth Flotilla—11 boats under Captain Goehle in *V28*

Sources

Admiralty. *Battle of Jutland, Official Despatches with Appendices.* 2 vols. London: HMSO, n.d.

Bacon, Admiral Sir Reginald. *The Jutland Scandal.* Rev. ed. London: Hodder and Stoughton, 1929.

———. *The Life of Earl Jellicoe.* London: Cassell, 1936.

Baker, Ray S. *Woodrow Wilson, Life and Letters.* Garden City, NY: Doubleday, Page and Company, 1935.

Barnett, Corelli. *The Sword Bearers.* New York: William Morrow, 1964.

Bassett, Ronald. *Battle Cruisers: A History 1908–1948.* London: Macmillan, 1981.

Beatty, Charles. *Our Admiral.* London: W. H. Allen, 1980.

Beatty, David. *The Beatty Papers.* 2 vols. Edited by B. McL. Ranft. London: Navy Records Society, 1989–1993.

Beesly, Patrick. *Room 40: British Naval Intelligence, 1914–1918.* London: Hamish Hamilton, 1982.

Bell, A.C. *A History of the Blockade of Germany, 1914–1918.* London: HMSO, 1961.

Bennett, Geoffrey. *The Battle of Jutland.* Barnesly, South Yorkshire: Pen & Sword Books, 1999.

Bernsdorff, Count Johann von. *My Three Years in America.* New York: Eric Sutton, 1936.

Bethmann-Hollweg, Theobald von. *Reflections on the World War.* London: Butterworth, 1920.

Borchard, Edwin, and W.P. Lage. *Neutrality for the United States.* New Haven, CT: Thomas Ward, 1937.

Breyer, Siegfried. *Battleships and Battle Cruisers, 1905–1970.* New York: Doubleday, 1973.

Burt, R.A. *British Battleships of World War I.* Annapolis: U.S. Naval Institute Press, 1986.

244 Sources

Butler, Daniel Allen. *The Age of Cunard: A Transatlantic History, 1839–2003.* Culver City: Lighthouse Press, 2004.

———. *The Lusitania—The Life, Loss, and Legacy of an Ocean Legend.* Mechanicsburg: Stackpole, 2000.

Carnegie Endowment for International Peace. *Official German Documents Relating to the World War.* 2 vols. New York: Oxford University Press, 1923.

Chickering, Roger. *Imperial Germany and the Great War, 1914–1918.* Cambridge, U.K.: Cambridge University Press, 1998.

Churchill, Winston S. *The World Crisis.* 6 vols. New York: Charles Scribner's Sons, 1926–1931.

Compton-Hall, Richard. *Submarine Boats: The Beginnings of Undersea Warfare.* New York: Arco Publishing, 1984.

Dönitz, Grand Admiral Karl. *Memoirs: Ten Years and Twenty Days.* Annapolis: U.S. Naval Institute Press, 1959.

Fawcett, H. W., and G. W. W. Hooper. *The Fighting at Jutland: The Personal Experiences of Forty-five Officers and Men of the British Fleet.* London: Macmillan, 1921.

Fisher, Admiral of the Fleet John Arbuthnot. *Fear God and Dreadnought: Correspondence of Admiral of the Fleet Lord Fisher.* 3 vols. Edited by A. J. Marder. London: Jonathan Cape, 1952–1959.

———. *Memories and Records.* London: Doran, 1920.

Freiwald, Ludwig. *Last Days of the German Fleet.* London: Constable, 1932.

Frost, Wesley. *German Submarine Warfare: A Study of Its Methods and Spirit.* New York: D. Appleton and Company, 1918.

Gilbert, Martin. *The First World War, a Complete History.* New York: Henry Holt and Company, 1994.

Goodenough, Admiral Sir William. *A Rough Record.* London and New York: Hutchinson, 1943.

Gordon, Andrew. *The Rules of the Game: Jutland and British Naval Command.* Annapolis: U.S. Naval Institute Press, 1996.

Gray, Edwyn A. *The U-Boat War, 1914–1918.* London: Leo Cooper, 1994.

Haythornewaite, Philip J. *The World War One Sourcebook.* London: Arms and Armour Press, 1992.

Horne, Charles F., ed. *The Great Events of the Great War.* 7 vols. N.p.: The National Alumni, 1921.

Horton, Edward. *Submarine.* New York: MacMillan, 1963.

Hough, Richard. *The Great War at Sea, 1914–1918.* New York: Oxford University Press, 1983.

Howard, Michael. *The First World War.* New York: Oxford University Press, 2002.

Hubatsch, Walther. *Die Ära Tirpitz: Studien zur Deutschen Marinepolitik 1890–1918.* Göttigen, Federal Republic of Germany: Musterschmidt Verlag, 1955.

Jane, Fred T. *Jane's Fighting Ships, 1914.* London: Hodder and Stoughton, 1914.

———. *Jane's Fighting Ships of World War I.* Reprint, London: Random House, 1990.

Jarausch, Konrad H. *The Enigmatic Chancellor: Bethmann-Hollweg and the Hubris of Imperial Germany.* New Haven: Yale University Press, 1973.

Sources

245

Jellicoe, Admiral of the Fleet Sir John. *The Grand Fleet 1914–1916.* London: Cassell, 1919.

———. *The Submarine Peril.* London: Cassell, 1934.

———. *The Jellicoe Papers.* 2 vols. Edited by A. Temple Patterson. Navy Records Society, 1966.

Kahn, David. *The Code Breakers.* New York: MacMillan and Company, 1967.

Keegan, John. *August 1914: Opening Moves.* New York: Ballantine, 1971.

———. *The First World War.* New York: Alfred A. Knopf, 1999.

———. *The Price of Admiralty.* New York: Viking, 1989.

Kennedy, Paul. *The Rise and Fall of British Naval Mastery.* Malabar, FL: Robert E. Krieger, 1982.

———. *The Rise of Anglo-German Antagonism.* London: Allen and Unwin, 1982.

———. *Strategy and Diplomacy, 1870–1945.* London: Fontana, 1984.

Koop, Gerhard, and Erich Mulitze. *Die Marine in Wilhelmshaven.* Koblenz: Bernard und Gräfe Verlag, 1987.

Legg, Stuart. *Jutland.* New York: John Day, 1966.

Link, Arthur S. *Wilson: The Struggle for Neutrality.* Princeton, NJ: Princeton University Press, 1960.

London, Charles. *Jutland 1916.* Oxford: Osprey Publishing, 2000.

Macintyre, Captain Donald. *Jutland.* London: Evans Brothers, 1957.

Manchester, William. *The Arms of Krupp.* Boston: Little, Brown and Company, 1968.

———. *The Last Lion, Winston Spencer Churchill: Visions of Glory, 1874–1932.* Boston: Little, Brown and Company, 1983.

Marder, Arthur J. *From the Dreadnought to Scapa Flow.* 4 vols. Oxford: Oxford University Press, 1964–1970.

———. *The Anatomy of British Seapower.* New York: Octagon Books, 1976.

Massie, Robert K. *Castles of Steel—Britain, Germany and the Winning of the Great War at Sea.* New York: Random House, 2003.

———. *Dreadnought—Britain, Germany and the Coming of the Great War.* New York: Random House, 1991.

May, Ernest R. *The World War and American Isolation.* Cambridge, MA: Harvard University Press, 1959.

Middleton, Drew. *Submarine: The Ultimate Naval Weapon, Its Past, Present and Future.* Chicago: Playboy Press, 1976.

Millis, Walter. *Road to War, America, 1914–1917.* Boston: Houghton, Mifflin and Company, 1934.

Moorehead, Alan. *Gallipoli.* London: G.B. Harper, 1956.

Oakeshott, Ewart. *The Blindfold Game: "The Day" at Jutland.* London and New York: Pergamon Press, 1969.

Padfield, Peter. *The Battleship Era.* London: Rupert Hart-Davis, 1972.

Patterson, A. Temple. *Jellicoe: A Biography.* London: Macmillan, 1969.

Paxon, Frederic L. *The Pre-war Years, 1913–1917.* Boston: Houghton, Mifflin and Company, 1936.

Phillbin, Tobias R. *Admiral von Hipper: The Inconvenient Hero.* Amsterdam: B.R.

Gruner, 1982.

Reuter, Rear Admiral Ludwig von. *Scapa Flow: An Account of the Scuttling.* London: Hurst and Blackett, 1940.

Ritter, Gerhard. *The Sword and the Scepter: The Problem of Militarism in Germany.* 4 vols. Coral Gables: University of Miami Press, 1972.

Rosskill, Captain S. W. *Earl Beatty: The Last Naval Hero.* New York: Atheneum, 1981.

Ruge, Vice Admiral Friedrich. *Scapa Flow 1919: The End of the German Fleet.* London: Ian Allen, 1973.

Scheer, Admiral Reinhard. *Germany's High Seas Fleet in the World War.* New York: Peter Smith, 1934.

Sidman, Charles F. *The German Collapse in 1918.* Lawrence, KS: Coronado Press, 1972.

Smith, Gene. *When the Cheering Stopped: The Last Years of Woodrow Wilson.* New York: William Morrow, 1964.

Spector, Ronald H. *At War at Sea: Sailors and Naval Combat in the Twentieth Century.* New York: Viking, 2001.

Spindler, Rear Admiral Arno. *Der Handelskrieg mit U-Booten.* 5 vols. Berlin: Ernst Mittler und Sohn, 1932–1966.

Strachan, Hew, ed. *World War I: A History.* New York: Oxford University Press, 1998.

Tarrant, V. E. *Battlecruiser Invincible.* Annapolis: U.S. Naval Institute Press, 1986.

———. *Battleship Warspite.* Annapolis: U.S. Naval Institute Press, 1990.

———. *Jutland: The German Perspective.* Annapolis: U.S. Naval Institute Press, 1995.

———. *The U-boat Offensive, 1914–1945.* Annapolis: U.S. Naval Institute Press, 1989.

Taylor, J. C. *German Warships of World War I.* London: Ian Allen, 1969.

Terraine, John. *The U-boat Wars, 1916–1945.* New York: Putnam, 1989.

Tirpitz, Grand Admiral Alfred von. *My Memoirs.* New York: Hurst and Blackett, 1919.

Tuchman, Barbara. *The Guns of August.* New York: MacMillan and Company, 1962.

———. *The Zimmerman Telegram.* New York: MacMillan and Company, 1958.

Van der Vat, Dan. *The Grand Scuttle.* Annapolis: U.S. Naval Institute Press, 1986.

Vincent, C. Paul. *The Politics of Hunger: The Allied Blockade of Germany, 1915–1919.* Athens, OH: Ohio University Press, 1985.

Waldeyer-hartz, Captain Hugo von. *Admiral von Hipper.* London: Rich and Cowan, 1933.

Wegner, Vice Admiral Wolfgang. *The Naval Strategy of the World War.* London: Rich and Cowan, 1933.

Wilhelm II. *My Memoirs, 1878–1918.* London: Cassell, 1922.

Winton, John. *Jellicoe.* London: Michael Joseph, 1981.

Yates, Keith. *Flawed Victory: Jutland 1916.* Annapolis, U.S. Naval Institute Press, 2000.

Index

Note: Flag rank officers are indexed under the most senior grade attained when appearing in the narrative. Also, only ships mentioned in the body of the text are listed.

Ancona, 25
Arabic, 25
Arbuthnot, Rear Admiral Sir Robert, 165–166
Asquith, H.H., 64, 88, 133, 196, 219

Balfour, Arthur, 133, 189
Beatty, Admiral Sir David, 73, 85, 89, 106–107, 108, 112, 114, 115–117, 119–120, 121–122, 134, 135, 136, 138, 139, 187, 204, 221–222; at Jutland, 140, 141, 143–144, 149, 151, 153–154, 155–156, 159–160, 161, 163, 164, 173, 177, 183–184; character of, 86, 87–88, 218–219; early career of, 86–89; leadership of, 106–107, 144–145, 154–155, 160
Behnke, Rear Admiral Paul, 156, 160–161, 164
Ben Cruachan, 22
Bernstorff, Ambassador Johann von, 128, 199, 200
Bethmann-Hollweg, Chancellor Theobald von, 9, 26, 125–127, 128, 132, 191, 192–193, 194–196, 209–211
Bingham, Commander Edward ("Barry"), 151–152
Bonaparte, Napoleon, 2, 4, 50
British Expeditionary Force (BEF), 9–10, 11

Chalmers, Lieutenant William, 147
Chatfield, Captain Ernle, 106–107, 145, 151
Churchill, Winston, ix–x, 16, 63–64, 70, 84, 88–89, 93, 94, 99, 114, 207; as First Lord of the Admiralty, 16, 40–42, 99, 133; and Gallipoli Campaign, 133–134
Collingwood, Admiral Cuthbert, 222
Craig, Captain A.W., 146
Cruiser Rules, 22–23, 25, 125, 130, 132

De Roebeck, Rear Admiral Sir John, 133
Doenitz, Admiral Karl, 20–21
Dogger Bank, Battle of, 76, 118–124, 125, 127, 132, 134, 143, 150

Duff, Rear Admiral Alexander, 205, 206–207
Dyer, Captain Frederic, 163

Eckhardt, Ambassador Hugo von, 200
Edward VII, 37
Evan-Thomas, Rear Admiral Hugh, 141, 149, 156, 157, 164, 166, 181

Falaba, 23
Falkenhayn, Field Marshall Erich von, 128–129, 130, 191, 193
Falmer, Signaller Charles, 148–149
Ferdinand, Archduke Franz, 8
Fisher, Admiral Sir John, 32, 36, 37, 42, 66, 69, 77, 85, 132; early career of, 32–34; designs first battlecruisers, 42, 44–46; designs HMS *Dreadnought*, 37–38
Flying Kestrel, 225, 226
Foch, Field Marshal Ferdinand, 212
Francis, Petty Officer Earnest, 150
Fremantle, Admiral Sir Sydney, 225, 227

Gallipoli Campaign, 132–133
Goodenough, Commodore William, 99, 100, 102–103, 105–106, 114, 116, 117, 139, 153–154, 180
Green, Captain John, 141

Hall, Captain Reginald, 18–19, 201
Hamilton, General Sir Ian, 133
Harvey, Major Francis, 147
Hase, Commodore George, 149, 151
Heligoland Bight, Battle of, 94, 100–109
Hesperian, 25
Hindenburg, Field Marshall Paul von, 191, 193, 196, 197, 210
Hipper, Vice Admiral Franz von, 73, 82, 101, 104, 107, 110, 112–113, 114, 115, 116–117, 118, 119, 121, 185, 210–211, 214, 220–221; at Jutland, 140, 141, 143, 149, 150, 152–153, 154, 155, 159–160, 164, 167–168, 174–175, 183; early career of, 81–82; personality of, 82

Holtzendorff, Admiral Henning von, 83, 129, 191, 192, 193, 195–196, 197, 209, 210, 224
Hood, Admiral Horace, 161, 166–167

Imperial German Navy, 8, 9, 16–17, 47–48, 49–50, 58–61, 62–65, 68–69, 75, 77, 80–81, 110, 210; German Admiralty, 57, 58, 60, 77, 81; High Seas Fleet, 4–5, 9, 16, 19–21, 27, 47, 49, 51, 70–71, 72, 75–77, 82, 83, 92, 95, 106, 123–124, 133, 135, 136, 155, 159, 163, 164, 171, 173, 174, 177–178, 179–181, 183, 185–186, 189, 208, 210–212, 213, 214–218, 229; Naval High Command, 5, 20, 47, 49, 57, 68, 94, 97, 113, 124, 136, 190, 193, 208; Ships: *Ariadne*, 104, 107; *Baden*, 212; *Bayern*, 49, 137, 226, 228; *Blücher*, 110, 112, 113, 118–119, 120–121, 122–123; *Bremse*, 229; *Cuxhaven*, 211; *D-8*, 101; *Derfflinger*, 111, 112, 113, 118, 119, 136, 144, 145, 149, 150, 151, 167, 168, 175, 186–187, 228, 229; *Deutschland*, 47; *Dresden*, 214; *Elbing*, 140, 166, 167, 180, 183; *Emden*, 216, 225, 227; *Frankfurt*, 166, 167, 227; *Frauenlob*, 101–102, 109, 180, 185; *Friedrich der Grosse*, 137, 139, 159, 164, 181, 185, 186, 214, 216, 226, 228, 229; *G-9*, 101; *G-39*, 168, 174–175; *G-194*, 101; *Goeben*, 50, 51; *Grosser Kurfürst*, 156, 157, 187, 228, 229; *Helgoland*, 48–49, 212; *Hindenburg*, 226, 227, 228, 229; *Kaiser*, 49, 228; *Kaiserin*, 212, 228, 229; *Kölberg*, 119; *Köln*, 104–105, 107, 109; *König*, 136, 137, 156, 157, 160–161, 187, 212, 214; *König Albert*, 228; *Kronprinz Wilhelm*, 156, 157, 212, 228; *Lützow*, 50, 136, 137, 143, 144, 145, 148, 161, 164, 167–168, 174, 182, 185; *Mackensen*, 214; *Magdeburg*, 18; *Maintz*, 104, 105, 109; *Markgraf*, 156, 157, 187, 211, 228; *Moltke*, 50, 51, 110,

112, 113, 118, 119, 120–121, 145, 148, 149–150, 151, 168, 174–175, 183, 187, 228; *München,* 190; *Nassau,* 47–48, 49, 180; *Nürnberg,* 227; *Ostfriesland,* 181, 183, 187; *Pillau,* 166; *Pommern,* 177, 182, 185; *Posen,* 177, 180; *Prinzregent Luitpold,* 228, 229; *Regensburg,* 151; *Rheinland,* 180; *Rostock,* 180, 183, 185; *S-33,* 101; *S-35,* 175; *Schlesien,* 177; *Schleswig-Holstein,* 177; *Seydlitz,* 50, 110, 112, 113, 118, 119, 121, 123, 136, 137, 145, 148, 150, 152, 157, 168, 174, 175, 177, 182–183, 186–187, 213, 228; *Strassburg,* 104; *Strasslund,* 107, 116; *Stettin,* 101–102, 103, 104; *T-33,* 101; *Thüringen,* 181, 212; *V-1,* 101; *V-27,* 152; *V-29,* 152; *V-187,* 103, 109; *von der Tann,* 50, 110, 111, 112, 113, 118, 145, 148, 149–150, 152, 175, 186–187, 228, 229; *Westfalen,* 180, 181; *Wiesbaden,* 166–167, 171, 185; *Yorck,* 110; strategy of, 20–22, 23–24; U-boats: *U-9,* 19–20; *U-17,* 19; *U-20,* 24, 25; *U-21,* 22; *U-24,* 25; *U-28,* 23; *U-38,* 25; *U-47* (1940), 86

Imperial Russian Navy, 18, 75

Ingenhol, Admiral Friedrich von, 17, 75, 76, 98, 104, 114, 115, 116, 117–118, 125, 135

Jackson, Rear Admiral Thomas, 139, 180

Jagow, Gottfried von, 191

Jane's Fighting Ships (1914), 35

Jellicoe, Admiral Sir John, 73, 85, 93, 98, 108, 111, 114, 115, 133, 135, 138, 187, 204, 213, 218–220, 221–222, 223; at Jutland, 140, 141, 145, 149, 154, 161–162, 170–171, 173, 175, 176, 177–178, 179, 181; character of, 90, 92; early career of, 90–92; leadership of, 98, 161–163; strategy of, 93–95, 170

Jerram, Vice Admiral Sir Martyn, 177

Jervis, Admiral Sir John, Earl St. Vincent, 2, 4

Jutland, Battle of, ix–x, xi–xii, 25, 61, 72, 77, 81, 125, 132, 140, 162–169, 184, 185, 189, 213, 217, 221, 222, 223–224; aftermath, 185–189, 218, 221–222, 223; battlecruiser action, 143–146, 148–152, 155–162, 164–165; "Death Ride" of German battlecruisers, 175–177; first German turn-away, 169–170; first meeting of battlefleets, 167–170; night action, 178–182; second German turn-away, 175–177; second meeting of battlefleets, 173–175; strategic consequences, 189–190, 192, 193–194, 223

Karpf, Captain Johannes von, 183

Keyes, Commodore Sir Roger, 98–99, 100, 102–103, 105–106, 108, 123

Lansing, Robert, 25

Lloyd George, David, 38, 196, 219–220, 222, 226

Ludendorff, General Erich von, 56, 191, 196, 197, 209, 221

Lusitania, 24–25, 82, 128, 130, 131, 192

Maass, Rear Admiral Liebricht, 104, 107, 109

Mahan, Rear Admiral Alfred Thayer, 16, 53–54, 55, 59, 60, 64, 71, 208

Mauve, Rear Admiral Franz, 137, 177

Moore, Rear Admiral Sir Archibald, 122, 123

Müller, Admiral George von, 127

Nelson, Vice Admiral Horatio, 1–2, 4, 32, 53, 66, 86, 222

Oliver, Rear Admiral Henry, 17

Pelly, Captain Thomas, 121

Pohl, Admiral Hugo von, 17, 23, 76–77, 81, 125–128, 135, 191

Prien, Kapitanleutnant Gunther, 86

250 Index

Prinzip, Gavrillo, 8

Raeder, Captain Erich, 168
Reuter, Rear Admiral Ludwig von, 214,
 216, 226, 228
Room 40, 18–19, 113, 114, 115, 119, 137,
 138–139, 180, 190, 193, 201
Royal Navy, 2, 4–5, 7–8, 10, 17, 19–21,
 27, 29, 32, 44, 46, 49, 50, 51, 61, 62, 64,
 65, 70–71, 72, 80, 81, 85, 87, 89, 90, 91,
 92, 93–95, 107, 108, 132, 133, 163, 176,
 197, 214, 229; Admiralty, 2, 16, 19, 22,
 29, 37, 38, 40, 67, 69, 70, 71, 84–85, 94,
 99–100, 107, 108, 113–114, 117, 184,
 188–189, 205–207; Grand Fleet, ix–x,
 4–5, 7, 16, 20–21, 33, 42, 46, 69, 71–
 72, 73–76, 80–81, 83–85, 92–95, 98–
 99, 104, 109, 110, 111–112, 113–114,
 115, 117, 123, 135, 136, 138, 155, 161,
 164, 169, 171, 173, 176, 177–178, 179–
 181, 183, 189, 204, 208, 220; Ships:
 Aboukir, 19–20, 109; *Acasta,* 167;
 Achates, 180; *Agamemnon,* 35;
 Agincourt, 181; *Ajax,* 114; *Arethusa,*
 100–102, 104, 105–106, 107; *Aurora,*
 119; *Australia,* 188; *Badger,* 167;
 Barham, 136, 149–150, 156, 157;
 Bellerophon, 46, 47; *Black Prince,* 181,
 184, 188–189; *Broke,* 180; *Canterbury,*
 173; *Cardiff,* 213; *Centurion,* 114;
 Chester, 166; *Conqueror,* 114; *Cressy,*
 19–20, 109; *Defender,* 103; *Defence,*
 165, 166, 184, 188–189; *Doon,* 114;
 Dreadnought, 33, 37–39, 45–46, 48–49,
 50, 51; *Dublin,* 180; *Falmouth,* 173;
 Faulknor, 181; *Fearless,* 101–102, 104;
 Fortune, 180; *Galatea,* 140, 141, 161;
 Halcyon, 110; *Hercules,* 181; *Hogue,*
 19–20, 107, 109; *Indefatigable,* 46,
 148–149, 152, 157, 160, 184, 185, 187,
 188–189; *Indomitable,* 119, 122, 166,
 188; *Inflexible,* 50, 166, 188; *Invincible,*
 44–46, 50, 99–100, 102, 166–167, 184,
 185, 188–189; *Iron Duke,* 40, 138, 161,

162, 163, 167, 173, 175, 177, 181, 183;
 King George V, 40, 177; *Laertes,* 105–
 106; *Laurel,* 101, 106; *Liberty,* 106;
 Lion, 46, 106, 107, 119–120, 121–122,
 139, 140, 141, 143, 145, 146, 147, 148,
 151, 152, 156, 161, 162, 188; *Lively,*
 110; *Liverpool,* 105; *Lord Nelson,* 35;
 Lowestoft, 102, 103; *Lurcher,* 102;
 Malaya, 149–150, 157, 181;
 Marlborough, 170, 174, 181, 183, 184,
 187, 188; *Monarch,* 114, 175; *Neptune,*
 39, 46, 49, 162; *Nestor,* 151–152; *New
 Zealand,* 99–100, 102, 119, 122, 141,
 148, 151; *Nomad,* 152, 165;
 Nottingham, 102, 103; *Obedient,* 182;
 Orion, 39, 114, 175; *Pathfinder,* 19;
 Princess Royal, 46, 107, 119–20, 122,
 141, 148, 151, 156, 177, 188; *Queen
 Elizabeth,* 40–42, 46, 49, 139, 143, 157,
 158, 164, 188, 214; *Queen Mary,* 46,
 107, 141, 148, 150–151, 152, 157, 160,
 184, 185, 187, 188–189; *Revenge,* 170,
 181; *Royal Oak,* 86; *Royal Sovereign*
 (battleship, 1880), 47; *St. Vincent,* 161;
 Shark, 167; *Southampton,* 100, 102–
 103, 108, 153, 180, 181; *Spitfire,* 180;
 Thunderer, 183; *Tiger,* 46, 107, 119–
 120, 121, 122, 141, 146, 147, 148, 151,
 156, 188; *Tipperary,* 180; *Valiant,* 157;
 Vega, 226; *Vespa,* 226; *Warrior*
 (armored cruiser, 1906), 165–166,
 184, 188; *Warrior* (ship of the line,
 1860), 29, 34, 47; *Warspite,* 149–150,
 157, 164, 165–166, 184, 185, 188;
 strategy of, 54–56, 65–66, 71–72;
 Submarines: *D-5,* 110; *D-6,* 110; *E-4,*
 103; *E-6,* 103, 108; *E-9,* 100–101; *E-10,*
 110

Scapa Flow, 74, 83–85, 225, 229
Scarborough Raid, 94, 111–117
Scheer, Vice Admiral Reinhard, 73, 135,
 138, 139, 185–186, 189–190, 191, 193,
 195–196, 208, 209, 210–211, 212, 220–

221, 224; at Jutland, 140, 155, 159, 163, 164–165, 168–169, 170–171, 173, 174, 175, 176, 178, 179–180, 183; character of, 77, 79–80; early career of, 77–79; strategy of, 80–81, 126, 136–137; succeeds to command of High Seas Fleet, 77, 81

Schlieffen, General Alfred von, 13, 14

Schlieffen Plan, 9, 10, 13, 14

Schwieger, Kapitan-Leutnant Walther, 24, 25, 82

Seymour, Rear Admiral Sir Edward, 92

Seymour, Lt. Ralph, 117, 122, 123–124, 147, 157

Sims, Admiral William S., 205

Somme, Battle of the, 13, 15, 193

Spee, Rear Admiral Maximilian von, 16, 111

Stirling, Captain Anselan, 181–182

Storey, Midshipman Jocelyn, 150

Submarines and submarine warfare, 19–22, 23–27, 67–68, 69, 125–126, 127–128, 129–131, 191–198, 200–201, 203–208. *See also* Imperial German Navy, U-boats

Sussex, 26, 131

Telconia, 17

Tirpitz, Admiral Alfred von, 16–17, 23, 50, 67, 98, 125–127, 130, 159, 191; early career and rise of, 56–59; strategy of, 17, 60–61, 62–65

Trafalgar, Battle of, 1, 3–4, 30, 32, 53, 66, 108, 134, 164, 191, 223

Treaty of Versailles, 216–217

Tyrwhitt, Commodore Sir Reginald, 98, 99, 100, 102–103, 105–106, 108, 115

Verdun, Battle of, 13, 129, 193

Villeneuve, Admiral Pierre, 1, 2–3, 4

Waldeyer-Hartz, Captain Hugo von, 116

Warrender, Rear Admiral Sir George, 114, 115–117

Weitzacker, Lieutenant Ernst von, 168–169

Wemyss, Admiral Rosslyn, 213

Whitehead, Robert, 66

Wilhelm II, 17, 25, 26, 59, 60, 61, 62, 75–76, 98, 117–118, 126–127, 128, 129–130, 132, 186, 197, 209, 210, 211, 212

Wilson, Woodrow, 24–25, 26, 128, 131–132, 192, 194, 195, 197, 199, 200, 201–203

Yarmouth Raid, 109–111

Ypres, First Battle of, 12–13

Zimmermann, Arthur, 199–200

"Zimmermann Telegram" 200, 201–202

About the Author

DANIEL ALLEN BUTLER is the author of *"Unsinkable": The Full Story of RMS Titanic, The Lusitania: The Life, Loss and Legacy of an Ocean Legend, Warrior Queens: RMS Queen Mary and Queen Elizabeth in World War Two,* and *The Age of Cunard: A Transatlantic History, 1839–1999.*